RADICAL
RIGHT-WING
POPULISM IN
WESTERN EUROPE

Also by Hans-Georg Betz

POSTMODERN POLITICS IN GERMANY:
The Politics of Resentment

RADICAL RIGHT-WING POPULISM IN WESTERN EUROPE

Hans-Georg Betz

St. Martin's Press
New York

First published in the United States of America 1994

Printed in the United States of America
Book design by Acme Art, Inc.

0-312-08390-4 (cloth)
0-312-12195-4 (paper)

Library of Congress Cataloging-in-Publication Data

Betz, Hans-Georg, 1956-
    Radical right-wing populism in Western Europe / Hans-Georg Betz.
        p. cm.
    Includes bibliographical references and index.
    ISBN 0-312-08390-4. — ISBN 0-312-12195-4 (pbk.)
    1. Political parties—Europe. 2. Elections—Europe.
3. Conservatism—Europe. 4. Populism—Europe. 5. Radicalism—
Europe. I. Title
JN94.A979B48 1994
324.94'0559—dc20   94-6696
                                                        CIP

For Sabina

CONTENTS

LIST OF TABLES

PREFACE

This book grows out of a long interest in the economic, social, and cultural transformation in Western Europe. I first started to think about its consequences for West European politics when I thought about the origins of the German Greens in the late 1980s. During my research I had the opportunity to talk to Harald Neubauer, at the time the general secretary of a little known, mostly Bavarian party, the Republikaner. The result was an article on the politics of resentment in Germany and a chapter in my book on "postmodern politics in Germany" in which I tried to show that both Greens and Republikaner were the products of larger changes in German society. During my work on the Republikaner I became increasingly interested in similar parties in other parts of Western Europe. When I had the chance to live in Italy for two years in the early 1990s I had the opportunity to witness first hand the dramatic rise of the Lega Nord in northern Italy.

This book deals primarily with the political aspects of radical right-wing populism and its causes in Western Europe. Those who search for answers accounting for the growing violence against foreigners or the spread of neo-nazism among young people will be disappointed. As heinous and deplorable as these phenomena are, they are the acts of relatively small minorities in Western Europe. By contrast, radical right-wing populist parties have attracted sizeable portions of the West European population; their deputies and representatives sit in local, regional, national, and European parliaments, their leaders have appeared as guests on talk shows. This book is an attempt to explain how it was possible that hardly forty-five years after the end of the Second World War the radical Right could have become a significant factor in West European politics.

Initial financial support for this project was provided by the Bradley Institute for Democracy and Public Values, Marquette University. I am grateful for its support. I would like to thank my graduate assistant, Åke Densert, for his invaluable help in dealing with Scandinavian sources and Susanne Bennman in giving me her time to translate Danish material. I am particularly grateful to Linda Merrill, who awakened my interest in the French Right. I also want to thank Jørgen Goul Andersen, Marcus J. Schmidt, Marc Swyngedouw, and Peter Ulram for sharing their work and sources with me. Survey data on Norwegian attitudes toward immigrants were provided by the Norwegian Social Science

Data Service, which delivered the data, and the Norwegian Central Bureau of Statistics, which did the field work. I would like to thank Bjørn Henrichsen and Knut Kalgraff Skjåk for their help.

I would especially like to thank John Felice for his continuous support while I was at the Loyola University Rome Center of Liberal Arts. Final thanks go to my wife, Sabina Bhatia, for her patience and encouragement. It is to her that this book is dedicated.

RADICAL RIGHT-WING POPULISM IN WESTERN EUROPE

1

Radical Right-Wing Populism and the Challenge of Global Change

In the decades immediately following the Second World War, the liberal democracies of Western Europe enjoyed a remarkable degree of social and political stability. Sustained economic growth, growing individual affluence, and the expansion and perfection of the welfare state each contributed to a social and political climate conducive to political compromise and consensus while eroding support for extremist solutions on both the Left and the Right. However, stability and consensus were only short-lived. The resurgence of ideological and political turbulence in the late 1960s, rising social conflicts in the early 1970s, and the spread of mass protest by new social movements and citizen initiatives in the 1980s were symptoms of a profound transformation of West European politics. Its contours were increasingly becoming visible in the late 1980s and early 1990s. What heightened and accentuated these developments were a number of factors: the decay of the grand ideologies of modernity, exemplified by the fall of the Soviet empire, and the ensuing destabilization of a world to which the majority of West Europeans had readily accustomed themselves; a new awareness of the finiteness of natural resources, the growing visibility of the economic and social consequences of environmental destruction and the population explosion in the developing world; and mounting uneasiness and ambiguity with regard to new technological projects.

It should hardly come as a surprise that these developments left deep traces in the political order of advanced Western democracies. Politics does not operate in a vacuum; it reflects as much the state of society as it seeks to influence and shape its direction. This became particularly obvious by the end of the 1960s when opposition to the American war in Vietnam and widespread political discontent combined into an explosive mixture that threatened to destroy the postwar political settlement. However, although the 1960s challenge to the established political institutions marked the beginning of a fundamental turn in Western culture and politics, it failed to break with their basic logic. The protest movements of these years still "took the idealistic and utopian promises of the 'affluent society' at their word, measured them against (inferior) reality, and emphatically demanded the promise as reality. But the still unbroken, optimistic belief in progress also nourished trust in technocratic solutions to existing problems 'from the top' or the fundamental changeability of existing structures 'from below'" (Brand, 1990, p.31).

Twenty years later, this optimism had all but evaporated. The political climate of the 1980s was characterized by disenchantment with the major social and political institutions and deep distrust in their workings, the weakening and decomposition of electoral alignments, and increased political fragmentation and electoral volatility. Concomitantly, new political issues emerged, promoted by new social actors outside and often against the established political institutions. Growing awareness of environmental degradation generated rising ecological protest; advances in general welfare and education led to demands for social equality and greater opportunities for women and minorities in politics; technological mega-projects such as nuclear power and nuclear waste reprocessing plants, new airports, and super highways evoked growing opposition from an increasingly sensitized and involved citizenry.

It was expected that each of these conflicts would benefit the Left, even if the demands of students, women, minorities, and engaged citizens appeared not necessarily compatible with those of the traditional Left. Indeed, the 1980s saw a significant fragmentation of the Left. Distancing themselves from what they considered the growth-oriented "old politics" of socialists and social democrats, Green, left-socialist, and similar left-libertarian parties succeeded in establishing themselves in the party systems of a number of advanced West European democracies (Kitschelt, 1990). Left-libertarian parties have not been the only ones to benefit from the political transformation of the past years.

Table 1.1

Electoral Results for Radical Right-Wing Populist Parties (in %)

	LN	AP	FN	REP	ND	FP(D)	FP(N)	FPÖ	VB
1980									
1981						8.9	4.5		1.1
1982									
1983									
1984			11.0*			3.6			1.3*
						3.5*			
1985							3.7		1.4
1986			9.8					9.7	
1987		2.6				4.8			1.9
1988			14.4**			9.0			
			9.7						
1989	1.8*		11.8*	7.1		5.3*	13.0		4.1*
1990				2.1		6.4		16.6	
1991		5.1			6.7				6.6
1992	8.7								
1993							6.0		
1994	8.4								

* = European elections; ** French Presidential Election

LN (Lega Nord); AP (Autopartei); FN (Front National); REP (Republikaner); ND (Ny Demokrati); FP(D) (Fremskridtpartiet, Denmark); FP(N) (Fremskrittspartiet, Norway); FPÖ (Freiheitlichen Partei Österreichs); VB (Vlaams Blok)

Increasingly, West European democracies have come under heavy pressure from a radical Right that in terms of its programmatic challenge and electoral potential represents the potentially most dynamic, and disruptive, political phenomenon of the 1990s. Their massive breakthrough in the late 1980s and early 1990s in a variety of West European countries has been one of the most significant signals of a fundamental transformation of politics in advanced Western democracies. Distancing themselves both from the backward-looking, reactionary politics of the traditional extremist (i.e., neo-fascist and neo-nazi) Right as well as its proclivity for violence, these parties are posing the most significant challenge to the established structure and politics of West European democracy today.

Generally, the majority of radical right-wing populist parties are radical in their rejection of the established socio-cultural and socio-political system and their advocacy of individual achievement, a free market, and a drastic reduction of the role of the state without, however, openly questioning the legitimacy of democracy in general. They are right-wing first in their rejection of individual and social equality and of political projects that seek to achieve it; second in their opposition to the social integration of marginalized groups; and third in their appeal to xenophobia, if not overt racism and anti-Semitism. They are populist in their unscrupulous use and instrumentalization of diffuse public sentiments of anxiety and disenchantment and their appeal to the common man and his allegedly superior common sense. In short, the majority of radical right-wing populist parties tend to blend a classical liberal position on the individual and the economy with some elements of the socio-political agenda of the extreme and intellectual New Right (and here especially the French *nouvelle droite*) and deliver it in a concentrated and simplified form to those voters who are disenchanted with their individual life chances, with the direction of societal developments, and the political system in general.

Recent electoral trends illustrate the dramatic rise, diffusion, and expansion of radical right-wing populist support in Western Europe. During the past several years most of these parties have been able to expand and multiply both votes and parliamentary representation, thus threatening to render the formation of governments increasingly difficult (see Table 1.1). In order to understand the significance of these developments it is necessary first to discuss the origins and evolution of these parties.

SCANDINAVIAN POPULISM: PROGRESS AND NEW DEMOCRACY

The first parties to gain significant electoral support under a radical right-wing populist banner were the Danish and Norwegian Progress parties. Unlike a majority of radical right-wing populist parties in Western Europe, these parties celebrated their first significant electoral successes in the early 1970s. Their origins go back to a short television interview on Saturday, January 30, 1971, the evening Danish families were busy preparing their tax returns. The hitherto fairly unknown tax lawyer and millionaire Mogens Glistrup, who had "built up a successful laywer's practice in the 1960s which specialized in the formation of limited companies for the sole purpose of avoiding income tax," disclosed on Danish national television that he had no intention of paying any income tax and that this was quite legal (Christiansen, 1984, p. 21). He challenged

Denmark's socio-cultural consensus by asserting that no one had to pay more taxes than they wanted. He even went so far as to praise tax evaders as heroes comparable to the groups that had resisted German occupation during World War II.[1] Predictably enough in a country with some of the highest taxes in the whole world, Glistrup's statement created quite a stir and made him an instant celebrity. But when Glistrup sought to cash in on his fame by offering himself as a candidate to the Conservatives for the 1971 elections, the party declined the offer. In response, Glistrup started to toy with the idea of organizing his own political party.

The Progress party was launched in August 1972 in a restaurant in Copenhagen's Tivoli amusement park. To the surprise of most political observers, support for the party grew rapidly. Within a few weeks in 1973, polls showed an increase in support from 4 percent in February to about a quarter of the electorate in April. Despite internal problems the party registered for participation in the upcoming election, which turned into the greatest political landslide in Danish post war history. The Progress party received 15.9 percent of the vote, which made it the second largest party in the Danish parliament behind the Social Democrats (c.f. Aimer, 1988; Harmel and Svåsand, 1989).

At about the same time in Norway, Anders Lange, the publisher of a magazine that mixed information on dogbreeding with conservative political commentaries, started to pay attention to the rise of "glistrupism" in Denmark. In the past, Lange's views had already attracted some groups on the far right of Norwegian societies. However, it was not until the rise of glistrupism in Denmark, that his plans for forming a party started to take on concrete forms. In April 1973, Lange called for a public meeting in an Oslo movie theater during which he launched the "Anders Lange's Party for a Strong Reduction of Taxes, Social Contributions, and Public Intervention." With this "ludicrously cumbersome," but "admirably explicit" name, Lange gained 5 percent in the 1973 election (Aimer, 1988, p. 2).

Despite significant successes in the early and mid-1970s, the electoral fortunes of both Progress parties declined considerably in the late 1970s and early 1980s. One of the reasons for the decline was the disappearance of both leaders from the political scene. In the Norwegian case, Lange's death in 1974 left the party disorganized. It was not until the charismatic Carl I. Hagen was elected chairman of the party (since 1977 renamed the Progress Party) that its fortunes started to improve, albeit only slowly and gradually. The first time that its potential importance became clear was in the aftermath of the 1985 general election. Although the center-right government under Kare Willoch was re-elected, it lacked a clear majority in parliament and thus depended on the support from the two deputies the Progress Party had managed to elect. The silent cooperation did not last long. In April 1986 the Progress Party supported the Labor opposition against the bourgeois government on a question regarding the raising of taxes, thus causing its fall and paving the way for a Labor government (Bjørklund, 1988, p. 215).

The party's breakthrough came in a landslide victory in the 1987 local election. With 12.3 percent of the vote in the county council polls it more than tripled its result from the general election of 1985. The party's rise was further confirmed in the 1989 general election where with 13 percent of the vote it received its best result ever. This translated into 22 seats in parliament. This made the party not only the third largest group in parliament, but left it once again in a crucial position between the bourgeois and socialist blocs, neither of which gained a decisive majority.

In Denmark, the Progress Party's decline in the late 1970s and early 1980s was largely due to the fact that the justice system finally caught up with Mogens Glistrup. He was convicted in 1978 of tax evasion and sentenced to pay a heavy financial penalty. In 1983, after a prolonged period of litigation, he was found guilty again and sentenced to a three-year prison term. But already before, Glistrup's weakened position as party leader had led to growing factional struggles within the party's parliamentary group between a radical wing dedicated to Glistrup's intransigent position and a moderate wing led by Pia Kjærsgaard. By 1979, the internal opposition had enough support to come out and call for a modification of the party line in order to allow the Progress Party to cooperate with other parties. In response to internal conflicts, between 1983 and 1984 a quarter of the party's deputies left the party (Harmel and Svåsand, 1989, p. 23). It was thus hardly surprising that by 1985 polls showed the party to have fallen close to the 2 percent threshold necessary to be represented in parliament.

Glistrup's return to politics after having partially served his prison term marked the revival of the party's fortunes. However, although he was returned to parliament in 1987, Glistrup was no longer able to assert control over the party against Pia Kjærsgaard, who had emerged as the new party leader. Her "relatively moderate, no-nonsense style" prevailed over Glistrup's radical and uncompromising position and gained the party new respect among the voters, but led to renewed tensions in the party (see Smith Jespersen, 1989, p. 193). When the Progress Party cooperated with the Conservative-led government on the budget in 1989, the strains within the party were becoming increasingly serious. In late 1990, Glistrup was expelled from the party and, after failing to get elected to parliament with a new party, fell back into political oblivion (Andersen, 1992, p. 194).

If radical right-wing populist parties have been part of the Danish and Norwegian political establishment since the early 1970s, it was not until 1991 that a similar party, the New Democracy, emerged in Sweden. The New Democracy party was founded in February 1991, seven months before the general election. The founders were Jan Wachtmeister, an aristocratic business-man and author of two highly successful satires on Swedish national life, and Bernt Karlsson, the director of an amusement park. Both were established media personalities. They entered the 1991 election campaign with the slogan "Life must be more fun." This was part of a broader marketing strategy to use unconventional methods to draw public attention to the new party. Thus, "the party program was available on answerphones and false parking tickets were doled out as part of the campaign against traffic wardens" (Arter, 1992, p. 366). With these gimmicks Wachtmeister and Karlsson managed to gain a respectable 6.1 percent of the popular vote in the general election.

NORTHERN ITALY: THE LEGA NORD

"I am the savior of Italy." With this bold claim Umberto Bossi, the undisputed leader of the Lega Nord, presented himself before the 1992 parliamentary election to the Italian voters. Two weeks later, the Lega captured almost 9 percent of the popular vote to become the fourth largest force in Italian politics. Those who dismissed the Lega's success as an impressive, but short-lived flash of popular protest against the scandal-ridden Roman *partitocrazia* soon had to revise their predictions. In September there were local elections in Mantova. Although of minor political importance, against the background of growing public disaffection and cynicism with the political system, the elections turned into a measure of whether and to what extent the political earthquake of April had affected the political landscape in northern Italy. Although the established political parties believed to be able to confine the political damage—after all Mantova was well known for its clean administration—the result of the election went beyond their worst expectations. Both Christian Democrats and Socialists lost half of their voters in the provincial elections of 1990. With a mere one fifth of the vote they landed far behind the great winner of the election, the Lega Nord. With 34 percent of the vote, Bossi's movement emerged as the strongest party in the city. The defeat was particularly bitter for the Socialists. With 7 percent of the vote they barely came out ahead of the Lega Alpina Lumbarda, a list headed by Bossi's estranged sister Angela, who had formed it primarily to take away votes from her brother's party.

Surveys conducted after the election confirmed that the results of Mantova were part of a trend, which was spreading like a brushfire throughout northern Italy. Had there been elections in northern Italy in the fall, the Lega would have received almost a third of the vote in Turin, Genoa, Venice, and Bologna, and one fifth in Milan. Even in Florence, where the Lega had virtually been nonexistent in the parliamentary elections, the party would have received one tenth of the vote and become the second largest party in the city. Even more impressive were the results in smaller Lombardian cities where surveys saw the Lega surpassing 40 percent of the vote.[2] Although the actual results of local elections in Varese and Monza in December 1992 proved these polls to have somewhat exaggerated the real extent of Lega support (the party received 37 percent of the vote in Varese and 32 percent in Monza), by the end of 1992 Bossi had become what one observer described as the person who "in only one year has done more to change Italian politics than anyone else has done in thirty."[3]

The historical roots of the Lega Nord go back to the late 1970s. The first regional leagues originated in the Veneto, a region in the northeast of Italy (Diamanti, 1992, Diamanti, 1993, ch. 3). They developed out of a regionalist linguistic association, which organized research seminars and courses on Veneto's culture, history, and language. When the Union Valdotaîne, a regionalist party from the French speaking Val d'Aosta, invited all regionalist movements to gather under a common banner for the 1979 European elections, the association presented one of its members as a candidate on the Union's list. The fact that its candidate received a significant number of preferential votes convinced the Venetian regionalists that there was electoral potential for regionalist ideas. This marked the beginnings of the Liga Veneta, which in the general elections of 1983 received enough votes to elect one candidate each to the Chamber of Deputies and the Senate. However, internal power struggles and scandals soon halted the Liga's ascent and threatened to condemn it to the fringes of Venetian politics, a fate from which it was only saved by the rapid rise of Bossi's Lega Lombarda.

The origins of the Lega Lombarda are closely associated with Umberto Bossi (see Bossi with Vimercati, 1992, 1993). In 1979, Bossi, a medical student at the university of Padova, met Bruno Salvadori, an activist for the Union Valdotaîne. During a discussion with Salvadori, Bossi, who had already been active in a number of left-wing political movements, discovered the notion of federalism. As Bossi put it in his autobiography, he realized that the "original sin" of the Italian political system was its "repressive bureaucratic centralism" (Bossi with Vimercati, 1992, p.33). In the early 1980s Bossi started to translate his thoughts into concrete politics. He wrote manifestos promoting the idea of Lombardian autonomy, founded *Lombardia Autonomista,* a political weekly, and finally in 1984 his own political movement, the Lega Lombarda. Like the Liga Veneta, the Lega Lombarda propagated ethno-regionalism as a political panacea. The magic word was autonomy; the enemies were found in the Roman *partitocrazia* and the immigrants from southern Italy and the Third World. The goals were anything but modest: extensive autonomy for Lombardy in a modern federal state modeled after Switzerland or Belgium; affirmation of Lombardian culture, history, and language; preferential treatment for the Lombardian population with regard to jobs, housing, social services, and positions in the public administration; a resolute campaign against organized crime; and the creation of a federated Europe of regions (Vimercati, 1990, pp. 151–153).

With this program Bossi campaigned for the local elections in Varese in 1985. He received 3 percent of the vote, sufficient for one seat on the city council. The Lega Lombarda's relatively successful showing encouraged Bossi to participate with the party in the parliamentary election of 1987. The Lega Lombarda received 3 percent of the vote in Lombardy, which translated into one seat in the Chamber of Deputies and one in the Senate, filled by Bossi. This marked the beginning of the *senatur's* rise to political prominence. Eight percent in the European elections of 1989 in Lombardy was followed by 19 percent in the regional elections in 1990.

The Lega Lombarda's success encouraged imitation. Regional leagues mushroomed throughout northern Italy. In 1989 Bossi succeeded in uniting them into one movement bound to the ideals of autonomy and federalism, the Lega Nord. After completing this project, Bossi also sought to extend the Lega to other parts of the country. Leagues were founded not only in the center, but even in the south. In the parliamentary elections, Bossi ran for a seat not only in Milan, but also in Rome and Palermo. However, the results remained disappointing. Whereas the Lega triumphed in the north, its candidates in the center and south found only minimal support. Yet in the north the Lega was well on its way to dislodging the Christian Democrats as the dominant political party, as shown by its electoral successes in the local elections in Varese, Monza, and a number of smaller communities in December 1992. These successes paved the way for the Lega's electoral triumph in the local elections in Milan in June 1993, where it received more than 40 percent of the vote and elected Marco Formentini as mayor. However, local elections in November and December 1993 showed the limits of the Lega Nord's capacity to translate support in the polls into political offices. Although the Lega strengthened its position as the dominant single party in northern Italy, it failed to elect its candidates as mayors in the important cities of Genoa and Venice. In both cases the Lega's candidates were only supported by their own party whereas the opposing candidates were supported by a broadly based coalition of left-wing parties.[4] This bode ill for the national elections in March 1994, which were held under new quasi-majoritarian rules (75 percent of the seats allocated in single-member districts, 25 percent proportionately). Given the fact that the Left (namely, PDS, Rifondazione comunista, La rete, Verdi) formed an electoral alliance before the election, the Lega's chances to win seats in all but their most solid strongholds in Lombardy and the Veneto appeared less than slim.

It is for this reason that Bossi decided to enter a strategic alliance with Silvio Berlusconi, the media magnate and leader of Forza Italia. Berlusconi, in turn, forged a tactical alliance with Gianfranco Fini's post-neofascists of Alleanza nazionale. Right from the start, Bossi's pact with Berlusconi was more of an alliance of convenience and irritation than of conviction. But it did serve its purpose for both Bossi and Berlusconi. Berlusconi's bloc won an absolute majority in the chamber and close to a majority in the senate. The Lega Nord received 8.4 percent of the vote. But because of the new electoral system, the Lega almost doubled its seats in both the chamber and senate. This put Bossi in a decisive position in the negotiations over the shape of the new government.

Bossi's strong position in parliament, however, obscured the fact that the Lega Nord's showing in the contest had at best been mixed. The party did manage to mobilize about the same proportion of the electorate as it had done in 1992. However, many voters who otherwise would have voted for the Lega Nord, voted for Forza Italia. In fact, Forza Italia surpassed the Lega Nord in all northern districts save for the Lega's stronghold in northern Lombardy. But even there, the Lega advanced by less than 2 percent. In Milan alone, the Lega lost 60 percent of the votes it had received in the local elections of 1993.[5]

In addition, there was the problem of the quasi-alliance with Alleanza nazionale. Fini's party gained 13.5 percent overall, thus surpassing the Lega by more than 5 percent of the vote. Most of its support came from southern Italy (including southern Latium), where in some areas Alleanza nazionale received more than 20 percent of the vote. Ninety-five of the party's 105 deputies and senators came from Rome or further south. Bossi interpreted this as a "declaration of war on the north" by the south, which sought to continue living off the north's rich pockets.[6]

Thus the outcome of the 1994 election had complicated Umberto Bossi's position considerably. On the one hand, the Lega was the first radical right-wing populist party to enter a national government. On the other hand, the elections also demonstrated that there were limits to the Lega's appeal, provided there was a credible alternative for the voters. They also showed, however, that the Lega could rely on a sizeable core of ideologically committed voters, which guaranteed that the Lega remained a significant force in Italian politics.

AUSTRIA: THE FPÖ

Whereas the Lega Nord had been a relative newcomer to Italian politics, the Austrian Freedom Party (Freiheitliche Partei Österreichs, FPÖ), played a significant role in Austrian politics throughout the postwar period. Founded in 1955, the FPÖ succeeded the League of Independents (Verband der Unabhängigen, VdU), which had been formed in 1949. The intention was to build a "Third Force" in form of a "centrist, reform party" between the socialist Left and the Catholic Right and thus to offer a political alternative to the considerable number of Austrians without firm commitment to either of the two large parties (Riedlsperger, 1993, pp. 21–22). Partly, the founding of the VdU was also a reaction to "the clumsy handling of Denazification by the government coalition," which resulted in the discrimination and exclusion of thousands of former NSDAP members from political life (Knight, 1992, p.291).

Despite significant gains in the 1949 elections the party soon declined as a result of internal conflicts between its liberal and German national wings as well as external denunciations and pressures. In response to these difficulties the VdU agreed in 1955 to fuse with other political organizations to form the FPÖ. In contrast to the VdU, the FPÖ initially consciously sought to revive the traditions of the national liberal political subculture (*Lager*), which had been an important part of the political landscape during the Monarchy and First Republic, and represent its interests against those of the Catholic and Marxist/Socialist *Lager,* which dominated Austrian post-war politics. However, the party's leadership soon recognized that the national-liberal *Lager's* association with Nazism had thoroughly discredited its German-oriented ideology. In response the party set out to establish a new profile without, however, completely abandoning its notion that Austria was a member of the German ethnic and cultural community. Relegated to the margins of Austria's political scene by the consensus politics of the two major parties, the FPÖ sought to sharpen its profile as a representative of the average citizen against the overwhelming power of the dominant parties (Riedlsperger, 1992, pp. 23–24).

With a new generation joining the FPÖ in the 1970s, the leadership increasingly sought to modernize the party by revitalizing and strengthening its commitment to liberalism at the expense of the remnants of the German-national wing. Particularly, when Norbert Steger, who represented the growing number of young and progressive party members, became party chairman in 1980 at the age of 36, the party's liberal wing gained increasing strength. One of its objectives was to establish a new balance between the liberal and national elements of the party program. This strategy largely succeeded, although even Steger's group could not eradicate the party's commitment to German nationalism completely (Pelinka, 1992, p. 104). As a result, the FPÖ was admitted into the Liberal International as a right-liberal party and, after the election of 1983, was invited by the SPÖ to form a coalition government under Chancellor Fred Sinowatz. However, a combination of blunders on the part of Steger, growing dissatisfaction with his leadership among the ranks of the party, and, particularly, a dramatic decline in voter appeal led to open revolt against the chairman. Instrumental behind the revolt against Steger was Jörg Haider, the chairman of the Carinthian party organization, who had emerged as Steger's most consistent and vocal critic (Riedlsperger, 1992, p. 25).

Like Steger, Haider had rapidly advanced through the party's ranks. He was discovered by Friedrich Peter, a former chairman of the FPÖ, in the late 1960s, after Haider had won a debating contest sponsored by the radical right-wing Austrian Gymnastic Federation with a contribution entitled "Are We Austrians Germans?" At the age of 25, Haider became secretary of the Carinthian FPÖ, at 28 a member of the Austrian parliament. In 1983, Haider was elected chairman of the Carinthian FPÖ, the strongest and most German-nationalist of the state party organizations. This position gave him a solid basis from which to start a campaign against Norbert Steger and the federal party organization. The conflict reached a first culmination point when Steger threatened to expel Haider from the party after Haider had threatened that he and the whole Carinthian party organization would secede from the FPÖ. After Haider managed to convince the Carinthian party leadership to support his position, the federal party organization preferred to seek reconciliation with Haider. This was a clear sign that the balance of power in the FPÖ had started to shift away from the liberal wing toward Haider's position. The confrontation between Steger and Haider in the stormy party convention in September 1986, which ended in Haider's election as the new chairman, served only as a confirmation of these developments.

Under Haider's leadership the party made a spectacular comeback. Polls conducted in the fall of 1986 had conceded the FPÖ not more than 1 percent support. After campaigning for 11 weeks, the party gained 9.7 percent of the vote in the national election (Plasser and Ulram, 1989, p. 153). These gains were followed by a series of successes in state elections, which gave the FPÖ seats even in those state legislatures where it had been absent for years (Riedlsperger, 1992, pp. 28-39). The party's successes culminated in the electoral triumph in the 1991 regional election in Vienna. With 22.6 percent of the vote the FPÖ became the second largest political force in the city, inflicting substantial losses not only on the conservative Austrian People's Party, but also on the Socialists, who had traditionally dominated the city. The situation was similar in Graz, Austria's second largest city, where in January

1993 the FPÖ gained more than 20 percent of the vote, inflicting heavy losses on both major parties.

These results were even more surprising given the fact that growing internal conflicts eventually led a number of leading party members (led by Heide Schmidt, the party's secretary and former FPÖ candidate for the Austrian presidency) to defect from the FPÖ and found their own party, the Liberal Forum. Observers expected that the new party would inflict heavy damage on the FPÖ. These expectations appeared to be met when in the state election in Lower Austria in May 1993, the Liberal Forum obtained more than 5 percent of the vote and gained two seats in the state legislature. However, despite this success, it soon became clear that the Forum could hardly seriously hope to challenge the FPÖ. Polls taken in late 1993 showed Haider's party running close to 20 percent. The result of state elections held in Carinthia, Tyrole, and Salzburg in March 1994 confirmed these trends. The FPÖ gained 16 percent in Tyrole, almost 20 percent in Salzburg, and 33 percent in Carinthia. The Liberal Forum, on the other hand, failed to gain a single seat in any of the three states.

FRANCE: THE FRONT NATIONAL

In the first turn of elections to the French National Assembly in March 1993 the Front National received nearly 12.5 percent of the vote, quite a bit more than preelection surveys had indicated. These results were evidence that the party had consolidated its electoral basis and established itself as a lasting element of the French party system. But they also showed that after a decade of steady electoral growth, the party had reached its limits, beyond which it could hardly expect to grow in the future. This marked a setback for Jean-Marie Le Pen, in the late 1980s the undisputed leader of the West European nationalist Right, who had dedicated most of his political career to bringing together the diffuse ideological and organizational elements of right-wing French radicalism and extremism in a party that he hoped would attract mass support.

The Front National was founded in October 1972, as a union of diverse right-wing radical and extremist groups each one of which jealously guarded its organizational structure and ideological identity. Initially the Front was dominated by members of the Ordre Nouveau, a group of militant national revolutionaries founded in the late 1960s in response to the student movement, but rooted in the ideas of the anticommunist, anticapitalist, militarist, and xenophobic French neo-fascism of the 1950s. They had two objectives: to subvert the existing democratic system through direct actions, such as agitation and terror, in order to create an authoritarian social and political order; and to establish a genuine European nationalism grounded in the notion of the superiority of Western civilization "in order to safeguard the cohesion of the Western bloc" (Buzzi, 1991, p. 34). It did not take long for the failure of this strategy to convince the leading representatives of Ordre Nouveau of the necessity to unite the different currents of the French radical and extreme Right in order to participate in the upcoming 1973 legislative election. Jean-Marie Le Pen became the president of the movement (Buzzi, 1991, pp. 34–35; Camus, 1989).

If Ordre Nouveau represented the militant, revolutionary wing of French nationalism, Le Pen represented its conservative populist wing, which had its origins in the populism of the Poujadist movement of the 1950s and the nationalist struggle of the early 1960s to maintain French control over Algeria. Le Pen could look back to a long career on the nationalist Right (see Vaughan, 1991, pp. 218–221). A law student in Paris between 1947 and 1953, Le Pen volunteered in 1953 as a parachutist in French Indo-China, without, however, seeing combat action. Back in France he met Pierre Poujade, the founder of the Union for the Defense of Merchants and Artisans (UDCA), which appealed to small shopkeepers and tradesmen threatened by economic modernization and urban growth with a platform that called for tax reform benefiting the self-employed. On its ticket Le Pen was elected in 1956 to the National Assembly. Between September 1956 and May 1957 Le Pen took leave from parliament to join his former regiment first in Suez, then in Algeria. Hardly back in Paris, Le Pen left the UDCA in 1957 after failing to "fashion it into a mass party of the extreme right which would defend the continuation of French rule in Algeria," but remained in parliament as an independent (Fysh and Wolfreys, 1992, p. 315). Soon after he founded the National Front for the Defense of French Algeria to fight de Gaulle's policy of decolonization. However, after the failure of the 1961 referendum in which the majority of the French approved Algerian self-determination and the failure of the attempted coup by members of the OAS, the nationalist opposition soon collapsed and Le Pen lost his parliamentary seat. In a last ditch attempt to unite the nationalist Right, Le Pen supported the candidacy of Jean-Louis Tixier-Vignancour, Le Pen's former law professor and a minister of information in the Vichy government, for the presidential election of 1965. It ended with a disappointing result of 5.2 percent of the vote, not least because of a scandal involving Le Pen's record company, which published a record with songs of the Third Reich that was charged with eulogizing war crimes.

It was not until the founding of the Front National that the radical and extreme Right sought to regain lost political terrain. However, the ideological contrasts between national revolutionaries and national populists proved too strong to allow for a durable alliance. Le Pen's personal ambitions exacerbated the tension between the members of the alliance. In response to the disappointing results of the 1973 legislative elections in which the Front obtained a mere 1.3 percent of the vote, the Ordre Nouveau group broke with Jean-Marie Le Pen. After the organization was dissolved in 1973, following a racist campaign against immigration, its members made a last effort to eliminate the Le Pen wing. When that proved a failure they founded a rival party with the identical name. It was not until a court order granted Le Pen's wing the right to call themselves Front National that the opposition wing organized a new party, the Parti des Forces Nouvelles (PFN). Under these conditions it was not much of a surprise that Le Pen's presidential bid in 1974 ended in disaster. Abandoned by his former Ordre Nouveau allies (who preferred to hire themselves out as security forces to V. Giscard d'Estaing's campaign) and other right-wing groups, Le Pen received a mere 0.76 percent of the first-round vote. The results of the legislative election of 1978 (0.3 percent) were even worse, and in the European election of 1979 the Front National even saw itself surpassed by its rival, the PFN. In 1981 the humiliation was complete: For the presidential election Le Pen failed to get the 500 signatures of elected officials necessary to put him on the ballot, and in the legislative election the National Front obtained not more than a minuscule 0.2 percent of the vote. The rapid decline of the Front National appeared to mark the end of both Le Pen and his party. Yet three years later the Front National had managed to increase its support to more than 11 percent of the vote in the European election of 1984, from roughly 25,000 to more than 2 million votes.

As Pascal Perrineau (1990, pp. 18–19) has shown, the rise of the National Front had begun before the 1984 election. As early as in the cantonal and municipal elections of 1982 and 1983, the party obtained significant results in several places (e.g., Dreux, Grande-Synthe). The most important result was the 11.3 percent obtained in 1983 in the 20th district of Paris (a largely working-class area with a large immigrant population), which translated into a seat on the district council. These results were a first expression of growing political and social discontent, which, however, in most cases got translated into votes for the traditional Right. The National Front did "not yet possess the political 'visibility' which would have allowed it to capitalize on its electoral potential" (Perrineau, 1990, p. 19). The party gained this visibility in the rerun of the municipal election in the fall of 1983 in Dreux, a dormitory town west of Paris, which was to become one of the party's strongholds in the 1980s (Gaspard, 1990; Bréchon and Mitra, 1992, pp. 71–74). Not only did the Front National gain 16.7 of the vote, but the center-right list composed of RPR and UDF chose to conclude an alliance with the Front National in order to defeat the Left in the second round. In compensation for the victorious showing for this alliance, the Front National received a number of seats on the city council, recognition from the established parties, and, most importantly, national publicity (Fysh and Wolfreys, 1992, p. 312).

The national breakthrough occurred one year later, in the European election of 1984 (see Bréchon, 1993). With 11 percent of the vote, the Front National became the fourth largest party in France. These results were largely confirmed in the cantonal election of 1985, where the party gained 8.8 percent of the vote and in the legislative elections of 1986. With almost 10 percent of the vote, the Front National surpassed the Communist Party to become the third party in France. Thanks to the proportional system of representation, introduced by the Socialists to limit the gains of the center-right, the Front National was able to elect 35 deputies to the National Assembly. For the first time since the success of the poujadists in the 1950s, the French far Right had thus gained parliamentary representation and with it a public tribune for its views.

The Front National had its greatest success in the presidential election of 1988. Particularly since Le Pen had been dismissed before the elections as a minor candidate, the fact that he came close to the results obtained by his competitors of the center-right with 14.4 percent of the vote, Chirac (19.9 percent) and Barre (16.5 percent), the leader of the Front National emerged from the first round of the election as the clear winner. Even if in the legislative election held at the same time the party fell far short of Le Pen's support, its result (9.9 percent of the vote) was only marginally below the one obtained in 1988. What was more important, however, was that the party succeeded in a number of cases to force the center-right alliance of RPR and UDF (called URC) to seek an alliance with its candidates for the second turn (by then the center-right had changed the electoral system back to a majoritarian system) or even to persuade a URC candidate to desist in favor of a Front National candidate (Bréchon, 1993, p. 43).

The results of the legislative elections indicated that its support had stabilized. This was confirmed in the municipal and European elections of 1989. Although the party obtained only 2.5 percent of the vote in the municipal elections, this was largely due to the fact that the party did not run in all communes. In those where it did run it received a considerably higher percentage than the national average. This was confirmed in the European election, in which the Front National obtained 11.7 percent of the vote, roughly a half percentage point more than in 1984 (Höhne, 1990, p. 82).

In 1989, two by-elections in Dreux and Marseilles suggested that the Front National was on the verge of a new electoral breakthrough. Although both cities are strongholds of the Front National (Loch, 1991), its shares of the vote in the first round (42.5 percent in Dreux, 33 percent in Marseilles) were unprecedented. In both instances the Front National candidates were women. Despite the fact that in the second round all political forces united in opposition to the Front National candidates, they could not prevent Marie-France Stirbois (whose husband had been the Front National's general secretary until his death in a car accident in November 1988) from gaining an absolute majority of 61.3 percent of the vote in Dreux, while they managed to barely defeat Marie-Claude Rousselin in Marseilles (she received 47.2 percent of the vote) (Bréchon, 1993, p. 52).

However, those who thought that these results were the beginning of a "new electoral trend in favor of the extreme right" (Bréchon and Mitra, 1992, p. 65) soon had to revise their expectations. It rather appeared that Dreux and Marseilles were exceptions, largely due to the particular circumstances of the two cities. This became clear in the regional and cantonal elections of 1992. With almost 14 percent of the vote in the regional and roughly 12 percent in the cantonal elections the party did considerably better than in the legislative elections, but remained substantially below its own expectations. In particular, the party failed to conquer a majority in its stronghold in the south, the region Provence-Alpes-Côte-d'Azur while remaining behind its own targets in the departments of Alpes maritimes and Bouches-du-Rhône (Mayer, 1992, pp. 4–5). Similar observations applied to the legislative election of 1993. The Front National improved its result of the legislative election of 1988 and gained the third position behind the victorious UPF alliance of RPR and UDF and the collapsing Socialists but ahead of both the Communists and the united Green list, even if it fell slightly short of its showing in the regional election of 1992. Most important of all, however, was the fact that due to the electoral system, the party failed to gain a visible presence in the National Assembly. Although a few of its candidates came very close to winning in the second turn (most notably in Dreux, Marignane, and Nice IV-VII, where FN candidates won 49.86, 49.52, and 48.42 percent of the vote), the party failed to elect even a single deputy to the National Assembly (Le Pen himself only received 42.06 percent of the vote in his district in Nice). Thus, despite having established itself as a permanent feature of the party system, the Front National continued to remain banished and confined to the margins of French politics. This was confirmed in the cantonal election of spring 1994. Although the party did better than was expected, it attained less than 10 percent of the vote and thus fell considerably below previous results.[7]

GERMANY: THE REPUBLIKANER

Compared to the dynamic rise of both Lega Nord and FPÖ the political evolution of the German Republikaner has been characterized by a number of setbacks, which more than once threatened to destroy the party. The Republikaner were founded in 1983 by Franz Schönhuber together with disgruntled members of the Bavarian Christian Social Union (CSU). The latter left the CSU after the Bavarian Minster-President and powerful CSU chairman, Franz-Josef Strauss, had secured the East German regime, until then the party's number one enemy, a billion mark loan (Betz, 1990a, p. 3). Schönhuber's motives were personal rather than political. For a number of years he had hosted a popular Bavarian television show, which gave ordinary citizens an opportunity to confront Bavarian politicians with their grievances. Despite excellent contacts with the CSU, Schönhuber was dismissed by the Bavarian broadcasting service after publishing his memoirs. In this book he recounted his days as a member of the Waffen-SS during World War II in a way which presented the Nazi period, and particularly the Waffen-SS, in a rather favorable light (Betz, 1990, p. 50).

The party scored only a modest three percent of the vote in the Bavarian state elections in 1986. However, compensation for the election campaign amounting to roughly 1.32 million deutschmarks allowed the party to organize almost throughout West Germany. This laid the foundation for the party's success in the 1989 state election in West Berlin where it scored 7.5 percent and gained immediate media attention. This was followed by 7.1 percent in the European elections and the expectation that the Republikaner might be on their way to become the fifth party to enter the German Bundestag (Roth, 1989; Pappi, 1990).

However, growing disenchantment among its supporters with the party's call to welcome German resettlers from Eastern Europe and the Soviet Union (to which the large majority were opposed) and above all Schönhuber's failure to respond quickly to the acceleration of events following the fall of the Wall, lost him much political support (Betz, 1990, pp. 54-55). Schönhuber's strategy to appeal to the fears of the expellees' organizations that the German government might recognize Poland's western borders remained largely unsuccessful. To make things worse, the Republikaner were prevented from participating in the first free elections to the East German Volkskammer in March 1990.

In the wake of these negative trends the party was shaken by violent internal conflicts that led a number of leading members to abandon the party (see Assheuer and Sarkowicz, 1992, pp. 41–54). Others were expelled. One of the main reasons behind these conflicts was Schönhuber's attempt to improve the party's image by drawing a clear line between the Republikaner and right-wing extremists, many of whom had joined the party during its rise to political prominence. The most prominent among them was Harald Neubauer, Schönhuber's designated heir and powerful head of the Bavarian party organization. Initially, it appeared as if Schönhuber's strategy would end in personal disaster. In early 1990, the anti-Schönhuber faction in the party presidium had gained enough strength to force Schönhuber to resign as party chairman and even threatened him with expulsion from the party. However, only a few weeks after his involuntary resignation, Schönhuber reemerged at a hastily convened party congress and regained his position as chairman. After the congress Schönhuber managed not only to have his opponents expelled, but also to fill the top of the party leadership with his followers.

Although Schönhuber had won the internal power struggle, his and his party's image had been severely tarnished. The result was a rapid decline in the polls. Thus the Republikaner failed, albeit only by a tenth of a percentage point, to enter the Bavarian Landtag in October 1990 and remained with 2.1 percent in the first all-German elections in December of the same year, far behind their own expectations. It appeared as if the Republikaner had fallen as rapidly back into politically obscurity as they had emerged from it in 1989 (Roth, 1990).

However, these expectations proved premature. Schönhuber's tenacity paid out: in the 1992 election in the important state of Baden-Württemberg the Republikaner received more than 12 percent of the vote, which made them the third largest party in one of Germany's most affluent states. The local elections in Berlin later that year and the local elections in Hesse in the spring of 1993 seemed to indicate that the tide had turned in Schönhuber's favor (Roth, 1993). In both elections the Republikaner received more than 8 percent of the vote. With that the Republikaner not only contributed considerably to the considerable losses of the two major parties, but also secured their position as the major party on the far right of the German party spectrum. However, state elections in Hamburg in September 1993 and in Lower Saxony in March 1994 showed that the party had reached its limits. Although the Republikaner made substantial gains in both states, they failed to overcome the 5 percent hurdle, thus leaving voters and pundits alike with the impression that the party had run out of steam.

FLANDERS: THE VLAAMS BLOK

The year 1991 also witnessed the biggest political success to date of the Belgian Vlaams Blok. The Vlaams Blok was founded in 1978 by two Flemish nationalist activists—Karel Dillen, a journalist, and Lode Claes, the leader of a Flemish nationalist splinter party—and former members of the Flemish regionalist party Volksunie (VU). What united them was their rejection of the Egmont Pact, the first step toward the transformation of Belgium into a federal state. In the early 1970s the confrontation between Flemings and Walloons had threatened to split the country. In an attempt to meet this threat, the major parties represent-ing the two linguistic communities decided on various reforms in May 1977 in the Egmont Pact. "The fact that as a member of the four-party coalition government of the time the VU was a party to this pact, was one impetus from which the VB was able to grow, since the Egmont Pact was far from universally popular, especially in Flanders, and indeed the issue split the VU, losing it both activists and voters to the benefit of the emerging VB" (Husbands, 1992, p. 135). Accusing the Volksunie of having betrayed the nationalist aspirations of the Flemish population, Dillen and his fellow Flemish regionalists decided to launch a genuine Flemish nationalist party (Fritzmaurice, 1992, pp. 304–305).

Although contesting parliamentary elections since 1978, the political success of the Vlaams Blok remained rather limited. In the 1978, 1981, 1985, and 1987 elections the party never received more than 2 percent of the vote. Its support came largely from the nationalist right wing of the Volksunie and from sympathizers of the Vlaamse Militantenorde (VMO), a semiclandestine circle of militants nostalgic for the days of Flemish collaboration with the Germans, which was formally banned as a private militia in 1983 (Vandermotten and Vanlaer, 1991, p. 5). It was not until 1988 that the Vlaams Blok emerged as a major political force in the Flemish part of Belgium.

This was largely due to its spectacular growth in Antwerp, Flanders' largest city, where the party had achieved its first local success in 1982 when it elected two of its members to the city council (see Husbands, 1992, p. 136). The next successes came in 1985, when it repeated its result of 1982 and in 1987, when it elected four councillors to the Antwerp provincial council. The breakthrough came in the 1988 municipal elections. The party gained 17.7 percent of the vote and elected ten members to the city council. This was followed by 20.8 percent in the 1989 European election. With regard to the whole of Flanders the Vlaams Blok almost tripled its support compared to 1984, attaining 6.6 percent of the vote (see Swyngedouw, 1991). This was enough to return Karel Dillen to the European Parliament where he joined the Technical Group of the European Right with the French Front National and the German Republikaner.

The party's spectacular rise in the latter part of the 1980s was largely due to the growing influence of member Filip Dewinter, an ardent admirer of Jean-Marie Le Pen. In 1987, at the age of 24 Dewinter became the youngest deputy in Belgian history.[8] An active member in a number of right-wing extremist organizations, he took on responsibility for party organization. Dewinter managed to rejuvenate the party leadership while at the same time moving its political program away from Flemish regionalist nationalism toward a xenopho-bic nationalist populism. With Dewinter leading the electoral campaign the Vlaams Blok emerged as the undisputed winner of the 1991 parliamentary election. With 6.6 percent of the overall vote, and 10.3 percent in Flanders, the party surpassed the Volksunie as the most significant representative of Flemish nationalist interests and was largely responsible for the heavy losses of the established political parties (Mabille, Lentzen, and Blaise, 1991). As had been the case in previous elections, the party was particularly successful in Antwerp, where it gained 25.1 percent to become the city's largest party. But unlike earlier elections, it also made significant inroads in other parts of Flanders. In Ghent it received 10 percent of the vote, in Louvain 5.6, and in Bruges 5 percent (Swyngedouw, 1992, p. 63).

SWITZERLAND: AUTOPARTEI AND TESSIN LEAGUE

The year 1991 was also a particularly good one for the Swiss Automobile party. The Automobile party was founded in February 1985 by Michael Dreher, a 41-year-old economic consultant and lawyer from Küsnacht, together with former members of the two major secular Swiss middle class parties, the FDP and the SVP (see Schiesser, 1992). Michael Dreher was hardly unknown to the Swiss political scene. In the early 1980s he founded a citizen action group that rode regular attacks in the media against too much state, too many and too high taxes, and especially against the supporters of measures that put restrictions on motorized traffic. Hardly surprising, Dreher conceived of the Automobile party primarily as a pressure group representing "the interests of motorized consumers" against Red-Green attempts to use the environment as a major means for imposing more and more limits on the freedom of Swiss citizens. Michael Dreher expressed the party's attitude toward environmentalists and Greens most drastically when he allegedly said at a formal reception of the Swiss Academy of the Humanities that Greens should be nailed to the wall and then torched with flamethrowers.[9]

The party's vehement and vocal hostility toward the established parties, the Greens, and the state bureaucracy did not deter a growing number of voters to support the party. In fact, with its radical populist strategy the party managed to surpass the established national-conservative National Action for the People and the Fatherland (NA) as well as the small traditional liberal party. The first success came in the national elections of 1987. The party received 2.6 percent of the vote, which was enough to elect two of its members to the Swiss assembly. The party's relatively good showing was even more impressive if one takes into consideration that it ran only in 10 out of 25 electoral districts. In 5 of these districts (Schwyz, Solothurn, St. Gallen, Aargau, and Thurgau) the party managed to reach or even surpass the critical 5 percent mark.

Following this first success, the party gained political strength in a number of cantonal and municipal elections in the German part of Switzerland. Between 1987 and 1991, the party altogether conquered 47 seats in cantonal parliaments, including 10 in Thurgau and 8 in Schaffhausen. By 1991 the party was thus well prepared for the crucial national elections. Its results went beyond the party's most optimistic expectations. With 5.1 percent the party emerged as one of the few clear winners of the election, quadrupling the number of its seats from 2 to 8, and in the process inflicting serious damage on the established parties. As in 1987, the party only ran in a limited number of electoral districts. In four of these districts (Aargau, Appenzell Ausser-Rhoden, St. Gallen, and Schaffhausen) it gained more than 10 percent of the vote. These electoral advances were, at least in part, a result of the fact that by the late 1980s, the party had made great efforts to shed its single-issue image and appeal to a broader range of concerns and resentments.

The other winner of the election was the Lega dei ticinesi. The Lega was founded in early 1991 by Giuliano Bignasca, a construction entrepreneur, and Flavio Maspoli, editor of the Lega weekly newspaper *Mattino della domenica,* which the party distributed free of charge to households in the Italian-speaking canton Tessin. Like the Automobilists, the Lega saw itself as a representative of the interests of the common people against environmentalists, the state, and the political establishment. Although modeled after the Italian leagues, the party had few contacts with its Italian counterparts. This lack of contacts reflected, at least on the part of the Swiss Lega's leadership, a hardly concealed disdain for the Italians living across the border.[10] The Lega gained its first success in the 1991 cantonal elections, in which it received 14 percent of the vote. The breakthrough came in the national elections. With 23.6 percent of the vote and two seats in parliament the Lega emerged as the third largest party in the Tessin. Flavio Maspoli received more personal votes than any other candidate running in the election.

EXPLAINING RIGHT-WING RADICALISM

Right-wing radical or extremist movements and parties are nothing new to postwar West European democracies. The Poujadist movement in France in the 1950s, the regional successes of the German National Democratic Party (NPD) in the 1960s, the significant rise of electoral support for the Italian Social Movement (MSI), as well as the (arguably radical right-wing) Danish and Norwegian Progress parties in the 1970s appear to support the suggestion that the potential for right-wing radicalism exists in all industrial societies and should be seen as a " 'normal' pathological condition" of modern democracies (Scheuch and Klingemann, 1967). However, these previous outbreaks of that pathology were sporadic instances, largely confined to individual countries. By contrast, the current wave of radical right-wing populist movements and parties represents a transnational phenomenon whose rise to political success has occurred contemporaneously and shares common traits.

This is particularly striking if we put the rise of right-wing radicalism in Western Europe in a broader context. Comparable movements and parties have achieved noteworthy political success in the United States, ranging from the nationalist populism of Pat Buchanan to the antiestablishment populism of Ross Perot. In India it has occurred in the form of the Bharatiya Janata Party's blend of free-market liberalism and (anti-Muslim) Hindu fundamentalism, and in Canada in the form of Preston Manning's Reform Party, the advocate of western Canada's vision of a new homogeneous Canada against the eastern and particularly francophone establishment and its vision of a multicultural society. We might even include the national populist rumblings of Vladimir Zhirinovsky's Liberal Democratic Party in Russia in this list, even if his threats of imperial reconquest and nuclear destruction clearly go beyond the ideological boundaries of radical right-wing populism elsewhere. This suggests that the wave of contemporary radical right-wing populism, unlike other right-wing radical or extremist movements in the postwar period, is a response to developments shared by all or at least most Western-style democracies. Seen from this perspective, the rise of the radical populist Right appears to share more similarities with the rise of fascism in the interwar period than with the sporadic outbreak of right-wing radicalism in the postwar period.

One of the central arguments in the literature on fascism was that fascism, and by extension all radical right-wing movements similar to fascism, represented a "revolt against modernity." The most influential example has been Seymour M. Lipset's well-known interpretation of fascism as an expression of middle-class extremism. For Lipset both fascism and postwar right-wing radicalism represented extreme responses of a middle class, which saw its social position and status, if not very existence, threatened by the process of modernization. In Lipset's view (Lipset, 1981, p. 489) fascist movements appealed to

> segments of the middle class displaced or threatened by the emergence of centralized, large-scale industry and the growing power and status of organized labor. Oppressed by developments fundamental to modern society, small entrepreneurs, small farm owners, and other insecure members of the middle strata were particularly prone to mobilization by fascist movements opposing both big labor and big capital. These developments represented in part a revolt against modernity.

In this interpretation, fascism was successful because it managed to exploit the middle class's immediate fears evoked by the economic crisis: the petty bourgeoisie's subjective fears of downward social mobility, of falling into the ranks of the proletariat, and the middle class's fear as a whole of the threat of a proletarian, socialist revolution. Fascist movements managed to appeal to the survival instinct of a class that the accelerated pace of industrialization, rationalization, and capitalist modernization in the early part of the twentieth century objectively threatened with extinction. Wolfgang Sauer put it perhaps most succinctly when he wrote that fascism was the "revolt of those who lost—directly or indirectly, temporarily or permanently—by industrialization. Fascism is the revolt of the déclassés" (Sauer, 1967, p. 417).

The social pressures on the middle class created by the process of modernization have also been held responsible for the rise and success of right-wing radical or extremist movements and parties in the postwar period. Particularly in the French context, observers have pointed to the social tensions created by the French state's attempts in the postwar period to modernize the country. This opened up opportunities for the radical Right and explains the spectacular success of middle class protest movements like the poujadists in the 1950s. In this view, the poujadists' success stemmed largely from the clash between two irreconcilable visions: Here a modern vision of a "dynamic France" advanced by civil servants "anxious to rationalize the economy" and by the public "who found cheaper goods in supermarkets and discount stores" (Blondel, 1974, p.78); there the desperate attempt on the part of merchants, artisans, shopkeepers, and the owners of small firms and farms to stop the industrialization and modernization of France and thus to avoid the fate of collective "extermination or suicide" (Eatwell, 1982, p. 70).

The rapid collapse of radical right-wing movements and parties in the postwar period lends some support to the argument that these parties were not much more than short-lived vehicles of protest. However, the middle-class protest thesis is less persuasive in explaining the rise of fascism. Recent studies by Thomas Childers and Jürgen Falter on the Nazi vote suggest that the social basis of the Hitler movement was considerably broader and more flexible than the middle-class thesis would suggest. This is not to say that these studies dismiss the old middle class's central role in the NSDAP's rise to political prominence in the Weimar Republic. Undoubtedly, small farmers, shopkeepers, and independent artisans were the "most stable and consistent components of the National Socialist constituency between 1924 and 1932" (Childers, 1983, p. 64). This supports the notion that the Nazis appealed most successfully to those groups among whom "the fear of social and economic displacement associated with the emergence of modern industrial society was most pronounced" and where the Nazis' "corporatist, anti-Marxist, and anticapitalist slogans struck the most responsive chord." These were the groups most likely to see themselves as the losers of modernization. Rather than expressing a short-term response to immediate economic difficulties, their support for the Nazis therefore was most likely to express "a congenital dissatisfaction with long-term trends in German economic and social life" (Childers, 1983, p. 264).

Further support for this interpretation comes from the fact that the Nazis' message found least resonance among the group whose fortunes depended most immediately on the modernization of society, the industrial working class (see Childers, 1976, p. 29). This is particularly striking with regard to the unemployed. Although radicalized and motivated to support extremist solutions, they failed in large parts to vote for the Nazis. In fact, "above-average unemployment rates not only tended to lower the NSDAP vote but also slowed down, on average, its stupendous growth in the July 1932 and March 1933 elections" (Falter, 1986, p. 202). If radicalized unemployed workers voted for a party at all, they voted for the Communists, the party that promoted a radically different, but thoroughly modern path of socioeconomic development.

If there is thus much evidence to support the validity of the middle class thesis, it fails, however, to capture the full complexity of the Nazi vote. As Thomas Childers and others have shown, besides appealing to lower middle-class voters the Nazis attracted a substantial number of voters from other social groups. Most significant among them were nonunionized workers without special skills and employed in handicrafts and small-scale manufacturing, new middle class voters, and here particularly civil servants and upper middle class university students, a substantial number of pensioners, and—particularly in the final elections of the Weimar period—a growing number of female voters. Based on these findings, one of the most prominent students of electoral behavior in the Weimar period concludes that as long as the NSDAP vote was relatively small, the party represented a "socially indistinct splinter group. When its electorate increased it eventually gained a somewhat more distinct social profile without, however, becoming the class-based movement portrayed so vividly by the middle-class hypothesis" (Falter, 1990, p. 71).

Rather, the NSDAP represented "the first genuine party of mass integration in German history" (Childers, 1983, p. 262). While evoking a vague vision of an elusive *Volksgemeinschaft*, the party offered concrete programs designed to respond to the specific demands of particular groups, and thus sought to transcend the traditional cleavages that informed German electoral politics (Falter, 1988, p. 496). Until 1928, the Nazis thus maintained a dual electoral strategy, which combined a social-revolutionary appeal to the anticapitalist sentiments of working-class voters with vehement assaults on Marxism and particularly Bolshevism designed to respond to middle-class anxieties.

By 1928, however, the party leadership recognized that its urban, working-class oriented strategy had largely failed. In response, it decided to shift attention to the rural electorate and the urban middle class. With this the leadership sought to attract those middle-class segments, which, "alienated by the traumas of the inflation and stabilization period," had become disenchanted with the established political parties and turned to various middle-class interest parties. The Nazis thus sought to gain from the "fundamental breakdown of voter identification with the traditional parties of the bourgeois center and right" (Childers, 1983, p. 127).

This strategic shift was reflected in a programmatic shift. Gradually intensifying its assault on Marxism, the party affirmed its general support of private property, sharpened its attacks on department stores and consumer cooperatives, and stepped up its efforts to penetrate existing middle-class organizations while organizing occupational associations of its own (Childers, 1983, p. 128). The middle-class bias associated with the Nazis was thus as much the result of strategic and programmatic choice as it was a reflection of socioeconomic developments. With it the party turned into a movement of middle-class protest without, however, completely abandoning its determination to become a party of mass integration.

The reinterpretation of the Nazi vote by Childers and Falter adds much to our understanding of the conditions under which radical right-wing parties are most likely to succeed. Like Lipset and others before them, they point to the crucial importance of social modernization in any explanation of the rise of radical right-wing movements and parties. In addition, their studies point to two factors neglected by those who interpret right-wing radicalism narrowly in terms of a middle-class protest. In Childers's and Falter's reinterpretation of the Nazi vote, the Nazis owed much of their success to two factors: on the one hand, a general breakdown of voter loyalties (or, in more recent parlance, a process of dealignment) on the center-right of the political spectrum; and on the other hand, an electoral and programmatic strategy on the part of the Nazis designed to mobilize a broad range of disenchanted and politically homeless voters.

The breakdown of voter loyalties was largely the result of the dramatic socioeconomic and sociocultural transformation of the 1920s, symbolized perhaps most vividly at home by the rise of organized labor, abroad by the rise of American capitalism. It is within this context that the rise of the Nazis gains its importance. By pursuing a catch-all strategy that transcended the established class cleavage lines, the Nazis represented a fundamentally new and thoroughly modern type of party, which radically departed from the traditional cleavage-based parties.

The interpretation of the rise and success of radical right-wing populist parties proposed in this book closely follows this model. The central argument guiding the analysis is that the political changes reflected in the emergence of the radical populist Right are largely a consequence of a profound transformation of the socioeconomic and sociocultural structure of advanced Western European democracies. In the literature this transformation is usually characterized as a shift from industrial to postindustrial capitalism. Although the notion of postindustrial capitalism fails to capture the full extent of global changes, it is useful enough to distinguish the contemporary period from the previous one.

POSTINDUSTRIAL CAPITALISM AND
SOCIAL FRAGMENTATION

During the last two decades advanced Western societies have been confronted by a fundamental restructuring of their economies, dramatic changes in their social structure and value system, and a major transformation of their culture. This has been a result of two revolutions. One is the final breakthrough of capitalism on a world-wide scale. With the collapse of Soviet-style state socialism, market capitalism has emerged as the only form to organize economic relations (Albert, 1993). Economic liberalization in Latin America and India, and the course of the Chinese economy are among the most vivid signs of the global triumph of capitalism. The second revolution has been the advent of a global economy, where capital and labor, production and markets, information and technology are organized across national boundaries. In the new economy, competition "is played out globally, not only by the multinational corporations, but also by small and medium-size enterprises that connect directly or indirectly to the world market through their linkages in the networks that relate them to larger firms" (Castells, 1993, p. 19). As a result, individual states and governments have seen their capacity to control national economies severely reduced (Scharpf, 1993).

The globalization of markets has been advanced and promoted by the rapid spread and diffusion of new information technologies. Computerized knowledge has quickly become the principal new force of production, changing the way knowledge is acquired, stored, transmitted, and exploited. This has had a dramatic effect on the composition of the work force of most advanced capitalist societies, reducing the number of factory workers while increasing the proportion of technical, managerial, and professional workers (Reich, 1992). What Daniel Bell predicted some 20 years ago appears finally to have come true: the majority of advanced industrial countries have become postindustrial societies characterized by a shift from the industrial to the service and information sectors, a shift from mass production to flexible specialization (Piore and Sabel,

1984), and from mass consumption to specialized consumption (Harvey, 1989; Featherstone, 1991).

These developments have allowed for new flexibility with respect to products, markets, and consumption patterns. They have created new sectors of production and innovative ways of providing financial services and greatly intensified rates of technological and organization innovation. The result has been a departure from the production of large-batch, standardized, disposable, mass-marketed and mass-consumed goods. In their stead the regime of flexible specialization has introduced products that distinguish themselves by their higher levels of quality, customization, and service content.

These changes in the macrostructure of modern Western economies have had a profound impact on the work force. Generally they have entailed a bifurcation of the labor market into core and periphery sectors, into highly demanding and attractive jobs and skill-poor and undesirable "junk-jobs" (Esping-Andersen, 1990, p. 204). The core encompasses flexible and, if necessary, geographically mobile employees aged 30 to 50 with formal professional education. They enjoy full-time, permanent positions with job security, increasingly "flexible, collegial forms of work organization in the typical form of autonomous project teams," relatively generous benefit packages, and good promotion prospects. Opposed to them is a marginalized periphery encompassing both full and part-time labor whose work "remains routinized, subject to control and direction by professional 'superiors', poorly rewarded, and insecure" (Cook, Pakulski, and Waters, 1992, p. 176). Possessing skills abundantly available on the market they contribute largely to the reserve army of the chronically under- and unemployed who are shut out of the core sectors of the economy (Room, Lawson, and Laczko, 1989, p. 172). These developments are particularly pronounced in the service sector. Its expansion has led to a sizeable occupational segment of "symbolic specialists," defined as professionals with higher levels of education in human- or culture-oriented organizations (Betz, 1992). Opposed to them are the swelling ranks of those performing menial and unqualified "Mcjobs" (Paci, 1992, p. 294; Howe and Strauss, 1993, pp. 74–75).

The economic transformation of advanced Western democracies is closely intertwined with developments in its social and cultural sphere. As Ulrich Beck has argued, high standard of living and high levels of social security have led to the dissipation of traditional class distinctions and subcultural class identities while setting in motion "processes for the 'diversification' and 'individualization' of lifestyles and ways of life" (Beck, 1987, p. 341). This is particularly pronounced with regard to education. In postindustrial society the higher levels and longer duration of education have increasingly come to be seen as the prime road to social mobility. Expanded educational oppotunities have accentuated the importance of individual effort and merit. "For it is after all only possible to pass through a formal education by *individually* succeeding by way of assignments, examinations, and tests. Formal education in schools and universities, in turn, provides individual credentials leading to individualized career opportunities on the labor market" (Beck, 1987, p. 344).

However, the spread of formal education has heightened the sense that qualifications are interchangeable, thus forcing individuals to advertise the individuality and uniqueness of their accomplishments. Self-promotion and the ability of self-discovery and existence design have become important preconditions for success in the postindustrial age. What enhances these tendencies is the rapid advance of free markets following the collapse of Soviet-style, centrally controlled economies. As Herbert Kitschelt has pointed out, markets "enable individuals to act on self-regarding preferences, because they stimulate the self-attribution of success and failure" (Kitschelt, 1993, p. 302). Markets and education thus form complementary bases for the emergence of new social groups, which share common experiences shaped by competition and the drive for self-promotion.

As a result of these developments, established subcultures, milieus, and institutions, which traditionally provided and sustained collective identities, are getting eroded and/or are being destroyed. Fixed identities are giving way to a "flux of contextualized identities," related to gender, ethnicity, sexual preference, and life-style. They find their reflection in the ambiguous imagery created by postmodern culture (Hutcheon, 1988). Its central features are the collapse of high into mass culture, advertising, and fashion, the emergence of various taste cultures, and the individualization of choice and of life-style. By hyping up the new, fleeting, and contingent in modern life, rather than the more solid values of the past, and by promoting individuality in choice and life-style, culture both fosters and reproduces the fragmentation of the economic and social spaces of postindustrial consumer society (Schulze, 1993; Vester, 1993).

THE INDIVIDUALIZATION OF RISKS

The transition from industrial to postindustrial capitalism is thus in large part characterized by a process of dissolution, fragmentation, and differentiation, which has its roots in a general acceleration of individualization processes. These create new challenges to the individual's capability to adapt to rapidly changing circumstances. This, in turn, puts a premium on cultural capital, individual entrepreneurship, and flexibility (Beck, 1987, p. 342). Individuals who possess these characteristics can be expected to be among the winners of postindustrial modernity. However, if the dominant feature of postindustrial society lies with an individualization of choices, life styles, and life chances, its flip side is a growing tendency toward the individualization of risks (Beck, 1987, p. 351). Whereas much of the literature on postindustrial and consumer society focuses on the glitzy world of the global shopping mall created by the emergence of new growth sectors, consumption patterns, and life styles (Featherstone, 1991), this is only part of the story. Though the emergence of postindustrial society has led to a significant expansion of jobs in human- and consumer-oriented services, it has also generated a seemingly permanent high level of structural mass unemployment, increasing underemployment, and a widening gray area between the registered and unregistered unemployed. Equally significant consequences are the rapid obsolescence of skills, continuous pressure on the individual to retrain and reskill, and slow and modest gains in real wages. Although the images of "high-tech elites ruling a jobless nation" or of "a world without jobs" appear exaggerated, they do point to real developments and trends common to all advanced capitalist societies (Reich, 1992).[11]

A number of studies suggest that unemployment affects particular social groups characterized by age, gender, education, and health status (see Room, Lawson, and Laczko, 1989). One case in point is youth unemployment. In 1990, roughly 16 percent of the under-25-year-olds in the European Communities were unemployed. Although this represented a considerable decline compared to the early and mid-1980s (in 1987 it was 21 percent), it was still considerably higher than adult unemployment rates. Thus "the burden of unemployment has been disproportionately heavy on the young" (OECD, 1989, p. 31). However, these data obscure the fact that youth unemployment has a considerable gender bias. In 1990, for instance, the unemployment rate among young males in the EC was 14 percent, but more than 18 percent for young women. Yet not only young women are at a considerable disadvantage compared to their male counterparts. Studies suggest that women have generally been considerably more exposed to unemployment than men, particularly if they are in their fifties and hold no formal degree (Tresmontant, 1991, pp. 47–48).

It is among those without finished education and professional training that unemployment is expected to grow as a result of diminishing demand for un- and semiskilled labor, especially in industry and offices. Unemployment statistics show that already in the 1980s, there was a close relationship between professional qualification and the likelihood of unemployment. In Germany, for example, in 1987 the proportion of unemployed unskilled labor was twice as high (18 percent) as that of skilled workers; that of skilled workers was roughly twice as high as that of persons with technical or master craftsmen certificates, which in turn was roughly twice as high as that of persons with university or polytechnical degrees (Wilke, 1990, p. 46). Similar trends have been found in France and Italy (Lacroix, 1990, p. 46; Caracosta, Fleurbaey, Leroy, 1991, p. 80). In Italy, in 1987, more than 75 percent of the unemployed were estimated to have at the most completed eight years of education, 45 percent not even those grades (Frey, 1988, p.38).

The demands of postindustrial society can only exacerbate these trends. Projections on the German labor market estimate that, compared to 1987, by the year 2010 the number of unskilled labor will have diminished by more than 2.2 million persons. At the same time the number of university trained personnel will have increased by roughly the same amount (Franke and Buttler, 1991, p. 120). During the next two decades the proportion of low-skill jobs is expected to decline to roughly 18 percent of the German labor force (in 1985 it was 27 percent). Highest qualified jobs (in organization and management, research and development, consulting and teaching, etc.) will increase to almost 40 percent (compared to 28 percent in 1985) (Stooß and Weidig, 1990, p.45).

These figures suggest that the labor market increasingly discriminates against and marginalizes a number of groups that have distinct characteristics. One typical example is the long-term unemployed. According to OECD data, in 1986 roughly one out of three unemployed West Europeans had been out of work more than 12 months (OECD, 1989, p. 32). By the early 1990s the situation had further deteriorated. In Belgium, for example, in 1991, 41 percent of the unemployed were out of work for more than two years, 63 percent for more than one year (Swyngedouw, 1992, p. 67). Long-term unemployment creates an especially serious problem not only because of the economic, social, and psychological repercussions it has on the individual. Long-term unemployment also tends to diminish considerably the chances for reinsertion into the active work force (Tresmontant, 1991, p. 43). The consequences can be expected to be particularly dramatic when the long-term unemployed eventually reach retirement age: "Their interrupted work and contribution records are likely to mean that the unemployment which separated them from the bulk of the working population during their working lives will during the coming decades turn them into the 'new poor' of the elderly population" (Room, Lawson, and Laczko, 1989, p. 173).

However, not all social groups are equally likely to be affected by long-term unemployment. The likelihood of reinsertion into the active work force diminishes considerably for several problem groups. Among them are persons without finished education and professional training, those in their fifties or older, those with health problems, and women 50 or older regardless of their education or training. In 1990 more than 80 percent of the long-term unemployed in Germany had at least one of these "risk factors." In addition, the likelihood of reinsertion decreases particularly for those groups with more than one risk factor. Of those German unemployed in 1990 who had more than one risk factor, 60 percent were unemployed for more than 12 months (Hof, 1991, p. 23, also Tresmontant, 1991, p. 48).

The unemployment trends are only one indication that a growing segment of the population of advanced postindustrial societies is confronted with deteriorating prospects with regard to their life chances. This supports the expectation that the "technological elimination of unskilled and semiskilled jobs means that a great many people will be caught in a world of despair, lacking marketable skills or hope for the future" (Hage and Powers, 1992, p. 41). This development has given rise to different sociological and/or ideological concepts such as "new poverty," "two-thirds-society," "dual society,' "two-speed society," or "underclass," which have emerged in almost all advanced postindustrial societies during the past decade, and which, despite their often polemical nature, capture significant aspects of the reality of advanced Western societies (see, for instance, Natter and Riedlsperger, 1988; Room and Henningsen, 1990). German statistics, for instance, show for the 1980s a consistent level of poverty around 10 percent. More than one fifth of the population lived between 1984 and 1991 at least once in conditions of poverty (Habich and Krause, 1992, p. 482; Krause, 1992, p. 9).

Among the groups that find themselves relegated to the bottom of Western Europe's emerging two-speed societies are, besides the long-term unemployed, young people without finished formal education, single-parent households (particularly if headed by a woman), immigrants and refugees and their families, old people living on minimal pensions, and the homeless (Room and Henningsen, 1990). In 1991, German statistics showed that 16.5 percent of those unemployed (compared to 3.3 percent of those employed), 9.8 percent of those without a degree (compared to 2 percent with a university entrance degree), and 26.2 percent of all single-parent households (compared to 2.3 percent of two-person households) were poor (Krause, 1992).

These figures suggest that the economic restructuring and social and cultural individualization processes characteristic of the current transition from modern industrial to postindustrial capitalism have left a sizeable portion of the population of advanced Western democracies in an increasingly precarious situation. Unable to cope with the acceleration of economic, social, and cultural modernization, these people are its most prominent victims. Those who have fallen into the underclass are threatened to "become superfluous and useless" for society. In Ralf Dahrendorf's words, they are "those whom the full citizens of society do not need" (cited in Schmitter Heisler, 1991, p. 460) because they do not have the skills necessary for a modern economy or because they do not fit otherwise into an increasingly ruthless postindustrial elbow society. Forming a rather heterogeneous group they are unlikely to organize themselves in order to be able to exert collective political pressure.

The emergence and growth of an underclass in most advanced societies show perhaps most convincingly that the transition from industrial capitalism to postindustrial capitalism has not only created profound social tensions, but has left society deeply split. The information revolution made possible by the rapid diffusion of new technologies has opened new venues for individual creativity and entrepreneurship. The education revolution of the past two decades enforced existing trends toward accelerated individualization. Individualization in turn has contributed to the dissolution of traditional subcultures and milieus. However, each of these developments has also engendered new pressures on the individual to be flexible in adapting to a rapidly changing world. This development favors those who possess a sufficient amount of cultural capital to take advantage of the opportunities postindustrial consumer capitalism affords. Those incapable or unwilling to adapt to a world in which all that used to be solid tends to melt into air, postindustrial consumer capitalism leaves anxious, bewildered, and insecure.

SOCIAL FRAGMENTATION AND POLITICAL CONFLICT

What emerges from our discussion of the transformation of advanced West European societies is that fragmentation and particularization have become central features of postindustrial capitalism. The acceleration of the modernization process that has dominated socioeconomic development during the past decade has but furthered these trends. Given the generally strong emphasis on consensus and on seeking collective solutions to individual problems characteristic of West European politics in the postwar period, the particularization of society cannot help but pose a serious challenge to West European political systems. Students of political sociology and electoral behavior have generally argued that Western European political systems were built upon broadly based and long-standing political divisions that emerged in the course of social and economic modernization (Lipset and Rokkan, 1967). These cleavages have traditionally been linked to two revolutions, the national revolution and the industrial revolution. The national revolution gave rise to two conflicts. A first conflict pitted interests of the secular national state against the claims of the church on the individual; a second pitted the centralized state against peripheral cultures. The industrial revolution gave rise to new conflicts. The first conflict set landowning, agrarian interests against the emerging urban, industrial bourgeoisie; the second pitted the interests of capital against those of the working class. Once established, these cleavages proved enduring and continued to shape electoral politics, even after the original conditions, which had led to their emergence and establishment, had vanished for a long time. The result was that West European political systems were characterized by a remarkable degree of stability, as new generations were socialized into their respective subcultures.

It was not until relatively recently that we have witnessed a marked decline in cleavage politics and at the same time a marked increase in issue voting (Franklin, 1992). In a number of West European countries, those parties of the Left and the Right most closely identified with traditional lines of conflict, have increasingly failed to mobilize their traditional clientele and as a result suffered serious losses at the polls. And even those parties that managed to retain their electoral strength have done so only by appealing to groups outside the confines of their traditional constituencies. Left-wing parties, for instance, have increasingly had to appeal to voters from the new middle class of private sector employees and civil servants in order to offset losses among working-class voters. For good reason, students of the evolution of electoral behavior have characterized this development as a process of liberation of the voter from the straight-jacket of political predestination.

There can be little doubt that the decline of cleavage politics and the concomitant rise in issue voting is related to the larger societal changes identified in the previous section. In fact, a recent study on electoral change in advanced Western democracies describes recent changes in electoral behavior in terms of a "particularization of voting choice." The authors explain this development as a consequence of the information revolution, which has turned the world into "a global city made up of interlocking electronic precincts" (van der Eijk, Franklin, Mackie, and Valen, 1992, p. 412). "In it, special-interest newsletters, papers, periodicals, and books, together with quite specialized programming on radio and television, cater to groups defined by values and concerns rather than by similarity in terms of a few broad social distinctions. Essentially what this means is that individuals can now choose the influences that they are subjected to, and can change those influences without the need to change their physical location."

This interpretation is consistent with broader notions of the transformation of advanced Western societies. From this perspective, the decline of cleavage politics is a result of the broader and more general processes of fragmentation and individualization characteristic of the transition to postindustrial capitalism. This interpretation is also consistent with the observation that issues have become an increasingly important determinant of voting behavior. As social identity becomes heterogeneous and fixed identities are giving way to contextualized identities, fixed political loyalties are giving way to differentiated and particularized values and priorities.

The decline of cleavage politics opens up new opportunities for new parties if they are able to monopolize a new issue and thus find a niche in the new space of postindustrial politics and if the established parties are unable or unwilling to compete with them on this issue. Given the particularization of electoral choice, the particularization of political supply in an increasingly decentralized political market should hardly come as a surprise.

In the chapters that follow we apply the theoretical model outlined so far to explaining the emergence of the rise of radical right-wing populist parties during the past 20 years. The central argument advanced in chapter 2 is that the political climate in Western Europe in the 1980s increasingly came to be dominated by sentiments of disenchantment and resentment. This was largely in response to the inability and/or unwillingness of the established parties to confront the new political exigencies of a rapidly changing socioeconomic and sociocultural environment. This created a window of opportunity for new parties ready to exploit popular political discontent. One of the central issues igniting political discontent was the question of immigration. As we will show in chapter 3, in the advanced societies of Western Europe, the reaction to immigration has on the whole been profoundly negative. Thus xenophobia was hardly a sentiment limited only to the supporters of the radical populist Right, even if it certainly was most pronounced among them. However, as we will see in chapter 4, although xenophobia was an important component of the program of all radical right-wing populist parties, it would be misleading to explain their appeal only in terms of their opposition to immigration. As we also point out in this chapter, a number of radical right-wing parties achieved a great deal of their support by promoting a radical neoliberal program. Only when this program lost its appeal, did they adopt anti-immigrant positions. Chapter 5 proposes that the shift from a predominantly neoliberal program to one with a stronger emphasis on immigration was largely an attempt to attract lower class voters. The final chapter summarizes the major points raised in this study and relates them to the theoretical model proposed in this chapter.

2

Resentment as Politics

During the past decade politics in Western Europe has increasingly come to be dominated by a climate of resentment and alienation. A majority of citizens in most Western democracies no longer trust political institutions that they consider to be largely self-centered and self-serving, unresponsive to the ideas and wishes of the average person, and incapable of adopting viable solutions for society's most pressing problems. As the public's confidence in the established political parties, the political class, and some of the most important social and political institutions has steadily eroded, a growing number of voters have chosen either to turn their backs on politics altogether or to use the ballot as a means of protest.

At the same time electoral alignments have decomposed, marking a decline in individual partisanship. This is hardly surprising in view of the tendencies of individualization and social fragmentation characteristic of postindustrial modernity. In fact, the "erosion of any sense of cogent political project or coherent political programme" might rather be a logical consequence of a process in which "the lives of individuals become increasingly merely a collection of discontinuous happenings" (Turner, 1989, p. 212). Particularly, mass-integration parties tend to be in a difficult position when it comes to "transporting and deciding vastly differentiated political demands. As a consequence, they will sooner or later frustrate the expectations of their members, activists, and voters in that respect" (Kaase, 1984, p. 305). It is thus hardly surprising that dealignment processes have been particularly severe for Western Europe's *Volksparteien* (see Wildenmann, 1989). Declining partisanship can also be interpreted as a consequence both of the increase in the number of voters who are better educated and of the media and information explosion (Dalton, 1984). From this perspective, better education has allowed a growing number of voters to approach the complexity of modern politics with greater sophistication; the greater supply of information has allowed them to keep abreast of important social and political developments. As a result, these voters no longer depend on political parties as primary sources of political information and guidance. This development has led to a shift from traditional "elite-directed" political participation to a new "elite-directing" mode of participation aimed at "affecting specific policy changes rather than simply supporting the representatives of a given group" (Inglehart, 1990, p. 339). As a result of the "participatory revolution" of the 1970s and 1980s medium-range, nontotalizing ideology (ideology that does not claim to be all-encompassing), issues and the personality and image of individual candidates have increasingly dominated electoral competition (Kaase, 1984).

As we have argued in the previous chapter, radical right-wing populist parties, which are relatively new to the political game, have been among the first to benefit from the decomposition of traditional electoral loyalties. It is less obvious which conditions predispose certain voters to vote for the radical populist Right rather than for any of the other new "designer parties," which have sprung up throughout Western Europe (for example, hunter and fisher lists, taxpayer parties, beerdrinker parties, and the like).

It is tempting to attribute the rise and increasing success of radical right-wing populist parties to voter alienation. From this perspective, radical right-wing populist parties are primarily interpreted as parties of discontent, which have managed to exploit voters' dissatisfaction and cynicism and to appeal to their sense of powerlessness by promoting strong authoritarian leadership. As one analysis of the rise of the German radical Right put it: "The recent electoral successes of the Right can be explained among others by the recent decline in the level of satisfaction with the political system. As a result, there is a wide basis for protest behavior among certain segments of the population" (Neu and Zelle, 1992, p. 5; see also Güllner, 1993). In what follows we present an analysis of the major aspects of political alienation and its relationship with the emergence of radical right-wing populism in Western Europe.

ELECTORAL PARTICIPATION AND PROTEST VOTE

During the past several years most major West European countries have witnessed a significant and persistent drop in electoral participation. At the same time there has been a pronounced increase in the number of voters who, albeit exercising their right to participate in the elections, cast blank or invalid ballots. In France, for example, in the 1993 parliamentary election only 69 percent of registered voters participated. Even if that represented a slight increase compared to 1988 when more than 34 percent abstained, it confirmed the recent declining trends in voter participation. For unlike the 1988 election, the 1993 parliamentary election did not follow a presidential election. (Presidential elections have traditionally tended to depress voter turnout in the parliamentary election.) When compared to the more "normal" parliamentary election of 1986, abstentionism actually increased by almost 10 percent. In addition, the 1993 election witnessed a record number of blank and invalid votes—more than 1.4 million in the first round, more than 2.1 million in the second (Hoffman-Martinot, 1993, p. 12).

The situation has been similar in Germany, Austria, and Italy. West German electoral results show a steady increase in the percentage of voter abstention. It started in the 1980s, and reached record proportions in the early 1990s. Despite its historical significance, the first all-German election in 1990 was no exception. Ten million eligible West German voters stayed at home—three million more than in 1987. At the same time the number of blank and invalid votes increased from roughly 358,000 to more than 380,000 (see Güllner, 1993). Some German observers even warned that the "party of the non-voters" was well on its way to becoming the largest party in German politics (Starzacher, Schacht, Friedrich, and Leif, 1992).

The development has been similar in Austria, where the number of non-voters increased between 1983 and 1990 from 394,000 to 780,000 and the number of blank and invalid votes from 69,000 to roughly 144,000 (Plasser and Ulram, 1992). In Italy, too, both the rate of abstention and the number of blank and invalid votes increased significantly starting in the late 1970s. Between 1979 and 1987 alone, the number of blank and invalid votes increased from roughly 1.5 to over 2.6 million votes (see ISPES, 1991, chapter 53). In the "historical" parliamentary elections in March 1994, only 86 percent of the Italian electorate turned out to vote, the lowest turnout in postwar electoral history.

Even if some West European democracies have been better than others in resisting these tendencies (and particularly the Scandinavian countries, although the 76 percent turnout in the 1993 Norwegian election was the lowest since 1927), the overall trend seems to support the notion of a growing alienation of West European voters from the political process. The question then is to what extent growing electoral abstention, protest votes, and support for radical right-wing populist parties are part of the same climate of political resentment that is characterized by wide-spread cynicism and alienation.

The decline in voter turnout especially lends itself to a number of alternative interpretations. As several American studies have shown, there is a strong link between electoral participation and partisan loyalty. The stronger partisan loyalty is, the higher the rate of participation. There are at least two major reasons for this. Strong and stable linkages between parties and their constituencies tend to reduce the costs of voting by allowing even relatively uninformed voters to decide on issues and candidates. At the same time, strong feelings of party identification make it easier for parties "to seek out supporters and mobilize them at election time" (Powell, 1986, pp. 14–15). An analysis of the 1991 national election in Switzerland—where turnout has traditionally been notoriously low—illustrates the point. Electoral participation among voters who had strong ties to a party, either as members or sympathizers, was more than twice as high as it was among nonpartisans. Whereas 91 percent of all party members took part in the election, only 24 percent of eligible voters who declared themselves to be nonpartisans "on principle" went to the polls (Longchamp and Hardmeier, 1992, p. 36).

In the past decade social fragmentation and individualization processes have increasingly come to prevail in all advanced Western democracies. One result of these processes has been an erosion of partisan loyalties. The recent trend toward declining voter turnout should therefore come as no surprise. A recent study of electoral participation in municipal elections in France illustrates this point. It shows that abstention rates are particularly high in towns that lack stable population structures and/or have a significant proportion of foreign residents who have not been integrated into the community (Hoffmann-Martinot, 1993, p. 10). Other studies indicate that nonvoters are generally less likely to be interested in politics, less close to political parties, and less likely to have strong political preferences (Bréchon, 1990; Ackaert, de Winter, Aish, and Frognier, 1991). Thus it seems that sociocultural changes account at least in part for growing electoral volatility.

This is not to say that dealignment is the only source of declining voter turnout. As American studies show, political alienation can have an equally strong impact on electoral participation (see Abramson and Aldrich, 1982, pp. 510–515). This holds even more true for the growing number of voters who take part in elections, but cast blank and invalid votes. Since these voters incur the costs of voting, but fail to get the potential benefit of seeing their favored candidate elected, their vote is most likely an expression of protest. The fact, as a Belgian study has shown (Ackert, de Winter, Aish, and Frognier, 1991, p. 222), that a significant number of voters who cast blank or invalid votes do so repeatedly, makes the protest hypothesis more plausible than the notion that blank or invalid votes are merely voter mistakes. The increase in these ballots is thus potentially a significant gauge of the extent to which voter disaffection, disenchantment, and discontent have come to characterize voting behavior.

A third source confirming these trends are surveys tracking support for the political system in West European democracies. They show that a growing number of citizens appear not only to believe that the established political class is no longer able to solve the most basic problems, but that politicians generally are too absorbed with themselves to be able to adapt to a rapidly changing world. Recent opinion polls abound in accusations that political parties and politicians are self-centered and completely oblivious to the problems they are supposed to solve. A growing number of voters charge politicians with lacking the competence, integrity, and vision necessary to respond effectively to the most urgent problems, be they environmental degradation, soaring unemployment, rising crime, or mass immigration.

Available evidence suggests that the climate of political resentment and disaffection that characterized much of Western Europe in the late 1980s and early 1990s has had various causes. Some can only be understood with reference to the unique characteristics of individual countries. Perhaps the most significant example is the impact of unification on the development of German politics. The importance of country-specific factors cannot be dismissed. But they should not detract from the fact that political alienation in the late 1980s stemmed largely from developments and experiences that were shared by the vast majority of advanced West European democracies. Some have to do with the stream of scandals that has shaken the political class in virtually all major West European democracies. But perhaps even worse than the experience that politics after all might be a rather dirty business was the recognition that, confronted with a profound socioeconomic transformation, most established political elites were at a loss for solutions. Their inability to restore the sense of security and prosperity, which steady material and social advances in the postwar period had led a majority of their citizens to expect from their leaders, has been a major cause of voter alienation and cynicism. Confronted with massive state deficits and mounting unemployment, a majority of West Europeans have come to sense since the late 1980s "that the very people they [had] chose[n] to solve their problems ha[d] been in power too long to steer a dejected Continent through the shifting shoals that mark the close of the 20th century."[1]

It is within this context of growing public pessimism, anxiety, and disaffection that the rise and success of radical right-wing populism in Western Europe finds at least a partial explanation. A brief discussion of the political developments in some of the countries in Western Europe where radical right-wing populist parties have made major gains serves to illustrate this point.

SCANDINAVIA

The first radical right-wing populist parties to benefit from voter disenchant-ment were the two Progress parties in the early 1970s. Glistrup himself interpreted the party's "principal line" as a protest against the fact that the established parties had not only misruled the country, but managed to deceive the population about their misrule and were generally "out of step concerning the rapid development of society." In his view, the party's success reflected "a democratic revolution coming from the hearts of the people."[2]

The growing distrust in the political establishment in Denmark and Norway in the 1970s was largely a result of growing public opposition to rising taxes and growing ambiguity toward the further expansion of the welfare state. In both countries, center-right governments were in office during what has been characterized as the period that witnessed the most dramatic expansion of the welfare state (Andersen and Bjørklund, 1990, p.198). Despite a clear mandate to act to the contrary, neither government effectively halted the growth of the public sector nor did they alleviate the tax burden (Olsen, 1984, p. 187). Quite to the contrary. Particularly in Denmark, this period witnessed both an accel-eration of the rise in income taxes and major improvements in the already generous welfare provisions, which made Denmark's the "world's most gener-ous cash-benefit program" (Borre, 1977, p. 7; Esping-Andersen, 1990, p. 175).

As a result of these developments, government collective consumption as a percent of GDP rose from 15 percent in 1965 to roughly one quarter in 1975 (Andersen, 1984, p. 115). At the same time, the percentage of persons employed in the public sectors dealing with administration, health, and education in-creased from 15 percent in 1968 to 22 percent in 1974 and 28 percent in 1980; the level of government expenditures for health and social welfare as a share of all public expenditures rose from 30 percent in 1960 to 48 percent in 1975 (Brettschneider, Ahlstich and Zügel, 1992, pp. 523–524). These increases came at a time when, as a result of the first oil shock, the Danish economy came increasingly under pressure. The result was declining real wages, growing public deficits, rising inflation, rising unemployment particularly among the young, and, starting in the mid-1970s, a dramatic rise in the number of social assistance beneficiaries (Marklund, 1990, p. 135).

As expenditures on the public sector expanded, bureaucrats and politicians came under increasing fire "for having exploited and alienated the general public." In 1973, 91 percent of the Danish population agreed that politicians were too generous with the taxpayers' money; 78 percent thought that politi-cians generally cared little about voters' opinions (Borre, 1974, p. 199). Both antitax and antiwelfare state sentiments and political alienation were particularly pronounced among Progress Party voters. Thus in 1973, virtually all citizens thought that politicians were wasting money; and roughly nine out of ten confessed little faith in politicians' responsiveness to public opinion (Nielsen, 1976, p. 149; see also Andersen, 1992, p. 111).

By the early 1980s, the Danish economy faced the most severe economic crisis since the 1930s. After the Danish government had financed the welfare state and the extension of the public sector largely by borrowing on the international financial markets, the country was facing financial disaster (Eysell and Henningsen, 1992, p. 7). However, with the formation of a four-party center-right coalition government in 1982, things turned around. Partly, this was the result of the fact that the new government introduced a number of crisis measures designed to improve Denmark's position in the international economy (Christiansen, 1984, p. 30). Partly, too, it was due to the fact that almost immediately after the new government had come to power there was a marked improvement in the international business cycle. The political fallout from the economic turnaround was a significant improvement in the public's trust in politicians, which even extended to Progress Party supporters (Andersen and Bjørklund, 1990, p. 203; Andersen, 1993, p. 14). Political trust, however, plunged in 1988 when the government called for new elections, which many Danes obviously considered unnecessary and only distracting from a resolution of pressing economic issues (Smith Jespersen, 1989). In 1989, political trust was lower than it had ever been in the 1970s and 1980s (Andersen, 1992a, p. 111). Not surprisingly, the Progress Party emerged as the winner of the election. However, the continued improvement of the economy (in 1990, Denmark closed the fiscal year with a budget surplus for the first time in 27 years) restored public trust and might, at least in part, have contributed to the Progress Party's losses in the 1990 election (see Andersen, 1992a, pp. 72-73).

Like Denmark, Norway witnessed a dramatic decline in political confidence in the early 1970s (Miller and Listhaug, 1990). As in Denmark, the supporters of the Progress Party were by far the most alienated from the political system. However, the start of a primarily oil-based investment and consumption boom appeared to provide a solution to the country's mounting problems. As a result, the Norwegian public's attitude toward the political establishment improved considerably. In no group was this improvement more pronounced than among Progress Party supporters. For example, between 1973 and 1985, the proportion of Progress Party supporters who believed politicians were largely incompetent declined from 66 percent to 34 percent (Andersen and Bjørklund, 1990, p. 203).

However, by the end of the 1980s, confidence in politics had sharply declined and, as Henry Valen noted, "contempt for politicians" had "become a household expression in public debate" (Valen, 1990, p. 289). Not surprisingly, the Progress Party reemerged in 1987 as a significant factor in Norwegian politics. This showed that oil and the progressive "Americanization" of Norwegian society in the 1980s (Lafferty, 1990, p. 85) had not been able to restore political stability to the country (Fagerberg, Cappelen, Mjøset, and Skarstein, 1990). Although the oil revenues allowed for new social reforms, public sector expansion, and high wage increases in the late 1970s, these measures came at the cost of rising inflation and growing deficits. This led to a swing to the right in the early 1980s (Kuhnle, Strom, and Svåsand, 1986, p. 466). The Right made the question of deregulating the domestic credit market a central issue of its political campaign, hoping that deregulation would break up the traditional bases of Social Democratic support. "The miscalculation was that, without a strongly restrictive monetary policy to break the underlying demand for credit, the deregulation could only spell further chaos" (Notermans, 1993, p. 143).

The new policy initiatives that aimed at deregulation, restraint on public sector growth, and tax reductions for high incomes contributed to growing budget surpluses, but also caused an explosion of borrowing, stock market speculation, and consumer spending. "Between 1984 and 1987, Norges Bank virtually lost control over the economy. In those years, credit overruns exceeded 100%" (Notermans, 1993, pp. 143–144). The result was a rise in interest rates and a surge in housing prices. Confronted with growing deficits following the end of the oil boom in the mid-1980s, the Left, which returned to power in 1986, was forced to keep interests high, pursue a restrictive wage policy, and abandon the party's commitment to full employment while increasing public expenditures. At the time of the 1989 election, the inflation rate had come under control, but at the cost of rising unemployment.

As a result of the economic and political developments of the 1970s and 1980s, Norwegian society experienced profound socio-cultural changes (Kuhnle, Strom, and Svåsand, 1986). The emergence of a consumer society led to the disintegration of "the cultural bonds of the closed corporate community" and their replacement with more individualistic values (Lafferty, 1990, p.86). It led to a growing private tertiary sector dominated by financial and business services, while the manufacturing sector stagnated or even declined. At the same time, public sector employment increased, accounting for roughly one third of all employment. Thus between 1981 and 1987 social expenditures as a percentage of GNP increased from 22 to 26 percent, per capita expenditures increased by 28 percent (Kuhnle, 1992, p. 17).

The postindustrialization of Norwegian society demanded its price. Most significant was the growth in unemployment. Between 1987 and 1990 alone, unemployment shot up from 2.1 percent to 5.2 percent. By 1989 it surpassed for the first time the level of 1933, the year unemployment peaked in the prewar period (Bjørklund, 1992, p. 340). By 1992 it topped the 8 percent level (including those participating in employment programs), affecting particularly the younger generation (Kuhnle, 1992, p. 16). As a result, Norway witnessed growing pockets of poverty, including old-age pensioners, young unemployed, and working-class males (Marklund, 1990, p. 136).

The relative deterioration of life chances might at least be a partial explanation for the marked decline in political trust in the late 1980s. Thus between 1985 and 1989, the share of Norwegians who were pessimistic about the future of the Norwegian economy increased from 11 to 45 percent. At the same time, the proportion of those who feared to become unemployed increased from 15 percent to 32 percent (Listhaug, 1993, p. 31). It is perhaps not surprising that in 1989 political trust was only marginally higher than it had been in 1973. And as in 1973, distrust was particularly pronounced among Progress Party supporters: in 1989, 58 percent said they thought many politicians were rather incompetent. This had a certain effect on voting behavior: those voters who thought in 1989 that politicians were untrustworthy were more than twice as likely to vote for the Progress Party than those who generally trusted them (Strom and de Rotstein, 1991, p. 12).

Despite the success of the two Progress parties in the 1970s and 1980s, it was not until 1991 that a similar party emerged in Sweden. One reason that has been suggested is that in Sweden, unlike in Denmark and Norway, the Social Democrats remained in office until 1976, thus until after the most expansive growth of the welfare state. Voters disenchanted with the Social Democrats thus could still express their discontent by voting for the bourgeois parties. In addition, in Denmark and Norway, the emergence of the Progress parties came at a time of profound political turmoil following the referenda on membership in the EC in 1972, which led to splits within the established parties and weakened voter loyalty. It was not until the 1980s that a similarly divisive issue emerged in Sweden with the question of nuclear power (Andersen and Bjørklund, 1990, p. 198). Others have explained the absence of a "welfare backlash" in Sweden as a result of Sweden's universal welfare programs, its high level of monetary transfers, and the large number of "welfare producers" and "welfare consumers" among the electorate (Hinrichs, 1988, pp. 583–584). Neither of these explanations appears very plausible, particularly given the fact that in the 1970s and 80s voter disenchantment and alienation in Sweden has been far more pronounced than for example in Norway (Miller and Listhaug, 1990, p. 360; 1993, p. 168). Between 1973 and 1991, for example, the number of Swedes agreeing with the statement that those sitting in Parliament and making decisions don't care very much what the ordinary people think increased from 53 to 70 percent. And the number of those who agreed that parties are only interested in votes, not opinions, increased from 46 to 68 percent (Gilljam and Homberg, 1993, p. 170). Available evidence also suggests that disenchantment and distrust was increasing among all Swedish voters, irrespective of their party affiliation (see Holmberg and Gilljam, 1987, pp. 236–239). However, in the early 1990s, it was particularly pronounced among New Democracy voters. In 1991, 79 percent of the party's supporters said they had little or very little confidence in Swedish politicians (Gilljam and Homberg, 1993, p. 173).

It seems more plausible to trace the absence of a radical right-wing populist challenge in Sweden to the relatively successful policies of successive governments in the 1970s and 1980s to restore and improve Sweden's international competitiveness without abandoning the commitment to full employment (cf. Hinrichs, 1988; Jonzon and Wise, 1989). The latter goal was initially achieved through a mixture of subsidies to the ailing steel and shipbuilding industries and the expansion of the public sector on the local level at the cost of growing budget deficits and rising inflation. However, a drastic devaluation of the Swedish crown in 1982, which coincided with the beginning of a world-wide economic recovery, together with specific programs designed to combat rising youth unemployment soon led to growing exports. Growing exports, in turn, lowered unemployment, reduced inflation, and, at least for a short time, balanced the budget. However, by the late 1980s it became increasingly clear that the mid-1980s had only marked a temporary suspension of a profound challenge to the Swedish model set in motion by the fragmentation of what used to be a compact system.[3]

In part, this fragmentation was due to the growth of the service sector, which led to a profound transformation of the labor market. By the end of the 1980s, more than two thirds of the Swedish working population were employed in private and particularly in public services (Hinrichs, 1988, p. 577; Jahn, 1992; Lindbeck et al., 1993, pp. 226–227). In part it was due to growing conflicts between private- and public-sector unions over the question who should set the benchmarks for wage increases (Hernes, 1991, pp. 254–255). In part it was due to the boom in the export-oriented sector, which led to an increasingly tight labor market, and prompted employers to seek to escape the constraints of centralized bargaining (Notermans, 1993, p. 147). In part, finally it was due (just like in Norway) to the deregulation of the financial markets, which led to an explosion in real estate prices and a building boom.

It is against this background that the Swedish model entered a profound crisis in the late 1980s, which could no longer be remedied using the traditional formula. The main factors behind the severe deterioration of the Swedish economy were rising inflation, a precipitous decline of household savings following financial deregulation, and the international business slowdown that started in 1990, which affected high-cost countries particularly hard (Lindbeck et al., 1993, p. 222). Given the breakdown of centralized bargaining in the 1980s, which destroyed the unions' capacity for wage moderation in an overheated economy, increasing budget deficits, and already extremely high taxes, which made it impossible to expand the public sector any further, the government was forced to resort to abandon its commitment to full employment (Hinrichs, 1988, p. 583). Instead it embarked on a monetarist program, which led to the "deepest recession in post-World War II history" with unemployment rates soaring to unprecedented levels (Notermans, 1993, p. 141). By the end of 1993, unemployment rates had reached 9.5 percent with another 5 percent temporarily parked in job retraining and/or workfare schemes. This was a result of the rapid deterioration of Sweden's position in the world economy, reflected among others by the fact that by the end of 1993 the national dept was projected to reach about 70 percent of GNP (The *Economist*, October 9, 1993). Undoubtedly, by the early 1990s the Swedish model had fallen apart (see, among others, Jenson and Mahon, 1993, pp. 91–100).

ITALY

In no other Western European country have political parties and the political establishment in general been more discredited in recent years than in Italy. And in no other country is the success of the radical populist Right so intimately connected to the almost complete delegitimation of the party system. Polls taken in the early 1990s showed that only one out of ten Italians had confidence in parliament and the government, and less than 7 percent in political parties.[4] This was hardly surprising considering the seemingly endless series of corruption scandals, which erupted in 1991 in Milan and soon spread throughout the whole country (on the situation in Milan see Bocca, 1993). By 1992 there was hardly a day in which the Italian public would not see a prominent entrepreneur or politician being led away in handcuffs for interrogation by the Milanese magistrates. In Milan alone, more than 40 politicians, most of them Christian Democrats and Socialists, and more than 30 entrepreneurs were arrested in 1992; others (among them Giuliano Andreotti and Bettino Craxi) were under investigation. By mid-1993, the magistrates were actively investigating more than 150 members of the Italian parliament, the great majority of whom were members of the Christian Democrats and the Socialist party.[5] The success of the Lega Nord was thus foremost a reflection of wide-spread disaffection and disenchantment with the established political institutions, which the public held responsible for the socioeconomic and sociocultural crisis of Italian society (see Pasquino, 1993). As a result, the Lega found itself in a position "to hold a monopoly in a political market where distrust vis-à-vis the system of parties and the public institutions had become the main point of reference for the citizens" (Diamanti, 1993, p. 88).

However, popular disaffection and political scandals are not sufficient to explain the extent to which northern Italy has turned to the Lega Nord and away from the established political parties. At least partly, the Lega's success must also be seen as a reaction of the affluent north to the inability of the Italian state to respond to the new situation created by the collapse of the Soviet threat and the acceleration of the modernization process throughout Western Europe (Cavazza, 1992). Thus it is in large parts a response to the unwillingness and/or inability of the established political parties to come to terms with the end of an era.

The postwar settlement left Italy with a peculiar situation. In the presence of the strongest Communist party in Western Europe, the Christian Democrats were virtually assured a position of political dominance. No longer forced to compete for political power, Christian Democrats developed a "multifaceted system of governance by blending clientelism, distributive politics and ideological appeal to a disparate constituency" (Woods, 1992, p. 57). This strategy was soon copied by other political parties (notably the Socialist Party under its omnipotent secretary Bettino Craxi), which created their own patronage networks (Cavazza, 1992, pp. 232–234). Clientilistic structures developed particularly in the south, which became the recipient of a massive transfer of funds from the more developed north. However, the result was disappointing. While much of the money spent in the south either ended in the pockets of corrupt politicians or mafia families, or were wasted on grandiose projects of more than questionable value, the south remained underdeveloped and became increasingly dependent on the state for funds and employment (Micossi and Tullio, 1992, pp. 57–62). These funds came largely from the affluent north. In 1989, almost 60 percent of all taxes came from four northern regions (Lombardy, Piemont, Veneto, and Emilia Romana), but only one third of public transfer payments returned to them. Meanwhile the south contributed one fifth of all taxes, but received one third of all public transfers.[6]

The success of the Lega has to be seen against this particular situation. It represents above all a revolt against a political class that was determined to maintain an outmoded system of political representation, which in the past had guaranteed its hold on political power (Biorcio, 1991/1992; Pasquino, 1991, pp. 558–560). As Dwayne Woods (1992, p. 58) has pointed out, what accounts for the Lega's appeal is the perception that "the Italian state does not embody the principles of a modern society—that is, the separation of public and private spheres of interests and bureaucratic rationality—but the parasitic aspects of a clientilistic state." With the profound changes underway in the advanced societies of Western Europe, this system had not only become dysfunctional and obsolete but threatened to destroy the socioeconomic foundation that made northern Italy one of the most prosperous and affluent areas in Western Europe.

In this sense the growing support for the Lega Nord in northern Italy was as much "a reaction to the failure of political modernisation in Italy" (Woods, 1992, p. 58) as it was an expression of deep-seated fears that Italy might once again miss its connection with developments happening elsewhere in Western Europe. As one observer in Mantova noted in 1992, one voted for the Lega "out of a survival instinct, not to end up like the south, which ended in the hands of the mafia, to stay in Europe instead of sliding down into the Third World."[7]

Available surveys confirm to what extent Northern Italian voters had come to resent the established political parties and the political class in the early 1990s. Thus between 1985 and 1991 the number of respondents who disagreed with the statement that parties are necessary for democracy increased from 19 to 38 percent. At the same time the number of Northern Italians who agreed "very much" that all parties were the same increased from 25 to 54 percent (Mannheimer, 1992). Not surprisingly, political distrust was particularly prevalent among Lega supporters. Thus in 1992, only 5 percent of Lega supporters said they had confidence in the political parties, 8 percent in the government, and another 8 percent in parliament. Two thirds of Lega Nord supporters agreed "very much" that the established parties were all the same (Mannheimer, 1992). Other polls show to what degree this disaffection with the established political parties was tied to perceptions of fiscal irresponsibility, corruption, and waste: In 1993, 78 percent of the Northern Italian population, and 90 percent of Lega Nord supporters, agreed that taxes should primarily be invested were they were raised (Diamanti, 1993, pp. 102-103). A study of the Lega's supporters in Milan showed to what degree the Lega profited from public disaffection with the political establishment. In 1991, more than 50 percent of Lega voters said they had voted for the party to protest against Rome and the *partitocrazia* (Mannheimer, 1991, p. 145).

AUSTRIA

The rise of the Austrian FPÖ in the late 1980s has to be seen in the context of the profound transformation of Austria's consociationalist system. This system was created after the war in order to integrate Austria's Catholic-conservative and Socialist-secular subcultures. It found its political reflection in the ÖVP-SPÖ grand coalition governments, which dominated Austrian politics until 1966, and developed an extensive system of influence and interests, which included the public administration at all levels, the education system, as well as the state-controlled industrial sector. "The so-called *Proporz* system was based on dividing the spoils proportionately between the parties. The awarding of jobs, housing, and government contracts was undertaken according to party affiliation and served to strengthen party loyalty and *Lager* culture." As a result, the parties gained considerable power over the lives of ordinary citizens whose living conditions, jobs, and chances of social advancement depended on them. Together with social and economic corporatism, this system allowed for the integration of the great majority of the relevant groups into the political arena. The result was that "the political and especially the party system enjoyed high levels of stability and public support—from stable voting patterns to the almost complete absence of social unrest" (Plasser, Ulram, and Graushuber, 1992, pp. 18–19).

During the past two decades, however, Austria began to experience profound socioeconomic changes, which were to have far-reaching consequences for its sociocultural and sociopolitical system. As in other advanced Western European countries, the demands of a modernizing economy led to the evolution of postindustrial structures. This meant above all a significant decline of the population employed in the agrarian sector, a stagnant industrial sector, and a steady advance of the service sector, which by 1981 employed half the work force. As farmers, old urban middle classes, and industrial blue-collar workers were decreasing both in numbers and importance, the ranks of a new middle class of civil servants and white-collar employees were steadily expanding. Together with secularization trends, which significantly decreased the number of citizens with strong church ties, the evolution of a postindustrial service economy in Austria led to an erosion of the traditional subcultures. This, in turn, led to an erosion of support for the established political parties identified with the *Proporz* system (Gehmacher, Birk, and Ogris, 1987, p. 160; Plasser, Ulram, and Grausgruber, 1992, pp. 20-21). As some of the leading observers of social trends in Austria noted: "An above average education level, high occupational qualifications, orientation toward social advancement, secularization and pluralization of social environments characterize a new type of voter who evades the conventional integrative, incorporative (sic) strategies of the political parties" (Plasser, Ulram, and Grausgruber, 1992, p. 43). These trends were not only reflected in the declining proportion of voters who identified themselves with one of the two major parties, but also in the declining number of voters who actually voted for them. Thus in the 15 years between 1975 and 1990, the two major parties' share of the vote declined from 93 to 75 percent (Plasser and Ulram, 1992; Pelinka, 1992).

As in other West European countries, in Austria, sociocultural moderniza-tion appears to have failed to lead to a higher degree of political satisfaction. On the contrary. In few other West European countries are citizen disenchant-ment with, and distance from, the political system as pronounced as in Austria. In 1989, three out of four Austrian citizens thought that the political parties were only interested in votes and that the average person had no influence on the government. Sixty-nine percent thought politicians were corrupt, and 55 percent disagreed with the statement that politicians were generally doing a good job (Plasser and Ulram, 1991a, pp. 113–115, 136). As a result, a growing number of voters considered corruption and privilege one of the most import-ant problems in Austrian politics (Plasser and Ulram, 1990a, p. 20). In 1992, for example, 44 percent of the Austrian public considered "the struggle against corruption and *Privilegienwirtschaft*" a very important political issue.[8]

At the same time there was growing disenchantment with the two main parties. In 1988, two years after the creation of a SPÖ/ÖVP grand coalition, between 30 and 40 percent of Austrian voters accused it of hushing up the growing number of scandals that were rocking the political establishment in the late 1980s, of perpetuating clientilism and patronage, and of having lost contact with the population (Plasser and Ulram, 1989, p. 158).

These results reflect a growing critique of, and emancipation from, the *Lager* mentality, which have been most pronounced among the younger generation (Bonengl, Horak, and Lasek, 1985, pp. 388–389; Plasser and Ulram, 1989, p. 156). Their main beneficiary has been the FPÖ. Surveys show FPÖ sympa-thizers (together with Green-alternative supporters) to be particularly disaffected and distrustful (Plasser and Ulram, 1991a, p. 137). Generally, FPÖ supporters were considerably less likely than the general public to believe that top positions were filled by the right persons, or that one could rely on the government and parliament to make the right decisions. In 1989, 47 percent of FPÖ supporters thought the political system in Austria was bad or very bad (compared to 28 percent for the whole population), and 17 percent thought that under certain circumstances a dictatorship might be better than democracy (5 percent of the total population) (Plasser and Ulram, 1991, p. 142). Like the Lega Nord, the FPÖ also benefitted from the growing distance between voters and established parties. Thus in 1986, a large proportion of new FPÖ voters explained their decision to vote FPÖ as a warning to the two major parties. Although this motivation was still quite strong in 1990, the FPÖ also increasingly benefited from the perception that it was the only party to fight against scandals and privileges (Plasser, 1986, p. 24; Plasser, Sommer, and Ulram, 1990, p. 49).[9]

FRANCE

The ability to appeal to growing voter disaffection and discontent has also been an important ingredient in the political strategy of Jean-Marie Le Pen's Front National. As early as the 1970s, "while interest in politics and willingness to engage in political activity remained as strong as ever, it appears that disillusionment with those who practise politics was growing, and attachment to established parties by the French electorate was diminishing" (Schain, 1987, p. 232). Thus those who felt that politicians were generally not concerned with what the average person was thinking increased from 42 percent in 1977 to 58 percent in 1985. These results reflected a marked decline in voter confidence, which was accompanied by growing cynicism toward the political class. This found expression in the growing conviction that politicians failed to deal with important issues concerning the lives of the French population (62 percent in 1982), that once elected politicians forgot the promises they had made (42 percent in 1984), and that politicians did not speak the truth (82 percent in 1985) (Ignazi, 1989, pp. 75, 80; Schain, 1987, p. 248).

Rising social tension was closely associated with the Socialists' conversion to market liberalism in 1983 after their initial economic program had dramatically failed (Uterwedde, 1991). After gaining power in 1981, the French Socialists had embarked on an ambitious attempt to build the foundation for a French model of democratic socialism. This included stimulating economic growth through a comprehensive policy of redistributive Keynesianism and unifying the working class through a reform of the industrial and labor-relations legislation in order to facilitate collective bargaining. Neither policy was overly successful. On the contrary, rather than "promoting economic growth and job creation, Socialist policies promoted economic dislocation and unemployment. Rather than promoting a virtuous circle of growth, redistributive policies promoted a vicious circle of inflation, international trade deficits, and a weakened franc." The failure of the Socialist policies stemmed partly from France's weak international competitiveness which even several successive devaluations of the franc failed to remedy. In part the failure stemmed from the negative effects of rising wages and a reduced work week on corporate profits (Lipietz, 1991, pp. 32–33). Although the labor reforms did improve labor's position, workers were increasingly threatened by rising unemployment, while employers continued their assault on trade unions, with little response from the government. And while the government did nationalize key industries and private banks, it failed to democratize the labor process so that nationalized industries "could hardly be distinguished from their privately owned counterparts" (Kesselman, 1992, pp. 222–223). Regardless of the reasons, by 1983 it had become apparent that "the economy of growth and prosperity" was giving way to an "economy of austerity and unemployment" (Vincent, 1985, p. 1773).

Confronted with a dramatic deterioration of France's international position resulting from their initial policies the Socialists performed a radical volte-face. In March 1983, the government introduced a package of austerity measures designed to reduce the budget deficit, defeat inflation, and restore confidence in the franc. The central factor was the decision to remain in the European Monetary System. This meant that France had to accept considerable limitations on its autonomy. Among others, France had to subordinate its targets for economic growth and demand to the imperatives of maintaining a balanced trade (Uterwedde, 1991, p. 18). As a result, the Socialists were forced to adopt policies that differed little from those of their liberal counterparts in other countries, such as reducing government regulations of private industries, reducing corporate taxes and keeping down wages in order to increase the profitability of French firms, and reviving and promoting private capital markets. These policies substantially improved the competitiveness of French firms. Yet they failed to reduce the growing rate of unemployment (Liepitz, 1991, pp. 34–35). On the contrary, between 1983 and 1985 alone unemployment increased by about 400,000. Since the mid-1980s unemployment remained at a persistently high rate of roughly 10 percent, despite numerous training, retraining, and other qualification measures and early-retirement schemes. "At the same time the segmentation of the labor market continued to proceed, the number of insecure forms of employment increased, social inequalities caused by mass unemployment deepened, and phenomena of marginalization began to develop which created growing problems for the state's social policy" (Uterwedde, 1991, p. 22).

At the time of the Front National's electoral breakthrough in the European election of 1984, French society had gone through a prolonged period of malaise. This was made worse by the economic recession, government-imposed austerity measures, mounting social tension over unemployment, and growing crime rates, which were increasingly associated with the Socialist government's policies (Shields, 1991). As a result, as Jean-Marie Vincent stated in 1985, for many segments of society, "disillusionment, even desperation, ha[d] replaced confidence in the future or the feeling that they were at least living under tolerable conditions" (Vincent, 1985, p. 1773). Surveys give an indication of the extent of anxiety and pessimism generated in the early 1980s. Thus between 1981 and 1984 the number of French citizens who thought that things tended to get worse increased from 40 to 70 percent, and the number of those who thought that France's position in the world was declining went from 32 to 44 percent (Ignazi, 1989, p. 80).

If the Socialists could not arrest the steady decline in the public's confidence in politics and politicians, or reverse the public's pessimistic dispositions, neither could the Right. In fact, although the policy failures of the Socialists increased hostility toward the Left, this did not automatically translate into greater confidence in the traditional Right. In the crucial period between 1982 and 1983, for example, when support for the Socialists was declining precipitously, support for the Right was rising only marginally (Shields, 1991, p. 78). This suggests that the French public was disaffected with all major parties and profoundly sceptical as to their ability to solve France's most urgent problems. Surveys taken in the early 1990s support this interpretation. When the French were asked in 1990 what they felt when they thought about politics, 47 percent said they felt distrust, 21 percent disgust. Most significantly, however, the number of respondents who said they felt hope declined from 49 percent in the election year of 1988 to 20 percent in 1990 (SOFRES, 1991, p. 280). By 1991, more than two thirds of the French population felt politicians cared very little if at all about the average person's opinions. Fifty-eight percent thought they were corrupt—an increase of 20 percent compared to 1977. More than three quarters thought that the economic situation had deteriorated during the past twelve months (compared to 36 percent in 1988). And more than half expected the economic situation to get even worse in the following year (compared to only 32 percent who thought so in 1988) (SOFRES, 1993, pp. 232, 234).

It is against this background of pessimism and political disaffection that the growing electoral success of the Front National and its message of "fear and exclusion, racial hatred and irrational fantasies" (Lipietz, 1992, p. 59) in the 1980s must be seen. Already in the mid-1980s National Front supporters were more pessimistic about the national economy (45 percent thought the national economy was getting "much worse"), more dissatisfied with the political system (34 percent said they were not at all satisfied with democracy in France; for 65 percent, democracy in France did not work well or worked not at all), and more cynical about the political class (71 percent agreed that politicians did not care about what the average French citizen thought; 72 percent thought that once in power politicians quickly forget the promises they made) than any other partisan group (see Lewis-Beck and Mitchell, 1993, pp. 121-122; SOFRES, 1985, p. 190; SOFRES, 1986, p. 241; SOFRES, 1990, pp. 163-164).

In the 1988 presidential election, National Front voters distinguished themselves by their propensity to feel that they had been better off before, and that things were not likely to be much better in the future. Fifty-two percent of voters who declared themselves very close to the Front National saw their decision largely as a protest against the political system (Mayer and Perrineau, 1992, pp. 131–132). Polls taken on the eve of the 1993 parliamentary election show that despite expectations that the period of Socialist hegemony was drawing quickly to a close, the attitudes of Front National supporters had remained largely negative. The party did best among voters who thought that democracy in France worked very badly (28 percent of them voted for the Front National compared to 6 percent among those who thought it worked very well) and those who were very concerned about their personal and professional future (25 percent compared to 9 percent among those who were completely confident about their future).[10] These results support the contention that the Front National's successes were at least in part a reflection of a profound malaise caused both by the economic crisis and the general direction of the evolution of French society (Bréchon, 1993, p. 55).

GERMANY

Perhaps in no other country in Western Europe is the public's attitude toward politics and the political system as extensively measured and as closely observed as in Germany. And perhaps in no other country has popular disenchantment and disaffection reached higher levels in the early 1990s than in the Federal Republic. By 1993, academics, pundits, and the population at large became more and more obsessed with analyzing the reasons for the dramatic rise in what came to be known as *Parteien-* and *Politikverdrossenheit* (disaffection with parties and politics in general), which was sweeping the country.

It would be tempting to blame the dramatic rise in political disaffection on the repercussions unification has had on the German population. However, this ignores the fact that political disaffection had already steadily increased in the 1980s, culminating in the dramatic gains of the Republikaner in 1989. Between 1980 and 1989, the number of respondents who thought that the political parties were only interested in votes and not in what the people thought increased from 63 to 75 percent.[11] At the same time, the number of Germans who thought they had no influence on politics increased from 48 to 63 percent (Neu and Zelle, 1992, p. 9). In 1989, 81 percent agreed that most politicians did not know what the average person thought; for 65 percent, the big parties were no longer capable of solving the problems confronting German society.[12]

Unification, instead of reversing these trends, only exacerbated them. Thus in 1991, 62 percent of the public believed politicians were lining their own pockets (*in die eigenen Taschen wirtschaften*). In 1980, only one third had held that view (Neu and Zelle, 1992, p. 9). At the same time, 59 percent of the population of former West Germany charged the parties with leading an inner life that no longer interested the average citizen; 59 percent agreed with the statement that the only thing that counted for politicians was their own power and money (Gluchowski and Zelle, 1992, p. 258). Finally, in 1993, more citizens (48 percent) were "very worried" about the fact that politicians were no longer capable of solving urgent problems than were very worried about immigration or the state of the German economy (Noelle-Neumann, 1993). It is hardly surprising that by 1992, merely one out of five former West Germans still had confidence in political parties (Wiesendahl, 1992, p. 4).

The extent to which cynicism had come to dominate public attitudes toward the political class is perhaps best illustrated by the fact that between 1979 and 1992 the number of respondents who said they liked it when a man (a woman) was actively engaged in politics dropped from 64 percent (63 percent for women) to 36 (45 for women) (Piel, 1992). These poll results suggest that despite initial public euphoria over the fall of the Wall, unification ultimately failed to reverse, or even halt, the decline in the public's distrust in parties or the political class. On the contrary, the impression had grown that if the government could not cope with the problems facing German society, neither could the opposition (Piel, 1992, p. 5). Thus in 1992, only 22 percent of the population thought the Social Democrats were united enough to represent a viable alternative to the governing center-right coalition (Köcher, 1992).

Evidence suggests that *Parteienverdrossenheit* has also affected public attitudes toward democracy itself. Throughout the 1980s the relationship between the German population and its most important social and political institutions was positive and rather stable (Stöss, 1990, p. 22, ipos, 1992, p. 40). It was not until 1992 that systematic studies showed a major decline in the public's trust in some of Germany's major social and political institutions: the federal and state governments, the Bundestag and Bundesrat, the unions, and the churches—in short, those institutions most closely associated with party competition and the political process (Gabriel, 1993, p. 10; ipos, 1992, p. 41).

Further support for this view comes from the development of public attitudes toward democracy and the political system in Germany. Again the trend has been quite clear. Generally, in the 1980s at least 70 percent of the population declared themselves satisfied with democracy. With 85 percent, political satisfaction reached its highest level in 1990, the year of German unification. However, unification also marked a watershed. Since 1991 satisfaction has declined rather precipitously. In 1993, only 54 percent of the population of former West Germany (41 percent in the East) declared themselves satisfied with democracy. What is more, compared to 1989, dissatisfaction with the political system markedly increased among the supporters of all major parties, including those who supported the governing center-right coalition parties (ipos, 1993, p.28).

Given Germany's strong position in the international economy throughout the 1980s, this sharp increase in *Politikverdrossenheit* might appear somewhat puzzling. In the early 1980s, German per capita growth was still among the highest in the world; Germany was still the number-two exporter only marginally behind the United States and way ahead of Japan; its rate of investment was still relatively high compared to its European competitors or the United States (Biedenkopf, 1990, p. 91; Heise, 1993, pp. 348–349). However, Germany's continued economic success in the 1980s obscured the fact that there existed deep structural problems that politics largely failed to resolve. These problems included growing mass unemployment, social bifurcation, which gave rise to what came to be known as a "two-thirds-society," and, perhaps most alarming, immobility and inflexibility in the face of Germany's declining competitiveness in a rapidly changing international economy. Burdened with high business taxes, overregulation, high labor costs largely due to burgeoning social costs guaranteed contractually through negotiations with the trade unions, and a rigid labor market, in the 1980s the *Standort Deutschland* threatened to lose its attractiveness. By the early 1990s the perception was growing that Germany was not only risking "losing its hard-won rank in world-wide competition" but was in danger of beginning "to lose out even in those areas where she was recently preeminent" (Lauk, 1994, pp. 62–63).

If, as Kenneth Dyson (1989, p. 153) has charged, the "pervasiveness of wealth and affluence helped to distract attention from structural problems," the government did its part to nurture public complacency in the face of the global challenge. Nothing perhaps illustrates this better than the government's response to unification. Instead of demanding sacrifices from the West German population in the face of a national emergency, the government decided to unify the country without imposing substantial financial burdens on the population (Katzenbach, 1992). Since then, growing structural problems resulting from unresolved challenges to German competitiveness in the 1980s were compounded by the fallout from unification, including the strengthening of the German mark. As critics rightly observed, unification was "only the occasion" by which Germany's structural weaknesses with regard to global competitiveness became visible (Lauk, 1994, p. 63).

Undeniably, however, unification exacerbated these weaknesses and compounded Germany's economic problems. One of the major reasons behind these problems was that the West Germans "exported their high wages, generous benefits, and stifling regulations to the east—just when this brand of capitalism was beginning to flag under global competition."[13] Confronted with a collapsing economy in the east, West German transfers to former East Germany rose from DM 50bn in 1990 to roughly DM 170bn in 1992, contributing to record budgetary deficits. It was not until the economy entered a deep recession in 1992 that some observers started to wake up. Germany's most widely read newsweekly *Der Spiegel* expressed the new anxieties perhaps best when it warned that Germany was on its way to becoming a second league player.[14]

Despite growing public awareness that things were perhaps not going as well as Germans had been consistently led to believe in the past, it took Chancellor Kohl and the German government until late 1993 to acknowledge that Germany was confronted with "structural problems that have accumulated over too long a period of time" and which would not be eliminated by economic recovery alone (see Bundesministerium für Wirtschaft, 1993, pp. 52–68). [15] Caught in the maelstrom of global competition, German industry started a massive downsizing campaign. By the end of 1992, more than 840,000 workplaces had been destroyed in an increasingly ruthless process of structural deindustrialization (Kühl, 1993, p. 4). In late 1993, almost 60 percent of German businesses predicted further cuts in their work force. Meanwhile, a third of western Germany's large and medium-sized companies were thinking about relocating at least part of their production outside the country.[16]

It is hardly surprising that the downturn of the German economy left many Germans deeply worried about their economic future. Available evidence suggests, however, that as early as the late 1980s the West German public was no longer fully convinced of the continued viability of steadily increasing affluence and prosperity. When asked in 1989 what kind of life their children would have in the future, only 20 percent of the West German population expected their children to have it better than they themselves did. Thirty-nine percent thought their children's lives would be worse. As in France, the supporters of the far Right were the most pessimistic. Fifty-two percent of Republikaner supporters agreed with the negative statement.[17] As German voters grew increasingly pessimistic about the state of the German economy, as well as their personal economic situation in the early 1990s, the electorate grew more and more disenchanted with the established political parties. A growing number of voters doubted the ability of all established parties to solve Germany's mounting problems, disagreed with their positions, and felt less and less represented by them (see Scheuch and Scheuch, 1992; Rattinger, 1993). Thus it appeared that in the early 1990s disillusionment was as widespread as in the early 1980s. "But unlike during the crisis of 1981/82 no-one expects better things from the opposition. Distrust and scepticism are directed against all parliamentary parties" (Feist, 1993, p. 179).

One might suggest that the German public's deep resentment toward the political class was caused by at least two interconnected factors: On one hand, the established parties' and politicians' failure to do the impossible and preserve the German model of stability and prosperity, and thus appease the public's anxiety about the future; on the other hand, their failure at least to show strong leadership, depart from the status quo, and show creativity and political innovation. The result has been sobering. As the German president, Richard von Weizsäcker, said: "Industry and the economy are stuck in a cost and innovation crisis, labor in an employment crisis, the political class in a credibility crisis and society in an orientation crisis."[18]

As elsewhere in Western Europe, in Germany the supporters of the radical populist Right have been most disaffected with the established political parties, politicians, and the political system. Thus in 1989, 88 percent of Republikaner supporters agreed with the statement that the established large parties were no longer capable of solving society's problems; 90 percent agreed that politicians did not know what the average person thought; and 94 percent agreed that the political parties cared only about getting votes.[19] In 1991, 85 percent thought politicians were lining their own pockets, and only 5 percent said they trusted political parties (Veen, Lepszy, and Mnich, 1992, p. 48). By 1993, only the supporters of the ex-communist PDS in eastern Germany were more disenchanted with the political system. Among Republikaner a mere 18 percent expressed satisfaction with the political system, 24 percent said they were "very dissatisfied" (ipos, 1993, p. 28).

RADICAL RIGHT-WING SUPPORT: BETWEEN PROTEST AND CONVICTION

The preceding analysis suggests that political alienation in Western Europe can at least partly be traced to the profound socioeconomic changes that have characterized Western Europe since the early 1980s. Confronted with a rapidly changing international and domestic environment, institutions more often than not distinguished themselves by their inertia. *Politikverdrossenheit* thus became part of a general malaise that reflected as much the futility of attempts to preserve a comprehensive socioeconomic system, which in the past had guaranteed security and prosperity, as it reflected a general pessimism about the future. The resulting climate of resentment and disaffection provided fertile ground for new parties ready to exploit the voters' alienation and appeal to their perceptions of powerlessness. The fact that alienation and pessimism were particularly pronounced among radical right-wing supporters appears to support a protest thesis. On this view radical right-wing voters are typical floating voters who don't understand "the intricacies of politics in postindustrial societies" and therefore fall prey to clever demagogues who dress up empty slogans as viable solutions to real problems (see Mayer and Perrineau, 1992, p. 132; Pappi, 1990, p. 37). Undoubtedly, much can be said to support this view. Right-wing radical supporters themselves have tended to explain their choice as an expression of protest. In Austria, both in 1986 and 1990, more than a third of FPÖ voters wanted their decision to be seen as a vote against the established parties (Plasser and Ulram, 1990; Stirnemann, 1992). Early studies of Lega Nord supporters in Milan presented a similar picture. Polls allowing for multiple answers showed that what motivated some voters to abandon the traditional parties and vote Lega Nord instead was their desire to express their "protest against Rome," "protest against the *partitocrazia*," or "protest against the inefficiency of the public services" (Mannheimer, 1991, pp. 143–145). Similarly, in France in the 1988 presidential election, more than half of those who declared themselves very close to the Front National saw the vote for Le Pen mostly as a protest against the political system (Mayer and Perrineau, 1992, p. 133).

Furthermore, evidence from France and Germany suggests that radical right-wing voters were no less skeptical toward their favored party than they were toward the established ones. Thus in 1988, only a quarter of Front National voters said they wished to see Jean-Marie Le Pen elected president of the republic. Less than half said they would be content, and a fifth even said they would be dissatisfied if he were elected (SOFRES, 1989, pp. 99, 102). In Germany, in 1989, only a minority of Republikaner voters thought the Republikaner were competent to solve some of Germany's most pressing problems. Only 40 percent had confidence in the party with regard to unemployment, 43 percent with regard to problems with housing, 18 percent with regard to the general state of the economy. Not surprising, the only exception was immigration where more than 80 percent thought the Republikaner would be able to solve the problem in a reasonable way.[20] Even in the Swedish case, 30 percent of New Democracy party voters said they had little or very little confidence in their own party's politicians (Gilljam and Holmberg, 1993, p. 173).

Studies on the electoral history of radical right-wing voters provide additional support for the protest thesis. They suggest that at least in the early stages of their rise and electoral consolidation radical right-wing parties have drawn support from a wide range of sources (see Table 2.1). Not surprisingly, between 40 and 50 percent came from former voters of the bourgeois center-right. In Northern Italy, for example, the Lega Nord received 45 percent of its support in 1991 from voters who in 1987 had voted either for the Christian Democrats, the lay center, or the MSI. It is quite striking that the latter party, which has traditionally been regarded as a neo-fascist, right-wing extremist party, contrib-

Table 2.1

The Political Origins of the Radical Right-Wing Electorate

	Lega Nord (1992)		REP (1989)		FPÖ (1986)			ND (1991)
DC	25	CDU/CSU	43	ÖVP	28	B*	41	
PCI/PSI	30	SPD	21	SPÖ	30	S	28	
PRI/PSDI/PLI	11	FDP	8	FPÖ	26			
Verdi/Radicali	8	Grüne	2	Grüne	0	Green	7	
others	18	others	6			others	2	
MSI	8	no vote	22	no vote	4	no vote	22	
				1st vote	12			

* B = Bourgeois parties, S = Socialist parties

Sources: DOXA poll, 1992; Veen, Lepszy, and Mnich, 1992; Plasser, 1986; Taggart, 1992.

uted only 8 percent to the Lega vote. What is perhaps more surprising is the extent to which radical right-wing populist parties have also drawn support from former left-wing voters. In Northern Italy, in Austria, and in Sweden three out of every ten voters for the radical populist Right reported to have previously voted for the socialist bloc. Finally, it is also noteworthy that radical right-wing populist parties have been rather skilled in mobilizing former nonvoters and/or first-time voters. Given the broad range of electoral experiences of their supporters, radical right-wing populist parties appear to bear a strong resemblance to that model of a "catch-all-party of protest," which Thomas Childers and others have advanced to explain the Nazi vote.

There are, however, good reasons to reject a pure protest interpretation. Survey data suggest that radical right-wing voters are hardly the politically disinterested voters the protest thesis might lead us to expect. On the contrary, at least in the Austrian and German case, the voters of the FPÖ and the Republikaner reported significantly higher levels of political interest than the average voter (see Table 2.2). This was particularly striking among the voters of the Republikaner. In 1989, Republikaner votes were by far not only the most likely group to show a strong interest in politics; they were also the most likely group (64 percent compared to 42 percent for the whole population) to express confidence in their political judgment (Noelle-Neumann, 1989). These results are surprising given the fact that high interest in politics and the

Table 2.2
Interest in Politics (in %)

	Austria			Germany	
	All	FPÖ		All	REP
very strong	9	12	very strong	13	29
strong	16	17	rather strong	27	37
some	39	47	average	41	28
hardly	21	16	less strong	14	5
none at all	14	8	none at all	5	0

All = all voters in survey

Source: Plasser and Ulram, 1991a, p. 110; EMNID poll, 1989.

ability to make political judgements are generally associated with cognitive mobilization. Similar results are reported for the supporters of the Front National. In 1984, 72 percent of Front National voters reported to be interested in politics (23 percent of them very much) compared to 61 percent of the general electorate (16 percent very much; Schain, 1987, p. 243). Further support for this observation comes from Ronald Inglehart who has noted that the Front National "draw their support largely from cognitively mobilized nonpartisans," which puts them into the same group as the supporters of left-libertarian parties (Inglehart, 1990, p. 368).

A second point regards the longevity of these parties. As we have seen, the Scandinavian Progress parties have been an enduring part of the Danish and Norwegian party system since the early 1970s. By the end of the 1980s, both parties had overcome a number of serious internal conflicts and major electoral setbacks and appeared to have consolidated their organization (Andersen and Bjørklund, 1990, p. 195). Since the other parties, with the exception of the somewhat special case of the FPÖ, represent fairly new creations, their potential for survival as a significant political force is difficult to appraise. However, even in some of the more recent cases we observe indications of increasing electoral stability. Electoral studies indicate that over a relatively short period of time both the Front National and the FPÖ managed to not only considerably expand their voter base but also to retain a substantial proportion of their electorate between elections. In France, for example, 86 percent of those who had voted Front National in 1986 reported to have voted for Le Pen in 1988;

81 percent of Front National voters in the 1989 European election reported to have voted Front National in the regional elections of 1992; and 91 percent of Front National voters in 1992 reported to have voted for the party in the parliamentary elections of 1993, despite the party's poor chances to elect any of its candidates to the National Assembly (Lewis-Beck and Mitchell, 1993, p. 125; Bréchon, 1993, p. 55; *Libération,* March 23, 1993, p. 4). Besides being among the most loyal of all party supporters, Front National voters have also been among the most determined. Both in the regional elections of 1992 and the parliamentary elections of 1993, more than 70 percent of Front National voters declared to have made their choice several months before the election, compared to 55 and 60 percent respectively for the average voting population (*Libération,* March 23, 1993, p. 4).

The evolution of the FPÖ vote after Haider's rise to the party's leadership confirms the French results. Whereas in 1986, the party lost almost one third of their 1983 voters, in 1990, it managed to retain 84 percent of its 1986 voters. The 1991 local elections in Vienna provided further indications that the FPÖ was consolidating its electoral basis. If in 1987, the party had lost 21 percent of those who had voted FPÖ in the 1983 local elections in Vienna, in 1991 it retained more of its voters (91 percent) than any of the other relevant parties. A comparison between the 1991 election in Vienna and the 1986 parliamentary election also confirms a second trend. Whereas in 1986 only 49 percent of FPÖ voters reported to have made their decision several weeks before the election, by 1991 that percentage had risen to 74 percent (see Plasser, 1986; Plasser and Ulram, 1990; Plasser and Ulram, 1991).

A number of radical right-wing populist parties have thus succeeded not only in expanding their electoral base but in retaining a growing proportion of their electorate between elections. At least in some cases, radical right-wing voters appear to have developed strong loyalties, identifying themselves and their interests with the radical populist Right and its programs. These are good reasons to reject the notion that these parties are merely parties of discontent, even if appealing to voter resentment and disenchantment is certainly part of their strategy.

A third aspect is the distinct ideological identity of the radical Right's constituency. Empirical evidence suggests that in a number of cases the supporters of radical right-wing populist parties distinguished themselves from the supporters of the established right-wing parties by their far-right position on the left-right continuum. In Switzerland, for example, in 1991 almost a quarter of the supporters of the Automobile party placed themselves on the far right of the political spectrum (compared to 5 percent for the whole sample and 3 to 8 percent for the bourgeois parties; Longchamp and Hardmeier, 1992, p. 23).

Similarly, in Germany, in 1993 more than a third of Republikaner supporters classified themselves as far right (compared to 3 percent of the whole sample) (see Noelle-Neumann, 1993).

A significant exception was the Lega Nord. Both in 1991 and 1992, Lega Nord voters placed themselves in the center of the political spectrum, close to the voters of the Christian Democrats (see Mannheimer, 1992; 1993, pp. 92–94). This might hardly come as a surprise given the fact that a great number of Lega Nord supporters had formerly voted for the Christian Democrats. However, the results of studies on the ideological self-placement of Front National voters at the beginning of the party's rise to prominence suggest that the Lega Nord results might be evidence of more profound differences between the Lega and other radical right-wing populist parties, which will be examined in chapter 4. Michael Lewis-Beck and Glenn Mitchell have recently pointed out that already in the mid-1980s Front National supporters were more extreme than the supporters of their competitors on the Right, the RPR and the UDF. Like the supporters of the Automobile Party or the Republikaner in the early 1990s, the supporters of the Front National in the mid-1980s were more likely to place themselves on the far end than any other group (Lewis-Beck and Mitchell, 1993, pp. 119–120; see also Mayer and Perrineau, 1992, p. 216). Because of our lack of comparative data on the ideological self-placement of the supporters of all radical right-wing populist parties in Western Europe, it is impossible to draw anything but tentative conclusions from these data. They do suggest, however, that radical right-wing populist parties might have managed to attract a rather distinct group of supporters who are fairly different from what one would expect of temporary protest voters.

BETWEEN PROTEST AND ISSUE VOTING

Ronald Inglehart (1990, pp. 275–279) is probably closer to the truth when he interprets the success of parties like the Front National as part of a secular shift in advanced Western democracies from class-based to issue-based politics. At least in part, available evidence supports this contention. What has most clearly distinguished the supporters of radical right-wing populist parties from the general voting public is the priority they give to two specific issues: immigration and law and order. In the European election of 1984, 30 percent of National Front voters mentioned insecurity among the two most important issues influencing their decision to vote Front National; 26 percent mentioned immigration compared to 15 and 6 percent respectively for the whole population (Le Gall, 1984, p. 44). The results were even more pronounced in the parliamentary elections in 1986 and the presidential elections of 1988. In 1986, immigration was the most important issue for 46 percent of National Front voters; for 18 percent it was insecurity (Perrineau, 1988, p. 26). Finally, in 1988 55 percent of Front National voters mentioned insecurity and 59 percent immigration as motivations for their choice, compared to 31 and 22 percent respectively for the whole of the voting population (Perrineau, 1988, p. 39; see also Mayer and Perrineau, 1992, pp. 131–132). At the same time National Front voters attributed less importance to unemployment than the general public (41 percent for Front National supporters, 45 percent for the general public). The contrast was even more pronounced in a survey conducted at the time of the municipal elections in 1989. When asked which two problems had counted most in the second round of the elections, 62 percent of Front National voters opted for immigrants and 58 percent for insecurity, but only 17 percent for unemployment. Survey evidence, however, also suggests that by the early 1990s anxiety over job security had increased dramatically among Front National supporters. Between 1987 and 1992 the proportion of Front National supporters who feared losing their jobs increased from 37 percent to 63 percent. Only Communist supporters were more anxious about their jobs (Dupoirier, 1994, p. 60). This might explain the shift in the Front National's economic policy in the early 1990s (see chapter 4).

The results have been similar for the supporters of other radical right-wing populist parties. Ever since their breakthrough in the 1989 elections, Republikaner supporters have been most concerned about two issues: the alleged abuse of Germany's asylum laws and the fight against crime in general and drug-related crimes in particular (see ipos, 1989, p. 11). In 1993, 92 percent of Republikaner supporters considered the prevention of the abuse of the asylum laws a very important political goal; 75 percent the fight against drugs. At the same time the concern about job security was not substantially higher among Republikaner supporters than among the general public (ipos, 1993, p. 11). In Belgium, in a survey conducted after the 1991 national election, two thirds of Vlaams Blok voters said they had voted for the Vlaams Blok because of its stance in the immigration issue (Swyngedouw, 1992, p. 64). Finally, in Sweden in 1991, New Democracy party voters distinguished themselves by their hostility toward refugees, immigrants, and development aid (see Gilljam and Holmberg, 1993, p. 155).

Immigration and drugs have also been among the most important problems for the supporters of the Swiss Automobile party and the Lega Nord. In 1991, 48 percent of Automobile party supporters identified the question of asylum and refugees as the most important political problem in Switzerland compared to 21 percent for the general public. For 8 percent, the most important problem

Table 2.3

Rating of Political Priorities, Austria, 1992 (in %)

	All	FPÖ	Greens
1. improve environmental protection	52	44	68
2. solve the foreigner problem	46	53	33
3. fight corruption and privileges	44	62	52
4. secure social security and pensions	42	36	23
5. prevent the waste of public funds	41	46	54
6. secure full employment	32	35	21
7. guarantee domestic order	26	25	20
8. preserve social peace	25	16	30
9. reduce tax burden	20	20	14
10. create more opportunity for public participation	20	21	31
11. secure living standard of the population	16	9	15
12. remove existing injustices in our society	15	15	23
13. Austria's EC membership	11	9	12

Source: Fessel+GfK, "Gesellschaftlicher Monitor," 1992.

was drugs (5 percent of the general public); for another 8 percent (2 percent of the general public) it was "traffic questions" (Longchamp and Hardmeier, 1992, p. 23). As for Lega Nord supporters, in a survey conducted in the winter of 1992/1993 in Lombardy and the Veneto, 61 percent of the respondents considered the immigrant question a very high priority compared to 53 percent of the population (Diamanti, 1993, p. 99).

A comparison of the political priorities of Green and FPÖ supporters in 1992 provides perhaps the best support for the thesis that issues rather than protest explain the appeal of radical-right wing political parties. As can be seen from Table 2.3, the supporters of both parties were considerably more concerned about fighting corruption and privileges than the general public. This would support the notion than both parties appealed primarily to voter protest. However, a closer analysis of the data reveals that what distinguished Green and FPÖ supporters was their response to two issues, environmental protection and immigration. The Greens were considerably more concerned about environmental protection than the general public, whereas FPÖ supporters attributed less importance to this issue than the supporters of any other party. The reverse was true with regard to immigration. Among FPÖ supporters more than half considered immigration a very important issue, among Green supporters only a third. Finally, the supporters of the FPÖ attributed relatively low importance not only to typically materialist issues, such as protecting full employment or securing the standard of living of the population, but also to typically authoritarian issues, such as securing internal order. These findings suggest that the sense of distrust that distinguishes a large majority of radical right-wing supporters represents more than a general disenchantment with political parties and the political system. Rather, their disenchantment stems from the perception that the established political parties have neglected to address certain issues that the supporters of the radical populist right deem to be essential preconditions for the revival and survival of advanced West European societies. Among these issues, the question of immigration appears to have become the central issue. The growing sense of insecurity and pessimism, the fear of crime and particularly drugs prevalent among radical right-wing supporters, are all related to the overarching question of the growing presence of foreigners in Western Europe. The fact, however, that for the supporters of the radical populist Right economic questions and unemployment appear to be of secondary importance does not necessarily imply that radical right-wing populist politics is essentially postindustrial, noneconomic politics. Rather, as James G. Shields has proposed, the questions of unemployment and economic decline present themselves as further symptoms of "a generalised climate of insecurity," or as one more consequence of immigration (Shields, 1991, p. 80).

The preceding analysis implies that the political climate of distrust and disenchantment that came to prevail in Western Europe in the 1980s was a significant precondition for the rise and success of radical right-wing populist parties. It contributed to a further weakening of traditional voter loyalties to the established parties and thus provided political entrepreneurs like Franz Schönhuber, Jörg Haider, or Umberto Bossi with the window of opportunity that would allow them to promote themselves as viable alternatives to the political establishment. By appealing to a limited range of new issues neglected by the established parties they managed to gain growing popular support.

Most studies on the contemporary radical Right put the emergence and rise of radical right-wing populist parties in the context of the rise of xenophobia and racism during the past decade. This corresponds with empirical evidence that suggests that the supporters of the radical populist Right are particularly concerned about immigration. This would suggest that the rise of radical right-wing populism is largely a result of growing xenophobia in response to the increasingly visible presence of immigrants and refugees in Western Europe. The following chapter explores this proposition.

3

Immigration and
Xenophobia

During the past several years the question of immigration has become one of the most significant social and political issues in a growing number of West European countries. Thus in 1990, the question of how to confront the problem of immigration ranked second (41 percent) only to the question of how to combat unemployment (66 percent) among the issues that the French population considered to be of top political priority for the next few years. At the end of 1991, more than 71 percent of the population of the western part of Germany regarded the question of refugees and foreigners a very important political issue. This was far more than they accorded environmental protection and unemployment (about 10 percent each).[1] This growing concern over immigration had come at a time when most West European countries already held a sizeable immigrant population while being confronted by a wave of new arrivals. In 1987, the 12 countries of the European Community were home to more than 13 million foreign nationals, 60 percent of whom were from nonmember countries. The vast majority of non-EC nationals lived in Germany, France, and Great Britain. Belgium and the Netherlands also had sizeable non-EC populations (see Table 3.1). Among nonmember states, particularly Switzerland, Sweden, and Austria have received considerable numbers of immigrants. In 1987, roughly 15 percent of the Swiss, 4.6 percent of the Swedish, and 3.9 percent of the Austrian population were foreign nationals. Since then, new immigrants, a growing number of refugees and asylum seekers, and

Table 3.1

Foreign Residence in the EC

1987	Total Population	(in 1,000s and % of total population) Immigrants EC	Immigrants non-EC
Bel.	9,864	533 (5.4%)	315 (3.2%)
Den.	5,102	27 (0.5%)	102 (2.9%)
Fr. (1982)	54,273	1,578 (2.9%)	2,103 (3.9%)
Ger.	61,171	1,377 (2.3%)	3,196 (5.2%)
Gr.	9,740	55 (0.6%)	31 (0.3%)
Ire.	3,543	62 (1.7%)	18 (0.5%)
It. (1981)	56,557	91 (0.2%)	112 (0.2%)
Lux. (1989)	384	102 (26.4%)	10 (2.7%)
Neth. (1988)	14,714	160 (1.1%)	435 (2.9%)
Port.	10,270	24 (0.2%)	66 (0.6%)
Sp.	38,832	193 (0.5%)	142 (0.4%)
U.K.	56,075	810 (1.6%)	1,651 (2.9%)
E.C.	**320,526**	**5,014 (1.6%)**	**8,179 (2.6%)**

Source: European Commission

(particularly in the case of Italy) better statistics have led to a considerable increase in the size of the reported number of foreign residents in Western Europe.

History shows that native populations have often looked upon new arrivals with a mixture of apprehension, suspicion, and disdain. As early as 1896, the French newspaper *La Patrie* welcomed immigrants with the following words: "They are like an invasion of locusts. . . . They are dirty, miserable, and in rags. . . . They work for minimum wages, play sometimes the harmonica, and sometimes with the knife" (cited in Knight and Kowalsky, 1991, p. 79).

Although the horrors of the organized extermination of millions of innocent human beings because of their ethnic origins sensitized the European public to the evils of racism and ethnic discrimination, hostility toward foreigners was far from disappearing completely in Western Europe. Since they were no longer *gesellschaftsfähig*, xenophobia, anti-Semitism, and racism were largely driven underground, relegated to the sidelines of beer-hall discussions and the lunatic fringes of the nostalgic extreme Right. The situation began to change with the economic crises of the late 1960s and early 1970s. Increasing unemployment and social marginalization caused a wave of resentment toward foreign workers. Political parties on the extreme Right and in some cases on the Left quickly seized upon the issue in order to exploit it for electoral gains. In Germany, home to one of the largest foreign populations in Western Europe, appeal to the growing hostility toward foreign workers was one of the reasons behind the electoral gains of the National Democratic Party in the late 1960s (Thränhardt, 1988, p. 11). In France, it was the Communist party that was largely instrumental in promoting a policy of race. This policy was directed primarily against non-European, particularly Muslim immigrants and nonwhite French citizens from the overseas departments, which the party regarded "as temporary residents who must be encouraged to return home" (Schain, 1990, p. 262; Hollifield, 1991, p. 134). In Switzerland, in the late 1960s and throughout the 1970s, antiforeigner parties repeatedly called for referenda to allow the population to decide whether something should be done to stop and reverse the threatened *Überfremdung* ("foreignization") of the country. Despite sizeable support for some of the referenda, all were defeated (Husbands, 1988, p. 715). Finally, in Great Britain, the early 1970s saw the emergence of the National Front, which sought to ride on the wave of growing hostility to immigration for political success. However, this first wave of xenophobic mobilization in Western Europe proved rather disappointing to its protagonists. Appeal to xenophobia and racism helped neither the German NPD, the British National Front, nor the Swiss antiforeigner parties to play more than a marginal role in national politics; nor could it halt or prevent the decline of the Communist Party of France.

Probably one of the major reasons of the failure of these parties to gain sustained support for their antiforeigner positions was that in most of the countries with large foreign populations the governments quickly adopted stringent measures to curb further immigration. Germany ordered a stop to the recruitment of foreign labor in 1973, and Belgium in 1975 (Vandermotten and Vanlaer, 1991). In 1974, France adopted a number of restrictive measures, which culminated in the complete closing of its borders to all immigrants except for seasonal workers, political refugees, and cases of family reunion (Schain, 1990, p. 256; Hollifield, 1991, p. 131). Similarly, Switzerland introduced stricter controls on the flow of immigrant labor after the first foreignization referendum in 1969 was almost approved by a majority of the population. In the British case, the demise of the National Front was linked above all to the fact that the Conservative Party quickly seized the immigration issue and "increasingly came to be viewed by the electors as the party most opposed to 'immigration'" (Eatwell, 1992, p. 186).

Despite efforts on the part of the established parties and the national governments to check growing hostility toward foreigners by setting strict limits to immigration, xenophobia and racism reemerged in the 1980s and early 1990s. There are at least two reasons for this development. One is found in the changes in the composition of immigrant groups. In the 1950s and 1960s the great majority of immigrant workers had been Western Europeans and Yugoslavs. The only important non-European groups were Turks, particularly in Germany, and Algerians in France. Starting in the 1970s, however, there was a steady decline in the proportion of European immigrant workers. At the same time, the number of workers from Asia and Africa increased considerably. A second reason is found in the dramatic increase in the number of political refugees in the 1980s. This was at least in part a result of the restrictive immigration policies in the 1970s. Since international law does not recognize unemployment and misery to be relevant reasons for seeking asylum, many would-be immigrant workers were forced to seek entrance into Western Europe as political refugees. The increase in the number of refugees, many of them coming from developing countries, added to the already growing non-European population in Western Europe. The result has been a profound apprehension on the part of Western Europeans "that some fundamental, unexpected and irrevocable changes have taken place because of recent large scale immigration," threatening "the historically given self-perceptions of European nations" (Hammar, 1989, p. 633).

IMMIGRANT LABOR

Postwar labor migration was a response to the labor shortage experienced in the northern industrial countries of Western Europe during the years of rapid economic expansion in the late 1950s and early 1960s (Bischoff and Teubner, 1991, pp. 31-34). In order to meet the economy's rising demands for fresh labor, a number of West European governments encouraged immigration, concluding recruitment treaties with a series of countries first in southern Europe, then outside Europe. Germany, for example, concluded the first treaty with Italy in 1955. Treaties with Spain and Greece (1960), Turkey (1961), Morocco (1963), Portugal (1964), Tunisia (1965), Yugoslavia (1968), and even Korea (1970) followed (Thränhardt, 1988). Recruitment was done either through "German commissions" of the Federal Bureau of Labor in the labor exporting countries or by the companies themselves (Bischoff and Teubner, 1991, p. 35). The situation was similar in France. As early as in 1946, in order to meet the anticipated need for labor for reconstructing the country, the French government established the National Office of Immigration (ONI) charged with recruiting temporary foreign labor and furnishing them with work permits. This system of recruitment worked well until the late 1950s when rapidly increased demand for labor caused many employers to recruit labor directly in the major labor-exporting countries and arrange their "regularization" after they were already in the country. "Thus a pattern of illegal immigration emerged during the 1960s, which was initiated by labour-hungry employers and openly tolerated by the state." As a result, by 1968, it was estimated that as much as 80 percent of immigrant workers had entered the country illegally (Schain, 1990, p. 255). In addition to tolerating active labor recruitment, the French government encouraged immigration from its former colonies Algeria, Morocco, and Tunisia. In 1962, "it agreed to accept an unlimited number of Algerians in France, although a quarter of the Algerian work force was already in France" (Schain, 1990, p. 256). As a result of rising demand for foreign labor, the number of immigrant workers significantly increased in the postwar period. In Germany, the number of registered foreign workers increased from roughly 280,000 in 1960 to almost 2.6 million in 1973. In Switzerland, the number of foreign residents with at least a one-year work permit increased from 330,000 to almost 600,000. And in Austria, the size of the foreign work force expanded from 21,000 in 1963 to more than 225,000 in 1973. At the same time the northern countries of Western Europe witnessed a dramatic increase in the overall foreign populations living within their borders. In Germany, their number increased from 690,000 in 1960 to 4.1 million in 1974, which constituted 6.6 percent of the population; in Switzerland, from 500,000 to roughly one million; in Austria, from 100,000 in 1961 to 310,000 in 1974; and in France from 1.8 million in 1962 to 3.4 million in 1975.

Although the measures to halt further immigration in the 1970s led to a stabilization and even decrease in the number of foreign workers, they failed to reverse the overall size of the resident foreign population. This was primarily due to family reunion, but also to the growth of a second generation of foreigners born to immigrant families. This was in line with a policy that on the one hand sought to stop any new immigration, but on the other hand sought to integrate immigrant families already settled into the host societies (Erichsen, 1988, p. 16; Schain, 1990, pp. 259–260). Thus Belgium recently adopted a law that granted automatic Belgian citizenship to third-generation foreign residents if both they themselves and their parents had been born in Belgium (Vandermotten and Verlaer, 1991).

One of the consequences of the immigration policies of the 1970s was a significant change in the structure of the foreign population. Whereas in the 1950s and 1960s the majority of immigrants had been (male) workers, starting in the 1970s a growing proportion of immigrants consisted of their (often nonworking) family members. In Germany, for example, in 1973 almost two thirds of the foreign population were active in the work force; by 1989 that proportion had fallen to one third. However, the immigration policies of the 1970s not only changed the internal composition of the foreign population. One of their unintended, but highly consequential effects was a considerable change in the national and ethnic composition of the foreign population. In the 1950s and 1960s, the great majority of foreign labor had come from neighboring European countries. In France, Europeans made up 90 percent of the foreign population in 1954 and still 86 percent in 1962 (Tribalat, 1986, p.34). The situation was not much different in Germany where it was not until 1973 that Turkish workers became the largest group of foreign workers (Thränhardt, 1988, p. 5).

However, a recruitment stoppage and incentives for foreign workers to return home had counterproductive effects: They reduced the number of both EC citizens, whose position was fairly secure, and Europeans in general. As a result, the proportion of non-Europeans among the overall foreign population increased considerably. In France, for example, the proportion of immigrant families from the Maghreb region increased from 23 percent in 1968 to 39 percent in 1982. At the same time the proportion of Europeans decreased from 86 percent to 48 percent (Tribalat, 1986, pp. 34–35; see also Hollifield, 1991, p. 127). The situation was not much different in Germany, where by the late 1980s Turkish nationals outnumbered foreign nationals from EC countries (33 percent to 27 percent).

By the late 1980s, developments in some of the smaller countries in Western Europe, but also in the new immigration countries of southern Europe (Italy and Spain), started to resemble those witnessed earlier in France. In Denmark, for example, between 1982 and 1991 the number of foreigners from Scandinavia and the EC countries increased slightly from 46,000 to 51,000. At the same time the number of Africans and Asians increased from 19,000 to over 45,000. In Austria, the 1980s saw a significant increase in the number of Turkish immigrants, which far surpassed the increase of the number of Yugoslavs who still represented the largest immigrant group in Austria (Eichwalder, 1991, pp. 165–166). But perhaps the most dramatic development occurred in Italy, where the government has only recently begun to compile detailed statistics on immigration. These statistics reveal a drastic change in the composition of foreign resident groups during the 1980s. Whereas as recently as 1980 the majority of foreign residents in Italy were Europeans, by 1991 the vast majority were from non-EC countries (so-called *extracommunitari*). Thirty-one percent came from Africa (more than half of whom were from the Maghreb region), and 26 percent from Asia and Latin America. Only one third of all foreign residents were Europeans, less than 20 percent from the European Community (ISPES, 1991, pp. 469–480).

Similar developments are beginning to occur in Spain, whose immigration population is still relatively low (in 1989 it was an estimated 400,000). In 1989, two thirds of the legally registered foreign residents came from Europe, a further 20 percent came from the United States and Latin America, with which Spain has traditionally had special links, and only 14 percent from Asia and Africa. However, over the last ten years the number of European residents has remained rather stable, whereas the number of Africans has increased sixfold and Asians have more than doubled. Thus in Spain, as in Italy, a growing proportion of new arrivals come from the developing countries, "some of which have not had any special links with Spain in the past" (OECD, 1991, p. 24). By contrast, Europeans still make up the vast majority of the foreign population in both Switzerland and Sweden. In 1991, almost 80 percent of all foreigners with permanent resident permits in Switzerland were citizens of EC or EFTA countries. A further 9 percent held Yugoslavian citizenship, and only 6 percent came from Turkey (Bundesamt für Ausländerfragen, 1991, p. 49). Similarly, in Sweden, in 1989 almost 60 percent of foreign residents came from Western Europe (a large proportion of them Finns). At the same time a growing number of immigrants came from Eastern Europe. Only 5 percent of the immigrant population were Turks (OECD, 1991, p. 147).

European statistics on immigrants show that despite entrance restrictions, incentive programs for foreign workers to return home, and growing hostility toward them the size of the immigrant population in Western Europe has remained fairly stable or has even increased. This confirms that some of the major assumptions and expectations of West European governments regarding immigrant workers were false. The most important of these assumptions had been that migrant workers were only attracted by economic gains. If "the economic gains to the migrants were reduced or ceased altogether, for example through unemployment," or "if their expectations of work and savings failed to materialise," they would return home. "Thus, in times of recession, policies to encourage repatriation would be both justified and successful." But despite economic recessions, despite mass unemployment almost everywhere in Western Europe, and despite the efforts of individual governments to curb immigration, "migrant workers have not only remained but have sent for their wives and children, have bought houses, and are showing every sign of settling as permanent members of their new countries" (Layton-Henry, 1990, p. 162).

As a 1985 German survey of (European and Turkish) foreign workers revealed, there are several reasons for this behavior. Although only a very small minority of respondents said they had no intention to return to their home countries, the rest found many reasons indefinitely to postpone their return. Some of these reasons were that there were no jobs in their home countries; that they liked their work in Germany; that their children were still in school or going through vocational education and training; that they had not yet saved enough money; or that they would not be allowed to reenter the country once they had left it. One fifth (44 percent among foreigners born in Germany) said they "felt good" in Germany (Bischoff and Teubner, 1991, p. 116). As the composition of the foreign population was gradually changing during the past two decades, one might presume that more reasons have been added. These are particularly the advanced state of the West European welfare state with its basic services unknown to most non-European labor exporting countries and the relative peace and tranquility, which stands in stark contrast to the situation in a number of developing countries. As a result, the majority of foreigners prefer to stay in their host countries rather than to return home. As one survey found, in 1990 almost two thirds of all foreigners living in France (54 percent Maghrebins and 36 percent Africans) would stay in France even if there were jobs available in their home countries (Le Gall, 1992, p. 131).

ASYLUM SEEKERS AND REFUGEES

Similar reasons also account for the growing number of foreigners who seek entrance into Western Europe as political refugees. During the past ten years all of Western Europe has witnessed a dramatic increase in the number of refugees. Between 1983 and 1989 alone, the number of asylum seekers and refugees more than quadrupled from roughly 70,000 to almost 320,000 (see Table 3.2). However, although all West European countries experienced substantially higher numbers of refugees in 1989 than they had in 1983, some countries clearly attracted more than others. Among these were France, Sweden, Switzerland, Austria, and above all Germany.

Because of its past, for a long time Germany had the most liberal asylum policy in Western Europe. It allowed virtually anyone to apply for asylum and required the state to take care of them while their claim was being processed. As a result, Germany attracted by far the largest proportion of refugees in Western Europe. In 1989, more than 120,000 refugees sought asylum in Germany. By 1991, that number had surpassed a quarter of a million. By the end of 1992, it reached almost half a million. This was more than the number of all refugees seeking asylum in Western Europe in 1988. In addition, as a result of the liberalization program in the Soviet Union and the eruption of

Table 3.2
Asylum Seekers and Refugees in Western Europe

	1983	1984	1985	1986	1987	1988	1989
A	5,898	7,208	6,724	8,639	11,406	15,790	21,882
B	2,937	3,666	5,340	7,640	5,995	5,078	8,021
DK	800	4,300	8,700	9,300	2,750	4,700	4,600
F	22,285	21,624	28,809	26,196	27,568	34,253	61,372
G	19,737	35,278	73,832	99,650	57,379	103,076	121,318
GR	450	750	1,400	4,250	6,342	9,316	6,474
I	3,050	4,554	5,423	6,478	11,032	1,366	2,240
NL	2,015	2,603	5,644	5,865	13,460	7,486	13,898
N	150	300	829	2,722	8,613	6,602	4,433
S	-*	-*	-*	2,819	3,714	4,494	3,989
SW	4,000	12,000	14,450	14,600	18,100	19,600	30,000
SWI	7,886	7,435	9,703	8,546	10,913	16,726	24,425
UK	4,296	3,869	5,444	4,811	5,160	5,263	15,530
Total				201,516	182,432	233,750	318,182

A = Austria, B = Belgium, DK = Denmark, F = France, G = Germany, GR = Greece, I = Italy, NL = Netherlands, N = Norway, S = Spain, SW = Sweden, SWI = Switzerland, UK = United Kingdom

*no Spanish data available for these years, and hence no meaningful total can be given

Source: OECD

domestic turmoil in Eastern Europe, Germany was confronted with a growing number of ethnic Germans seeking repatriation from the Soviet Union, Eastern Europe, and East Germany. Within three years, the number of resettlers more than quadrupled from 78,000 in 1987 to 377,000 in 1989 (*Daten und Fakten*, 1992, p. 36).

The right to asylum in Western Europe is laid down in The Convention Relating to the Status of Refugees, which was adopted in 1951. Initially, it was established in order to deal with the problem of refugees flowing from Eastern to Western Europe. Because of that, it was limited to the results of the postwar settlement in Europe. It was not until 1967 that an amendment abolished the closely circumscribed boundaries of the convention. Despite this extension, throughout most of the Cold War period the question of refugees in Western Europe was mainly a question of Eastern Europeans fleeing the sphere of Communist domination. Statistics on refugees seeking asylum in Austria and Switzerland reflect these developments. In the years 1956 and 1957, Austria altogether received almost 230,000 Hungarian refugees who fled the repression after the Soviet invasion of Hungary. In 1968/69 both Austria and Switzerland received more than 10,000 Czechoslovaks, leaving the CSSR after the Soviet invasion put an end to the Prague Spring. Finally, in the years following the declaration of martial law in Poland in 1981, both countries experienced a significant increase in the number of Polish refugees, which in the Austrian case amounted to more than 38,000 (Eichwalder, 1991, pp. 165-166; Bundesamt für Flüchtlinge, 1992).

The policy of many West European countries to grant asylum to East European refugees was not only a humanitarian gesture. Particularly in Germany, East European refugees, namely those fleeing East Germany, were held up not only as symbols of the desire for freedom repressed under Communist rule, but also of the moral superiority of the West. The question of asylum thus always also had an ideological and propagandistic dimension. One important aspect of this dimension was the demand that the Soviet Union and the East European Communist regimes grant the freedom of free movement to their citizens, which one might suppose included the right to choose where they wanted to live and work. Without a doubt Western pressure on Eastern Europe's Communist regimes to open themselves up to Western influences contributed to the political crisis and ultimate collapse of these regimes. Particularly, the influence of Western culture among the younger generation of Eastern Europeans was of great significance. However, the collapse of Communism in Eastern Europe confronted Western Europe with a new and unexpected challenge. It allowed a growing number of Eastern Europeans to leave their home countries for the first time and to migrate to the affluent consumer societies of Western Europe. As a result, in 1991 more than two thirds of all political refugees in Germany came from central and southeastern Europe. Among them were 40,000 Romanians, 12,000 Bulgarians, and 75,000 Yugoslav citizens (Biermann, 1992, p. 29; also Ronge, 1993, p. 20). The situation was similar in Austria, which in 1989 and 1990 saw itself confronted with a dramatic increase of Romanian refugees, and in Switzerland, which in 1991 registered more than 14,000 refugees from Yugoslavia. The great majority of these refugees fled political violence and ethnically motivated persecution, as in the case of Romanian gypsies or Bulgarian Turks (Müller, 1992). However, expectations were that in the future a growing number of Eastern Europeans would migrate to the West for economic reasons. These impressions were reinforced by opinion polls, which found a considerable number of Central Europeans and Russians intent on leaving their home countries within the next few years (see Biermann, 1992, p. 30). It is thus hardly surprising that in the spring of 1993, more than two thirds of the German population expected to be confronted with a large immigration/refugee wave "within the near future" (Noelle-Neumann, 1993).

Confronted with already drastic increases in the number of refugees and the expectation of more, rapidly growing public hostility toward the new arrivals, and in some instances spectacular gains of radical right-wing populist parties, a number of West European governments responded similarly to the way they had sought to halt immigration in the 1970s. Austria introduced visa requirements for East European citizens and deployed military personnel along its border with Hungary to stop the influx of illegal immigrants. Denmark and Sweden adopted stricter controls of refugees entering the country while Sweden even decided to expel asylum-seekers from Bulgaria charging that their fears of persecution were not well founded (Arter, 1992, pp. 358–359). Great Britain enacted new legislation drastically shortening the period within which authorities determine whether refugees qualify for political asylum, made it considerably more difficult to appeal refusals, and increased fines on foreign airlines that flew in foreigners without proper entry documents (Whitney, 1991, p. 8). In Germany there began a debate on whether the country should change its Basic Law, which ended in a compromise between the established political parties in late 1992 to toughen Germany's relatively generous asylum law. At the same time Germany reached an agreement with some East European countries in which these countries agreed to take back nationals (particularly gypsies) who had fled to Germany to escape alleged or real persecution. Finally, in France, the appointment of Charles Pasqua to the post of minister of the interior in the spring of 1992 was a clear sign of the political importance the new center-right government attributed to the question of immigration. Under Pasqua, France introduced a number of stringent measures designed to discourage all forms of immigration and eventually reach the goal of "zero immigration."[2] Even the relatively tolerant Italian government could be rather ruthless when it came to discouraging East European asylum-seekers. In the summer of 1991, thousands of desperate Albanians landed on Italy's shores. Unprepared for such an emergency, the Italian authorities detained them under police guard with a minimum of food or water in a soccer stadium in the port city of Bari. Inducing them with new clothes and a small amount of money to return to their country, they sent the majority back across the Adriatic Sea a few days later. Those who had refused these inducements were in some cases mistreated by the police, then promised a temporary permit to stay in the country and put on airplanes and returned to Albania.

The dramatic increase of East European refugees after the collapse of Communism suggests that the search for asylum is less and less motivated by purely political reasons. Most refugees flee a combination of problems ranging from abject poverty and near starvation to domestic turmoil and civil war to environmental destruction in their home countries. This is also reflected in the low rates of approval of asylum applications. In the early 1990s less than 10 percent of applications for political asylum were approved in Western Europe. The rest were considered to have entered Western Europe as "economic refugees" whose only means of bypassing the severe restrictions on immigration was to ask for political asylum. As most outside observers readily acknowledged, most refugees "want to build a better life for themselves, either here or, eventually, back home, and perhaps therefore are better described as immigrants." However, since most West European countries had barred immigration, "the only way to get a foot in the door is to sneak into countries like Spain [or Italy], which until recently did not even require visas of people coming over from Morocco, or to fly into an airport and to ask for asylum, then taking advantage of the time it takes to determine qualification to settle down and take root anyway" (Whitney, 1991, p. 8). Surveys confirm that this perception came increasingly to be shared by a growing number of West Europeans. Thus, in 1992, 75 percent of the West German population thought that most asylum seekers were abusing Germany's asylum laws (ipos, 1992, p. 93). And 78 percent thought the number of economic refugees allowed to stay in Germany should be drastically reduced.[3]

The dramatic increase in the influx of refugees in the late 1980s led to a new wave of resentment and hostility toward foreigners among large parts of the West European public. Confronted with the threat of an "invasion of the poor" (Werner, 1992) set on "storming Europe" (Ritter, 1990) a growing proportion of West European citizens turned against the new arrivals. Within a few years, the question of immigration and asylum had become one of the most important issues facing West European governments. In 1989 (the first year the question was asked) 54 percent of the German population said they considered it "very important" to prevent the abuse of the asylum law. By 1992, the number had increased to 67 percent, surpassed only by concern for the environment, the housing market, and the future of the pension system (ipos, 1992, p. 8). However, the dramatic increase in sheer numbers in the late 1980s is only one reason for the growing hostility toward refugees in Western Europe. Another is the fact that in the 1980s non-Europeans began to constitute a growing proportion of refugees in Western Europe. Refugees thus started to add to the large population of non-European immigrants reinforcing the impression that Western Europe is being "invaded" from developing countries (Werner, 1992).

The French situation once again provided a clue as to general trends in Western Europe. In 1982, European refugees accounted for no more than 12 percent of all refugees that year. More than two thirds came from Asia, most of the rest were from Africa. By 1989, Europeans accounted for a little more than 5 percent of all refugees. By contrast, almost four out of ten refugees came from Africa and half from Asia. Turks alone accounted for more than 50 percent of all Asian refugees and 28 percent of all refugees that year (Lebon, 1990, p.76). Germany and particularly Switzerland showed similar trends. Thus, in 1991, Europeans accounted for 44 percent of all refugees seeking asylum in Switzerland; 14 percent came from Africa, 31 percent from Asia, and 10 percent were from Turkey (Bundesamt für Flüchtlinge, 1992). In Germany, in 1991, Turks accounted for 9 percent of all refugees; refugees from Iran, Nigeria, Afghanistan, Vietnam, and Sri Lanka made for another 15 percent (*Daten und Fakten,* 1992, p. 35). As a result of these trends, even those West European countries which hitherto had not yet been exposed to major non-European immigrant populations, were increasingly confronted with a sizeable number of non-Europeans, whose physical differences made an impression beyond their number.

THE XENOPHOBIC BACKLASH

It should come as no surprise that the emergence and rise of radical right-wing populist parties in Western Europe coincided with the growing tide of immigrants and particularly the dramatic increase in the number of refugees seeking peace, security, and a better life in the affluent societies of Western Europe. The reaction to the new arrivals was an outburst of xenophobia and open racism in a majority of West European countries. This includes the most liberal ones, such as Sweden and the Netherlands. Upon closer analysis, however, many of the negative sentiments toward foreigners turned out to be little more than prejudices, which can easily be refuted. However, surveys indicated that these prejudices were wide spread among the population of most West European democracies. This has made it relatively easy for the radical populist Right to evoke, focus, and reinforce preexisting xenophobic sentiments for political gain.

Surveys from individual countries as well as EC polls suggest a number of common trends in Western Europe. Generally, a majority of Western Europeans think that the number of non-European nationals in Western Europe is too high. Within the European Community this opinion has been particularly

Table 3.3

Opinions of EC Citizens on the Presence of Non-EC Citizens,
Migrants, and Racist Movements in the EC

(IN % AGREEING WITH STATEMENTS)

B	DK	G*	GR	S	F	IR	I	L	NL	P	UK	EC

1. The presence of non-EC nationals is a bad thing/to some extent a bad thing for the future of the country:

B	DK	G*	GR	S	F	IR	I	L	NL	P	UK	EC
52	47	43	27	20	44	13	31	18	25	18	35	35

2. Completely approve/to some extent approve movements in favor of racism:

12	16	10	4	10	11	15	8	9	9	14	11	11

3. There are too many non-EC nationals in EC:

56	43	55	29	25	56	12	63	20	44	18	54	51

4. Do not accept presence of people from south of the Mediterranean:

34	25	25	26	11	33	12	15	17	28	7	26	23

5. Do not accept presence of people from Eastern Europe:

27	19	26	24	9	22	13	15	16	22	7	23	20

6. Do not accept presence of political refugees:

29	8	24	18	7	24	18	15	13	16	7	20	19

7. Non-EC nationals' rights should be restricted:

58	32	37	27	12	41	22	28	10	29	11	43	33

B = Belgium, DK = Denmark, G = Germany, S = Spain, F = France, IR = Ireland, I = Italy, L = Luxemburg, NL = Netherlands, P = Portugal, UK = United Kingdom

* questions 3-7: unified Germany

Source: Questions 1 and 2 from Eurobarometer 30, December 1988; 3-7 from Eurobarometer 35, June 1991

prevalent in Italy, France, Belgium, Germany, and Great Britain, whereas it is least frequently expressed in Ireland, Portugal, Luxemburg, Greece, and Spain. The population of the latter group of countries is also more likely to regard the presence of non-EC nationals as being positive for the future of their country than are Germans, Belgians, French, Italians, or British (see Table 3.3). Similar results have been found in Austria. In 1990, about two-thirds of all respondents agreed either completely or to some extent that there were too many foreigners in Austria. German surveys indicated that these sentiments were directed primarily against new arrivals (see Table 3.4). Despite the wave of attacks on Turks in the recent past, Germans have been relatively tolerant toward guest workers who generally have lived in the country for a considerable amount of time. Thus between 1980 and 1990 the number of Germans who said that guest workers should be sent back home when work places get scarce diminished from 38 percent to 20 percent. The number of those saying foreign workers should adapt their life-style to those of the Germans declined from 45 to 34 percent. And those who said guest workers should choose their spouse among their own people declined from 33 to 18 percent. In 1990, almost half of the German population thought the presence of guest workers had brought advantages for Germany; only one fifth considered it a disadvantage. (Statistisches Bundesamt, 1992, pp. 615–616). However, it is open to question to what degree these results were representative of broader trends in West European public opinion. Thus, in 1990, 58 percent of the Austrian public disagreed with the statement that foreigners represented an enrichment for their country (Plasser and Ulram, 1991, p. 321).

Surveys clearly reflected growing concern about immigration, and a substantial level of rejection of both resident foreigners and new arrivals. These surveys were particularly telling, since polls on immigration are rather accurate in reflecting changes in the public mood regarding foreigners in general. For example, between September and November 1991 German polls registered a significant drop in the number of respondents opposed to the large number of foreigners in Germany (from 54 percent to 36 percent).[4] However, this decline hardly meant that a large number of the population had suddenly discovered their sympathies for guest workers and asylum seekers (see, for example, Jäger and Wichert, 1993). In fact, by mid-1992, roughly three quarter of the German population thought that the great majority of refugees were abusing Germany's asylum law (ipos, 1992, pp. 93–94). Rather, the decline in hostility toward foreigners in 1991 was a response to the highly publicized outbursts of ethnically motivated violence against foreigners in the Saxon city of Hoyeswerda, which made respondents shy away from open expressions of xenophobia.[5] A similar decline in negative attitudes toward immigrants occurred after skinheads murdered a Turkish woman and two Turkish children in the city of Mölln in the fall of 1992.

In a similar way, the surprisingly high proportion of Italians concerned about immigration can be interpreted as a response to the rapid rise in the number of immigrants in the late 1980s. Individual studies found that the number of Italians who thought foreign immigration was causing only, or predominantly, problems increased from 49 percent in 1987 to 61 percent in 1991 (DOXA, 1991, p. 96). This also explains the seemingly high tolerance for foreigners in

Table 3.4

German Attitudes toward Various Immigrant Groups
(rated on a scale of -5 to +5, in %)

	Turks/ Guest Workers	Recognized Pol. Refugees	Economic Refugees	African Refugees	Gypsies
(-5)	8	6	18	9	15
(-4)	4	3	9	7	7
(-3)	7	6	13	9	12
(-2)	8	7	12	12	10
(-1)	8	8	8	12	12
(0)	33	31	24	27	25
(+1)	10	13	6	8	5
(+2)	10	11	5	6	5
(+3)	8	7	3	4	3
(+4)	2	3	1	1	1
(+5)	2	3	1	2	2
Average	**-0.4**	**0**	**-1.6**	**-0.9**	**-1.3**

Source: EMNID-Spiegel polls, October–December 1991.

Ireland, Portugal, Spain, and Greece where the size of the foreign population is still relatively small, and in Luxemburg, where the large majority of resident foreigners are EC nationals.

A second trend in Western European attitudes toward immigrants is a growing unwillingness to accept refugees unconditionally. In 1991, less than a quarter of the population of the EC were willing to accept even genuine political refugees without restrictions. About one fifth of the respondents said their country should not accept political refugees at all. German surveys show that this readiness to reject the concept of asylum altogether can in part be explained as a response to the dramatic increase in the number of refugees.[6] In 1990, between 19 and 28 percent of the German population thought Germany should accept all political refugees, between 14 and 30 percent thought none at all (ipos, 1990, p. 43; Statistisches Bundesamt, 1992, p. 621). The growing opposition toward refugees is also reflected in the increase in support for restricting the rights of immigrants in the EC. This became particularly evident during the debate on whether or not Germany should restrict the constitutional protection afforded refugees. In 1991, 69 percent of the population of the former FRG and 64 percent of the former GDR supported a change of the constitutional right to asylum, in order to deter and impede potential refugees from coming into the country.[7]

However, sheer numbers alone hardly explain the profound hostility toward new arrivals that has come to characterize the attitude of a sizeable portion of Western Europe's population concerning immigrants and refugees. Rather, this hostility is motivated by a combination of fear and resentment, which has emerged and spread in response to the uncertainties brought on by the social and cultural transformation of advanced Western democracies, of which foreign presence is one of the most visible pieces of evidence. These fears and resentments are reflected in the views that immigrants are contributing to unemployment and to the increase in violence and crime. They find expression in the view that foreigners take advantage of the democratic *Rechtsstaat* and exploit and abuse the system of social welfare.

IMMIGRANTS AND REFUGEES AS MIRRORS OF WEST EUROPEAN ANXIETIES

In his preface to the 1991 report on racism and xenophobia in the European Community, Enrique Barón Crespo, the president of the European parliament, suggested that although both were rooted "in the fear and insecurity of the individual facing the future" they found "nourishment in unemployment and poverty" (Parlement Européen, 1991, p. 3). A number of surveys support this conclusion. They suggest that a large portion of the West European public associate immigration with unemployment.

Thus, in 1991, 22 percent of the German population agreed completely and 35 percent in part that newly arriving foreigners were worsening the unemployment situation of the native population.[8] Similarly, in Austria, 51 percent of the population associated foreign immigrants with rising unemployment. Twenty percent agreed completely, and 29 percent in part that foreigners were taking away jobs from Austrians (Plasser and Ulram, 1991, pp. 314, 321). Even in Italy, 38 percent of the population associated the influx of non-EC nationals with "an inevitable increase in unemployment" (ISPES, 1991a, p. 131; similarly DOXA, 1991, p. 120). At the same time, a significant number of West Europeans supported measures to protect the native work force. Thus, 49 percent of the Norwegian population agreed with the notion that in difficult times Norwegians should have a priority in getting jobs. And in Germany, two-thirds of all respondents agreed that foreign workers should not be allowed to enter Germany for more than one year.[9]

Although a significant number of West Europeans not only recognize the contributions foreign workers have made to their economies,[10] but also that foreign workers perform many jobs that unemployed natives refuse to accept, they still see them as taking away scarce jobs from the native unemployed. Thus, in a 1990 Austrian survey, 38 percent of the population (and 48 percent of the Viennese) denied that Austria could do without "guest workers," and a fifth agreed that because of the lack of workers Austrians "should be glad that foreign workers were coming to Austria."[11] The number was even higher in Germany. In 1992, 67 percent of the West German population agreed that the German economy needed foreign workers. (However in the former East Germany only a third agreed with that statement [ipos, 1992, p. 83-84]). Finally, in Italy, which has consistently been plagued by high unemployment, 47 percent (and 52 percent among workers) agreed in 1991 with the statement that it was right to use foreign workers because many unemployed Italians refused to perform "low" jobs. Yet at the same time, 44 percent of the population thought that jobs should go first to the Italian unemployed (ISPES, 1991a, pp. 131, 137).

Surveys showed that the latter attitudes were as diffused among the younger generation as they were among the population in general. According to a 1982 study of Austrian youth, more than half of the respondents (young people under 20) agreed with the statement that foreign workers were taking away jobs from Austrians (Bonegl, Horak, and Lasek, 1985, p. 395). A 1987 study of Germans between 16 and 17 years of age found half of them agreeing with the statement "German vocational education and training posts only for Germans" (Heitmeyer, 1989, p. 117). And a 1992 survey of Italians aged 15 to 29 found 41 percent agreeing that it was not right that immigrants took away jobs from the unemployed in the country (Cavalli and de Lillo, 1993, p. 264).

The fear of losing one's job to immigrant competitors might be understandable in the face of the fact that in the past large companies have increasingly moved to developing countries, where workers are generally willing to work more for less. However, the situation of foreign workers in advanced West European democracies shows that these perceptions are hardly justified. In most of these countries, a majority of the immigrant labor force has low levels of education. Most perform un- and semiskilled labor, which the indigenous population has increasingly come to refuse, even though the West European population's attitude toward jobs appears to be changing (in 1993, 52 percent, compared to 38 percent in 1983, in France thought the French would accept the type of work foreigners were performing at the moment; 44 percent thought they would not[12]). In 1989, 61 percent of the foreign work force in Austria (84 percent of its Turkish workers) had no more than compulsory education compared to 28 percent of the native work force. As a result, the majority of foreign workers held low level positions (Eichwalder, 1991, p. 172). Surveys showed that Austrians were not only aware of that fact, but considered it a positive and desirable situation. In 1990, 42 percent (23 percent of the Viennese) thought that foreign workers should be used in un-skilled positions; 26 percent of the Austrians (32 percent of the Viennese) believed that they should be trained to become specialist workers. However, there was also agreement that new immigrants should be trained to become specialized workers to alleviate the growing shortage of trained workers. Only 14 percent thought immigrants should receive no training at all.[13]

The situation was similar in Germany and France, where immigrant workers had lower levels of education, fewer chances to advance from unskilled to qualified positions, and faced a considerably higher risk of losing their jobs than their German and French counterparts (Deplanques and Tabard, 1991; Maurin, 1991; Erichsen, 1988, p. 19). In 1992, two thirds of the foreign work force, but only one third of their French counterparts had not more than minimal formal training or no training at all. In Germany, in the mid-1980s, 60 percent of the foreign work force, but only 17 percent of the German work force, were un- and semiskilled workers (Geißler, 1992, p. 157). The situation was similar regarding unemployment. Between 1980 and 1992, the rate of unemployment among foreign workers increased from 9 to 19 percent, roughly double the increase among French workers. And as in other West European countries, unemployment particularly affected workers from non-EC countries: In 1992, 28 percent for Moroccans, 34 percent for Tunisians, 29 percent for Algerians (Marchand, 1992, pp. 77–78).

German studies suggest that the situation is not substantially different for the second generation of foreign workers. Generally, foreign youth tend to attain lower levels of education and are considerably less likely to complete professional education and training than their German counterparts (Geißler, 1992, p. 159). Thus, in 1990, one fifth of foreign youth left school without complete education compared to roughly 7 percent of their German counterparts. Whereas more than one third of German youth left school with a university or politechnical entrance degree (*Hochschul-* or *Fachhochschulreife*), only one in ten foreign students attained the same level of education. Young Turks and particularly young Turkish women were especially affected by a lack of professional qualification and thus unemployment. Of those employed, the majority of the foreign labor force was employed as un- or semiskilled workers. In 1989, 64 percent of foreigners were in this category compared to 16 percent of the German labor force. And although second generation foreigners made advances, they were still twice as likely to be unskilled workers and three times as likely to be semiskilled workers than their German counterparts (Hübner and Rohlfs, 1992, p. 64; Boos-Nünning, 1990, p. 22; Statistisches Bundesamt, 1992, p. 531).

These and similar studies from other countries indicate that foreign labor is generally most threatened by redundancy; "guest workers" are most likely to be among the first to be negatively affected by the rationalization and modernization drive characterizing advanced economies (Marchand, 1992, p. 79; Geißler, 1992, p. 158). This development suggests that immigrants do in fact contribute to unemployment in Western Europe, but less by taking away jobs from the natives than by adding to the overall rate of unemployment, because they lack the education and professional training necessary to compete successfully in a changing labor market. It is thus hardly surprising that particularly in times of economic transformation the number of foreigners who fall below the poverty line is considerably higher than is the proportion of the native population. In Germany, in 1987, for example, more than twice as many foreigners than Germans were officially considered poor (12.4 percent of the foreign population versus 5.4 percent of the German population; see Krause, 1992, p. 12; Geißler, 1992, pp. 172–173).

Fear of losing one's job to cheaper foreign workers is only one, if prominent, fear associated with immigrants. A second, and increasingly important one, is the notion that immigrants contribute significantly to the increase in violence and crime. Generally, during the past several years, Western Europeans appear to have become increasingly concerned about security. In the western part of Germany, for example, between 1990 and 1991 the number of those who felt threatened by crime rose from 56 to 67 percent (92 percent in the eastern part of Germany in 1991). At the same time those who believed that the threat to their safety was growing increased from 54 percent to 63 percent (91 percent in the east) (ipos, 1991, p.48). Surveys suggest that this increase is at least in part connected to the growing concern over immigration. Thus, in 1993, 53 percent of the French population considered immigration "a factor of insecurity."[14] In Italy, the number of those who considered foreigners a cause of delinquency and crime increased from roughly 4 percent of the population in 1987 to 12 percent in 1991 (DOXA, 1991, p. 120). These perceptions were even stronger in those countries with a longer history of immigration. Thus, in Norway, 46 percent, and in Austria, 64 percent, of the population associated immigrants with an increase in crime and violence.

These perceptions have been supported by official statistics that show disproportionately high crime rates for foreigners. Thus, in 1991, more than a quarter of those suspected to have committed a crime in Germany were foreigners, although foreigners constituted only 7.7 percent of the population.[15] Similarly, in Italy, in 1988, more than 11 percent of all prisoners were foreigners (Natale, 1990, p. 326). However, as it is increasingly recognized, these statistics are highly misleading. And this for a number of reasons. Most importantly, a large proportion of crimes committed by foreigners derive from their particular situation such as violations of the asylum law, illegal border crossing, or residence requirements. Secondly, foreigners are more likely to be denounced and detained. In Italy in 1988, more than 50 percent of all foreigners, but only 12 percent of Italians denounced of a crime were also detained (Natale, 1990, p.338). Finally, a disproportionate number of foreigners are young with low levels of education and training and, as a result, they have little chance for upward social mobility. They are threatening to become part of a growing urban underclass that is susceptible to petty crime. This is no excuse for the fact that 31 percent of all cases of murder and manslaughter and 36 percent of all cases of rapes registered in Germany in 1991 were committed by foreigners.[16] However, these facts should not lead to accusations of collective guilt. Most crimes committed by foreigners result from their particular situation and thus will decrease in numbers only if their situation improves.

Fear of unemployment and increasing crime has figured prominently among xenophobic sentiments in Western Europe for some time. Recently, they have been joined by a wave of resentments. Central to these resentments is the notion that immigrants and refugees exploit and abuse the generosity of Western democracy and the welfare state. As one opponent of Germany's asylum laws has interpreted the mood in Germany, the country's public is less "against giving asylum to the politically persecuted or the orderly immigration of other foreigners. But they are outraged by the continued and constantly growing abuse of a basic right. . . and the continued toleration of this abuse. The state demands from its citizens that they observe its laws and enforces them whenever they are not observed. Why then, the citizen asks, is there a difference when it comes to asylum seekers?"[17] These charges are driven by resentments against those who allegedly are granted privileges. Like similar charges against affirmative action in the United States, or the allegedly special treatment of the French-speaking population in Canada and Muslims in India, they belong to a culture of resentment, which has been a core component of the neo-conservative turn of the 1980s.[18]

As in the United States, Canada, or India, misgivings toward those who benefit, or are suspected of benefiting from preferential treatment by the state, figure prominently in the Western European culture of resentment against immigrants and refugees. As early as 1982, two-thirds of Austrian youth agreed with the statement that "foreigners with their many children often come to

Austria only to get the high Austrian child allowance which we pay with our taxes" (Bonengl, Horak, and Lasek, 1985, p. 395). Particularly in the Scandinavian countries, resentment toward refugees focused on the welfare issue. Thus in 1985, 28 percent of the Danish population agreed completely, and a further 26 percent agreed to some degree, that immigrants represented an economic burden for Denmark since they used the welfare system while sending their earnings back to their home country.[19] And in 1993, 71 percent of the Danish population agreed that refugees did not want to leave Denmark even if the political situation improved in their home country because of the nice treatment they received from the Danish government.[20] But the resentment toward the alleged abuse of welfare benefits by refugees was perhaps most pronounced in Germany. In 1991, two thirds of the German population thought foreigners were abusing social welfare benefits.[21] In order to prevent these abuses, the German public supported not only a change in the asylum law, a majority (in 1989 more than two thirds) favored forcing foreign workers to leave the country after one year of unemployment.[22]

Public opinion in Western Europe has increasingly come to regard immigrants and refugees as a considerable social and economic burden. While some of these allegations are justified, most of them are not. There is some truth in the charge that refugees represent a net burden for the welfare state. According to German studies, the roughly 670,000 refugees who arrived in Germany between 1988 and 1991 cost the German taxpayer in 1991 an estimated six billion marks. However, this was largely due to the fact that refugees were not allowed to work. Had only a third of them been able to assume an average paid job, the costs for the other two thirds would have been covered by the taxes and contributions to the German social security system paid by the first group.[23]

The charge that immigrant workers represent a net burden to the advanced economies of Western Europe is a distortion of the truth. It disregards that immigrant workers have made significant contributions to West European societies. Recruited to fill vacant positions during the period of high economic growth, they played a vital part in laying the foundation for affluence and prosperity. Because of their generally low levels of formal education and training they tend to be the first ones to be dismissed in times of recession and thus form a "buffer" for the native work force.[24] Furthermore, immigrant workers are not only a work force but also consumers, taxpayers, and contributors to social security and pension systems. As German and French studies have shown, in both countries foreigners have contributed more to pension systems than they have claimed (Erichsen, 1988, p. 23; Knight and Kowalsky, 1991, p. 99). In Germany, in 1989, foreigners paid 12.8 billion marks into the pension system.

This constituted 7.8 percent of all contributions. But with 3.7 billion marks they received only 1.9 percent of all pension payments.[25]

The question of the future of pension systems and their relationship with immigration assumes increasing importance for West European societies. Because of falling birthrates, much of Western Europe is experiencing a significant change in the age pyramid. Projections are that by the year 2020 the youngest age group of the Italian population (0 to 14 years) will have diminished by some 41 percent compared to 1987, in France, by some 16 percent compared to 1985. At the same time the age group 65 and older is projected to have increased by some 47 percent in Italy and by some 64 percent in France (Fondazione Agnelli, 1990, p. 42). In Germany, by 2010 the youngest age group (0 to 15 years) will have decreased by some 12 percent compared to 1990, whereas the age group 65 years and older will have grown by about 20 percent (Hof, 1990). This is expected to have serious consequences both for the labor market and social security systems. Some have argued that in order to keep the labor force stable and to guarantee social security for a rapidly growing older generation it will be necessary to recruit new foreign labor (see Chesnais, 1993, pp. 110–113). French experts have projected that between the years 2000 and 2039 France very likely will have to recruit annually between 165,000 and 315,000 new immigrants to prevent a decline in the active population (Blanchet and Marchand, 1991). German experts expect that Germany will have to attract at least 400,000 immigrants annually in order to guarantee a stable labor force (Hof, 1991a). Thus, it appears that despite high rates of unemployment, "the need for large numbers of migrant workers will not greatly diminish, as is amply demonstrated by the present circumstances in Western Europe. In France, for example, immigration continues despite high youth unemployment. The young nationals prefer to stay cocooned in their families, or to get unemployment benefits, rather than accept menial jobs considered to be further degraded in status because they are increasingly held by low-skilled foreign workers" (Chesnais, 1993, p. 111).

This view has not remained unchallenged. Critics have pointed out that migration has at best little effect on rectifying the balance of Western Europe's age structure; at worst it impedes the modernization of Western Europe's economy while blocking the chances of disadvantaged groups (such as women, the long-term unemployed, and persons with health problems) from joining or rejoining the active labor force. Under these circumstances, "there seems to be little opportunity for large scale legal movements by migrants from less developed countries, either in the South or the East, into the European labor market. The West suffers high levels of unemployment, especially of the unskilled, of young people and of previous immigrants. Such jobs for which there are vacancies demand high levels of education and skill. Third World labor forces are mostly unskilled or semiskilled rural workers." By allowing them to import cheap labor and employ them for low wages, West European states encourage employers to evade their training responsibilities, which only aggravates Western Europe's low productivity problem. Instead of continuing to encourage immigration, Western European states need to give priority to training the substantial reserves of the employable work force (such as young people and married women) while retraining "the existing work force for a more demanding skilled labor market in the future" (Coleman, 1992, pp. 444, 455).

If the academic debate on the desirability of further immigration appears far from settled, the prospects that Western Europe's aging population might have to depend on immigrants have become a new source of anxiety and resentment. The reasons have already been mentioned. Whereas in the past, the vast majority of foreigners in Western Europe were other Western Europeans, in the future, the majority of new immigrants can be expected to come from developing countries. The French migration specialist Jean-Claude Chesnais, for instance, foresees a growing "Africanization" of Europe. According to his estimates, by the year 2010, the number of Africans residing in Western Europe will be somewhere between fifteen and thirty million. France alone will have become home to an estimated six to eight million Arabs. As a result, Islam will become Western Europe's second religion while Arabic might become its second language (Chesnais, 1993, p. 113). Nowhere in Western Europe are the imbalances in population growth more striking than in the Mediterranean region. Whereas on the northern bank of the Mediterranean fertility rates are among the lowest in the world, the southern bank continues to experience considerable population growth. By the late 1980s, birth rates in the Maghreb countries, although considerably lower than in the past, were still three to four times higher than they were in Italy, Spain, or Portugal.

THE CULTURAL ROOTS OF XENOPHOBIA

Numerous studies show that Western Europeans are particularly concerned about foreigners from developing countries. Studies on "otherness" reveal that a growing number of West Europeans associate otherness in terms of culture and religion with North Africans, Turks, and Muslims (Fuchs, Gerhards and Roller, 1993). When asked to rank various immigrant groups according to preference Western European respondents tend to particularly place the latter groups on the bottom of sympathy scales. A Danish survey of views on family reunion illustrates this point. In 1991, 89 percent of the Danish population generally agreed that the partners of foreigners living in Denmark should be allowed to come to Denmark in the context of family reunification. However, only 65 percent agreed on that for foreigners from Eastern Europe, 48 percent for Arabs, 49 percent for Asians, and 49 percent for Africans.[26] In Germany, the majority of the population had a predominantly negative view of gypsies, African refugees, economic refugees generally, and Turks and other guest workers (see Table 3.4). In France, in 1990, more than 50 percent of the respondents said there were too many North Africans, more than a third said there were too many sub-Saharan Africans, but only 13 percent said there were too many Spanish immigrants. French surveys also reveal growing public awareness of, and concern about, culture and religion. Asked to identify which differences made life with foreigners difficult, the most frequent answers in 1989 and 1990 were customs and religion (Le Gall, 1992, p. 126). Even in Italy, where xenophobia and racism have been less prevalent than in other West European countries, the population was considerably more hostile toward gypsies (49 percent in 1992), Arabs (18 percent), and *extracommunitari* (16 percent) than to foreigners in general (5 percent).[27]

The results of Western European surveys on foreigners reflect a growing concern about the growing visibility of non-European cultures. Probably, its most important result has been a lively debate about the emergence of a multi- or pluri-cultural society and its desirability (Cohn-Bendit and Schmid, 1992). At the core of this debate is the question of whether or not Western European societies should seek to integrate the foreign population without forcing them to abandon their traditions and cultures. This implies that immigrant minorities have enough possibilities to uphold and develop their cultures, identities, and social relationships. It also means that the relationship between foreigners and the native population is characterized by reciprocity and equality rather than assimilation and exclusion. It finally implies that the native population should make an effort to understand and tolerate alien cultures and if necessary contribute to their preservation (Schulte, 1990).

Available surveys raise doubts as to the willingness of Western Europeans to actively contribute to the preservation of foreign cultures. One of its preconditions would be to encourage foreigners to preserve their language. If Danish polls are representative of Western Europeans' views on this question, the expectation should be equally dim. In 1992, more than two thirds of the Danish population rejected the notion that local communities should instruct the children of foreigners in their native language.[28]

Furthermore, the native population can only be expected to make such efforts if it sees foreign cultures as a potential enrichment of its own culture. If the opinions of young Italians are any indication of larger trends in Western

Europe, the chances for this are rather dim. In 1992, only a third agreed that immigrants living in Italy contributed to the cultural enrichment of the country; for 28 percent the answer was "not at all" (Cavalli and de Lillo, 1993, p. 264).

Particularly in the case of Muslims the exposure of Western Europeans to a foreign culture has led less to appreciation than to open hostility. Disturbed by the spread of militant fundamentalism, a growing number of West Europeans associate Islam with intolerance and fanaticism, especially after the Iranian death threats against Salman Rushdie. Surveys reveal that this perception was widely shared among West European populations. As early as 1985 Danish surveys found that a considerable number of Danes (47 percent) thought that Muslims were too culturally different from the Danish population. Therefore there could not be a meaningful exchange of culture and ideas between the two communities. One quarter of those polled even considered Islam a threat to the survival of the Danish church.[29] At the end of the 1980s, the perception of an Islamic threat to Western European culture had grown considerably. In 1990, for example, 71 percent of the French population associated Islam with fanaticism (Mermet, 1990, p. 204). And although 63 percent of the population considered it "normal" that Muslims were allowed to build mosques to practice their religion, only 43 percent considered it "normal" if a mosque were to be constructed in their neighborhood. Forty-seven percent did not (Le Gall, 1992, p. 128). Similarly, in Denmark, in 1991 55 percent of the population rejected the notion that Muslims should be allowed to build a large mosque (*en stormoské*) in Denmark, but only 28 percent of the population supported the notion that Muslim girls should be forbidden to wear traditional cloths covering their face and hair in Danish schools.[30]

Even if Islamic fundamentalism is increasingly used to incite and justify growing anti-Islamic sentiments in Western Europe, the threat of Islamic fundamentalism is hardly the most important reason for the growing fears and anxieties that Islam has come to evoke among parts of Western Europe's population. There is good reason to believe that Muslims have come to stand for the profound changes in global demographic patterns and their averse effects on Western European society. In Western Europe, indigenous population growth has largely been halted, if not reversed. At the same time, many developing countries are experiencing a virtual explosion of their populations. The result is a growing preoccupation that within a few decades a progressively depopulated Europe will be confronted by a severely overcrowded South. For Europeans, South means above all Northern Africa, and Northern Africa means above all Islam. Some West European journalists, publicists, and academics dealing with demographic questions have increasingly become alarmist, seeking out Muslims who are ready to confirm their fears. Take for example an article written by an Italian sociologist for a series on sexual education published in stages by a prominent Italian daily newspaper. He cited an Egyptian professor who he claimed had told him that the West should stop trying "to convince the world that your way of organizing political and social life is better." Islam would win anyway because from "four Christians or four Communists derive two, whereas within only a few years four Muslims will turn into one hundred."[31] A German commentator came to similar conclusions: "If Islam encourages the high birthrates of the faithful while the Christians kill their children already in the womb, then mathematics shows that these peoples will soon numerically far surpass the Christians" (Ritter, 1990, p. 52).

With an expanding number of West European immigrants originating from developing countries, these words reflect growing concern that because of their large birth rates, immigrants and their descendants might eventually reduce the indigenous West European population to minority status in their own country. Danish surveys again illustrate the point. As early as 1985, 41 percent of the population agreed that there were too many immigrants and they would dominate Danish society within a few generations.[32] Statistics reveal a different picture. They show that over time the fertility rates of immigrant populations in Western Europe have markedly declined. Immigrants tend to assimilate their reproductive behavior to that of the indigenous population. Thus in France between 1968 and 1990 the number of children per a Portuguese woman declined from 4.9 to 1.9 approaching that of her French counterpart (1.7). During the same time period the number of children per an Algerian woman declined from 8.9 to 3.2, while the fertility rate of Moroccan and Turkish women between 1982 and 1990 (the majority of them arrived in France after 1975) declined from 5.2 to 3.5 and 3.7 respectively (Tribalat, 1986, p. 41; Haut Conseil à l'intégration, 1993, pp. 336–337). Despite these facts, public attitudes toward Western Europe's Muslim population are increasingly dominated by irrational phobias rather than a reasoned debate on the cultural advantages and disadvantages of a growing Muslim presence in Western Europe.

If the debate on the notion of multicultural society has shown anything, it is that it finds only support among a minority. In 1992, in Germany, only 23 percent of the population were in favor of multiculturalism; 49 percent did not even know what it meant.[33] Rather, a large minority tend to consider foreigners a threat to its way of life and identity. In 1990, 45 percent of the Austrian population agreed with that statement (Plasser and Ulram, 1991, p. 321). As German polls show, the threat of *Überfremdung* can lead to rather shocking reactions. Thus, in 1991, the notion that "we should take care to keep the German people pure and prevent the mixing of peoples (*Völkervermischung*)" found considerable support.[34] So did the statement that "it would get to the point that the Germans have to defend themselves against the foreigners" living among them. Between 1990 and 1992 those agreeing with that statement in former West Germany increased from 26 to 37 percent.[35]

Neither is there much support for assisting foreigners to sustain their traditional culture. In 1988, only 24 percent of the population of Norway, where the government has actively encouraged cultural pluralism, favored increasing financial support to immigrants' culture. Almost two thirds were opposed. Instead the majority of Western Europeans would like to see immigrants adapt to European customs and habits, if they don't outright support their departure. Thus in France in 1993, 83 percent of the population agreed that foreigners had to integrate themselves into French society and "abandon customs contrary to French legislation" (such as polygamy). Seventy-five percent thought it would be better if foreign workers lived in areas where there were also French families.[36] Italian polls reveal the extent to which West Europeans are ambiguous in their attitudes toward foreigners. When those who agreed that foreigners were contributing to rising crime were asked what could solve that problem, one third opted for barring entrance to foreigners without work, 38 percent for creating conditions for genuine integration (ISPES, 1991a, p. 152; see also Le Gall, 1992, p. 125).

The Italian data also reveal that xenophobia is only one part of a larger combination of feelings of resentment directed toward all groups that are "different." Thus, Italians also show considerable hostility toward homosexuals (40 percent in 1992), drug addicts (43 percent), and atheists (15 percent) (Dini, 1992, p. 129). Polls from other countries show that these and similar sentiments are fairly standard among the West European public. In 1992, in Germany, for instance, 67 percent of the population said they would not want to have neighbors who were drug addicts; 66 percent did not want as neighbors "people who were often drunk"; 64 percent did not want gypsies; 31 percent, homosexuals; 18 percent, Muslims; and 8 percent, "people with lots of children."[37] Since, ideally, the notion of multicultural society would include not only respect and support for foreign cultures but also respect for life-styles and personal preferences that differ from those of the majority of the population, the prospects for the development of multiculturalism in Western Europe are hardly bright.

Opinion polls suggest that the majority of Western Europeans are deeply ambiguous, if not outright hostile toward immigrants and refugees. Slogans such as "*Ausländer raus*" or "*fuori gli immigrati*" are not the isolated calls of a miniscule minority on the lunatic fringes of postindustrial Europe, but express and reflect the attitudes and opinions of a sizeable portion of the core of West

Europe's public. Yes, it might be exaggerated to equate hostility toward foreigners with racism. (Although the fact that almost 23 percent of the Italian public agreed in 1991 that there was a fundamental inequality [*disugualianza di fondo*] between various races [ISPES, 1991a, p. 179] and that 11 percent of the population of the EC approved in one way or the other of racist movements [see Table 3.5] is reason enough for concern.) Yet one thing is clear. There is a profound xenophobic streak running through Western European society. With the growing visibility and assertiveness of non-European cultures this xenophobic streak is bound to gain in political significance.

THE SOCIAL BASIS OF XENOPHOBIA

Immigrants and refugees from the developing South to the prosperous North represent perhaps the most visible and "tangible" signs of the current social and cultural transformation of advanced Western democracies. They confront the indigenous population of the West with the social realities brought about by the new age of global economic, ecological, and political interdependence and universal communication. Therefore, these people are particularly vulnerable to becoming the target of those persons who feel objectively or subjectively threatened by this transformation. We would expect to find prejudices and hostility toward foreigners to be particularly pronounced among persons with lower levels of education, among older generations, and perhaps also among blue-collar workers. These are the groups most likely to both have the greatest difficulties adapting to rapid social and cultural change and to respond to the challenge in a cognitively rigid fashion (see Scheuch and Klingemann, 1967; Hoskin, 1991, chapter 5). However, in the case of blue-collar workers, xenophobia might be checked by traditional solidarity with fellow workers, particularly among those who are unionized. On the other hand, working class groups are also most likely to see immigrants as outsiders eager to enter society and compete for increasingly scarce jobs. One might therefore expect working class groups to feel particularly threatened by their admission (Hoskin, 1991, p. 107).

Table 3.5 provides a number of survey results from the EC, from France, and from Italy. They indicate that negative attitudes toward foreigners correlate to a large extent with age, level of education, occupation, and value preferences (for a more detailed analysis of the 12 EC countries see Fuchs, Gerhards and Roller, 1993, pp. 250–251). Thus, in France, 46 percent of the youngest age group said they favored integrating immigrants rather than sending them back to their home country. Among the advanced age groups only a third supported integration; more than half came out in favor of immigrants' departure. The differences are even

Table 3.5

The Social Basis of Xenophobia

1. Percentage of EC Nationals Who Believe the Rights of Foreigners Should Be:

	Improved	Maintained	Restricted	No Reply
Total	30	39	18	13
Male	30	41	19	10
Female	29	37	18	16
Age				
15-24	34	41	13	12
25-39	35	36	18	11
40-54	30	37	20	13
55-	23	41	20	16
Education				
low	28	35	19	18
medium	26	43	20	11
advanced	39	40	13	8
Value Types				
Materialist	25	38	21	16
Mixed	28	40	20	12
Postmaterialist	45	36	11	8

Source: Eurobarometer Special on Racism and Xenophobia, 1991, p. 80.

2. France: Percentage of Population Believing in Integration/Departure of Immigrants

	Integration	Departure	No Opinion
Total	42	46	12
Male	44	45	11
Female	40	47	13
Age			
18-24	46	44	10
25-34	52	38	10
35-49	45	43	12
50-64	35	51	14
65-			
Education			
primary	29	55	16
secondary	43	43	14
technical/com-mercial	40	53	7
advanced	65	27	8

Table 3.5 (cont.)
The Social Basis of Xenophobia

	Integration	Departure	No Opinion
Occupation			
Farmers	36	46	18
Shopkeepers, Artisans, Small Business	40	45	15
Executives, Liberal Professions	56	36	8
Middle Management	61	31	8
Salaried Employees	46	41	13
Blue-Collar Workers	37	53	10
No Profession, Retired	31	54	15

Source: Le Gall, 1992, p. 125

3. Italy: Belief in the Statement that the Presence of Non-EC Foreigners has Led to an Increase in Drug Dealing (in %)

	True	Partially True	False	No Info.
Total	**24**	**45**	**30**	**1**
Male	24	43	32	1
Female	23	47	29	1
Age				
0-29	15	52	33	0
30-49	25	41	33	1
50-69	31	44	24	1
70-	56	26	16	2
Education				
none	41	28	25	6
elementary	40	35	24	1
primary	28	43	28	1
secondary	20	49	30	1
advanced	13	45	41	1
Occupation				
Small Business	31	39	29	1
Liberal Prof.	14	51	35	0
Employees	21	47	32	0
Workers	32	40	29	0
Teachers	13	49	38	1
Retired	35	42	20	3
Others	22	47	31	1

Source: ISPES, 1991a, p. 149.

starker with regard to education. Whereas less than 30 percent of those with only primary education favored integration, integration was supported by almost two thirds of those with advanced education. These results also help explain the large attitudinal differences between workers and farmers on the one hand and liberal professionals, executives, and middle-level management on the other (for earlier results see Humbertjean, 1985, pp. 85–86).

Similar results were obtained in the Italian case. There the most advanced age groups and those with primary degrees were at least twice as likely to associate the presence of non-EC foreigners with an increase in drug dealing, as were the youngest age group and those with advanced degrees. And as in the French case there were clear and significant attitudinal differences between workers on the one hand and liberal professionals and teachers on the other. These were also the groups most likely to hold postmaterialist values.[38] Other studies come to similar conclusions. In Norway, 65 percent of voters with primary, but only 22 percent of voters with advanced education, agreed in 1988 that in economically difficult times Norwegians should be given priority for jobs. Similar results were obtained regarding the desirability of a multicultural society: 76 percent of those with primary education, but only 58 percent of those with advanced education agreed that foreigners should adapt to Norwegian customs.

Curiously enough, there appear to be hardly any differences between female and male respondents in their attitudes toward immigrants. This is surprising since women have generally been much less likely than men to support right-wing radical and extremist parties (see Chapter 5). One reason for expecting that women might be more sympathetic to foreigners than are men is that women, like foreigners, have been the victims of discrimination. Yet surveys indicate that women are generally as likely as men to harbor negative attitudes toward immigrants. However, there are exceptions. If attitudes are associated with manifestations of open intolerance or violence, women are significantly less likely to agree with them than are men. In Italy in 1991, 46 percent of female respondents (and 44 percent of respondents with advanced degrees), but only 37 percent of male respondents said they considered such acts a clear expression of racism (ISPES, 1991a, p. 187). In this instance women belonged to the most liberal social groups.

The only other instance in which women's attitudes toward foreigners appear to be rather different from those of men is when age is taken into consideration. One Danish survey found that young women age 19 to 28 were considerably more opposed to sending back immigrant workers who were no longer needed than were men in the same age group (76 to 65 percent) (Svensson and Togeby, 1991a, p. 147). Similar differences emerge from a 1992

Table 3.6

Norwegian Voters' Views on Immigrants

(IN % AGREEING WITH STATEMENTS)

PrS	PuS	PrS Low Income	PuS Low Income	PrS High Income	PuS High Income
1. Priority for jobs should go to Norwegian unemployed					
50	39	58	46	46	28
2. Foreigners should adapt to Norwegian habits					
75	64	72	64	78	59
3. Increased financial support should be given to promote immigrants' culture					
17	30	20	24	18	36

PrS=Private Sector PuS=Public Sector

Source: Norwegian Study on Immigration, 1988

study of youth in the Eastern German state of Brandenburg. Forty-one percent of male respondents, but only 25 percent of female respondents, agreed with the statement that most criminals were foreigners; 48 percent of the males, but only 35 percent of the females agreed with the statement "Germany for the Germans—foreigners get out"; and 45 percent of the males, but only 31 percent of the females agreed that foreigners were responsible for unemployment in Germany (Dietrich, 1992, pp. 43–46). These results suggest that young women play a prominent and important role in sustaining left-libertarian attitudes toward immigrants and refugees.

In their study of the conservative resurgence in Norway, Lafferty and Knutsen (1984) found public-sector workers and employees in general, and particularly high level public sector employees, to be considerably more left-wing than those employed in the private sector. The results of a study of Norwegian voters indicate similar differences with regard to their attitudes toward foreigners (Table 3.6). Generally, those employed in the public sector tend to be more inclined than their counterparts in the private sector to oppose assimilation, to advocate financial support for immigrants' culture, and to reject giving priority for jobs to Norwegian unemployed. These differences become even more pronounced in a comparison between different levels of private- and public-sector employees (in terms of income): Low level public employees are at least as liberal in their attitudes toward foreigners as high-level private-sector employees. High-level public-sector functionaries in turn are more sympathetic toward foreigners than both their private-sector counterparts and the public sector as a whole.

What, then, appear to be the major factors determining citizens' attitudes toward immigrants and refugees? Gaasholt and Togeby's study of xenophobic attitudes of Danish citizens ranging from 18 to 37 years of age and based on a 1988 survey provides a comprehensive, if tentative answer (Gaasholt and Togeby, 1992). Like earlier studies from other countries, the two authors found a strong relationship between level of education and tolerance. Respondents with university entrance level education showed almost three times as high a level of tolerance toward immigrants as did respondents with lower levels of education (70 to 24 percent among men, 70 to 27 percent among women). As in the Norwegian case, the tolerance level among public-sector employees was considerable higher than among private-sector employees. It was particularly high among those employed in social services and among students in the humanities and the social sciences. Besides education and sector employment a third factor influencing attitudes on immigrants was a respondent's position toward a number of left-right issues. Generally, the more positive a person's attitude toward economic equality, the welfare state, and the regulation of private enterprise, the more tolerant he or she was likely to be toward immigrants. Because of a lack of comparable cross-national data, these findings have only limited validity. They are, however, quite suggestive, given the general free-market orientation of a majority of radical right-wing populist parties, if not their supporters (see Chapter 5).

XENOPHOBIA AND THE RADICAL POPULIST RIGHT

With the social and cultural transformation of advanced Western democracies, questions of immigration, foreign labor, and asylum have assumed a prominent place in the cultural and political discussion in Western Europe. So far, however, the results of this discourse have for the most part been negative. Western Europe is close to turning into a fortress for the already affluent and privileged. As one observer wrote a few years ago before the establishment of the European Union: "The 'fortress Europe' that Americans, Japanese and other outsiders fear when the European Community finally becomes a tariff-free, continent-wide market at the end of next year is already being built. But its walls are intended to keep out people, not commodities" (Whitney, 1991, p. 1). Attempts on the part of politicians and pundits to convince the public that the affluent democracies of Western Europe have, for all practical purposes, become countries of immigration like the United States, Canada, or Australia have largely failed. So has the appeal to support the creation of multicultural, multiethnic, or multiracial societies. Only a minority of highly educated and, in terms of their jobs, secure segments of the new middle class as well as a majority of young women are willing to face the challenge of a rapidly changing world. More so than ever, a majority of Western Europeans themselves are profoundly suspicious of new arrivals while reconciling themselves only hesitatingly to those who are already there.

An impressive number of surveys point to the same conclusion: In the 1980s, hostility toward new and resident immigrants was growing considerably throughout Western Europe. By the early 1990s, a majority of the Western European population supported a number of xenophobic views. At the same time, the "immigrant problem" became one of the most important political issues with governments and political parties coming under mounting public pressure to offer effective solutions.

Despite considerable support for racist movements, alarming numbers of physical attacks against immigrants and refugees, and a general increase in cases of historical revisionism such as the denial of the Holocaust and of outright anti-Semitism, it would be mistaken, however, to confound or equate contemporary xenophobia with the racism that characterized nazism or white supremacism. As the Swiss case demonstrates, xenophobia is not necessarily directed against persons and groups of different ethnic origins. All Swiss referenda on immigration were called at a time when the vast majority of foreign residents of Switzerland were West Europeans. Similarly, German hostility toward foreigners has hardly been limited to guest workers, immigrants, or refugees. In the late 1980s and early 1990s, it also reached ethnic German resettlers from the east (*Aussiedler*) and even German migrants from the former GDR. In 1991, only 13 percent of the German population was willing to accept all *Aussielder;* 43 percent thought their numbers should be drastically reduced.[39] At the same time, episodic accounts suggested that the West German population also turned against former East Germans.[40] The hasty conclusion of the currency union was largely an attempt to arrest the unrelenting flow of East German migrants into West Germany and curb growing West German resentment toward the newcomers.

These examples suggest that xenophobia is less an expression of the revival of racism. It rather reflects the desire on the part of the population of the affluent West European societies to protect their islands of prosperity against an outside world marked by poverty, environmental destruction, interethnic violence, and growing desperation. Confronted with a profound transformation of the economic and social infrastructure and with mass unemployment at home, Western European citizens are increasingly turning inward. Fatigued by the cultural and political battles of the past two decades, they appear little ready to face the new conflicts bound to arise over the changing cultural makeup of their societies. Faced with chronic deficits and growing public debts, they are no longer willing to allocate money to those who are outsiders to the ethnic, cultural, and social community. Thus, a majority of Western Europeans still consider foreign residents "foreigners," or at the most "guests," rather than fellow citizens. In Germany, in 1989, 26 percent considered these residents foreigners, 27 percent guests, and 44 percent fellow citizens (Veen, Lepszy, and Mnich, 1992, p. 60). And guests are expected to respect the customs of their hosts and, above all, not to turn into a financial liability. Yet, particularly the new arrivals from the developing world were being perceived as following neither of these rules. As a result, the notion that Western European governments should halt new immigration as well as reduce the number of the resident foreign population from non-Western European countries was steadily gaining ground.

Nowhere was this more the case than among the supporters of the radical populist Right. Not only did they generally consider the question of immigration by far the most important issue on the political agenda (see chapter 2), they were also the group that was by far most hostile toward immigrants and refugees. Representative survey results from France, Denmark, Norway, Germany, and Austria illustrate not only to what extent xenophobic attitudes define the supporters of the radical populist Right but also their range.

Given the importance Front National supporters have generally attributed to the question of immigration, it is hardly surprising that they show some of the most negative attitudes toward non-Europeans of any group in France and perhaps even Western Europe. Thus, in 1990, virtually all supporters of the Front National thought that the number of foreigners living in France was too large (compared to 68 percent of the population); and nine out of ten favored a policy that would lead to the departure of a large number of immigrants currently living in France (compared to 46 percent of the whole population; see Le Gall, 1992, pp. 121, 125). Polls taken in 1984 and 1985 show that these feelings were strong right from the beginning of the party's rise. In 1984, when asked which measure they thought would be most efficient to improve security, twice as many Front National supporters (62 percent) as supporters of any other political grouping chose "reduce the number of immigrant workers" (Humbertjean, 1985, p. 83). Similarly, in 1985, Front National voters (72 percent) were significantly more likely than the voters of other parties (the highest were RPR supporters with 55 percent; SOFRES, 1986, p. 220) to think that immigrants were far too different to be able to adapt themselves to French society. A poll taken in Grenoble in 1985 confirms this result. Asked about their opinion on North-Africans, 90 percent of Front National supporters agreed that they were too numerous. For 63 percent they constituted the principal cause of unemployment, and for virtually all the principal cause of crime (Bréchon, 1993, p. 43).

By the early 1990s, xenophobia was also one of the most important characteristics distinguishing FPÖ supporters from the rest of the Austrian population. In 1992, for example, FPÖ sympathizers were at least twice as likely as the general public to consider it unpleasant to have Turks, Romanians, or Jews as their neighbors. The differences were even more pronounced with regard to the FPÖ's proposals to curb immigration included in the 1991 petition. On average, more than three times as many FPÖ sympathizers as supporters of other parties came out in support of drastic antiforeigner measures such as enshrining it in the constitution that Austria was not an immigration country, or immediately halting all new immigration (see chapter 4).

In Germany, both in the late 1980s and early 1990s, Republikaner sympathizers showed by far the least sympathies of any politically relevant group toward immigrants, refugees, and even German resettlers from the former Soviet Union. In 1989, 90 percent of Republikaner supporters (compared to 58 percent of the whole population) thought Germany did too much for the latter group.[41] Undoubtedly, however, resentment was highest with regard to refugees. Thus, in 1993, almost three quarters of the German population, but only one out of two Republikaner supporters, considered it a good thing that Germany gave those who faced political persecution in their home countries the right to asylum. The numbers were reversed when Germans were asked whether or not they thought it was okay that there were many foreigners living in Germany, or whether they agreed that people coming from different cultures would invariably remain alien to each other. Whereas the population was generally split on both questions, an overwhelming majority of Republikaner supporters chose the xenophobic answer. Perhaps nothing could have better illustrated to what degree xenophobia distinguished the sympathizers of the radical Right from other groups in German society than the fact that, in 1989, half of all Republikaner supporters agreed with the notorious statement that the Germans should take care to keep the German character pure and prevent the mixing of peoples.

Danish surveys come to similar results. They show that in the late 1980s and early 1990s those sympathizing with the Progress Party distinguished themselves from the supporters of other political parties by their pronounced resentment toward foreigners. In the 1987 and 1988 elections, for instance, the overwhelming majority of Progress Party voters agreed that immigrants represented a threat to Danish national identity and that refugees had to assimilate to Danish culture and the Danish way of life (Borre, 1987, p. 354; Andersen, 1992, p. 200). In 1993, 97 percent of Progress Party supporters agreed that the Danish government treated refugees too well; 83 percent thought the majority of those seeking political asylum were in reality economic migrants (compared to 54 percent of the population); and 58 percent thought immigrants and refugees were more likely to commit crimes than Danes (compared to 34 percent of the whole population). When asked which foreigners should be allowed to enter Denmark to join their relatives, 57 percent answered flat out "none" (compared to 27 percent of the population).[42]

What differentiates the supporters of radical right-wing populist parties most from average citizens is the former's consistently negative attitudes on all aspects associated with immigration and asylum. Against that, the general population is far more selective. Thus, in the late 1980s, the average Norwegian citizen hardly differed from the average Progress Party supporter when it came to questions of assimilation, or giving immigrants financial support so that they could preserve their own culture. The two groups diverged, however, much more visibly on statements that could either be construed as having racist overtones (for example, that immigrants represent a threat to national identity), or that might have implied drastic consequences (such as immigrants' access to their country should be limited).

Despite these caveats, the Norwegian results generally reinforce the central argument of this chapter. The rise and spread of xenophobia in Western Europe in the 1980s and early 1990s was hardly restricted to small minorities in the population. Large majorities believed that there were too many foreigners residing in their countries, that immigration had become the most important political problem facing Western European societies, and that governments should act decisively to stem the tide. Undoubtedly, radical right-wing populist parties owed much of their success to this climate of growing resentment and anxiety, which the question of immigration invariably engendered. However, this is not to say that radical right-wing populist parties were, above all, antiforeigner parties. As the following chapter seeks to demonstrate, radical right-wing populist parties distinguished themselves not only in terms of the importance they attributed to immigration in their programs, but also with regard to how they justified their opposition to immigration.

4

The Two Faces of Radical Right-Wing Populism

One of the central points in the debate on the transformation of political behavior in advanced Western democracies has been the argument that modern voters increasingly tend to privilege issue- and value-oriented forms of participation over ideology-oriented ones. In the past, political parties distinguished themselves from each other by offering to the voters competing conceptualizations of a future ideal society and the different ways to get there. In the "postmodern" present, where the ideological foundations of the modern age are fundamentally questioned, and where idealism has largely been displaced by skepticism, ideology appears to have given way to a pragmatism of common sense. Populist parties are generally held to lack grand visions or comprehensive ideological projects. Instead, they are presumed to appeal to the common sense of the common people, seek to divine the mood swings of an increasingly volatile electorate, and shape their political programs accordingly. It seems then hardly surprising that radical right-wing populist parties have been relatively successful in attracting significant electoral support among the growing number of disenchanted and skeptical voters more interested in voicing their grievances than in evaluating alternative approaches to solving pressing societal problems.

Although this conclusion might appear plausible, it is also rather incomplete and misleading. As happens so often, reality is rather more complex than theory would suggest.

There is no denying that some radical right-wing populist parties in Western Europe offer very little of any programmatic substance. The Swiss Automobile party, for instance, for years restricted its programmatic output to a ten-point program, which it distributed in the form of a flyer. Others, however, have developed relatively coherent political programs, which, in a few cases at least, are grounded in a rather comprehensive right-wing ideology. Particularly, the Front National and, to a lesser degree, the Lega Nord and the FPÖ have developed programs that represent serious and radical alternatives to those advanced by the established political parties.

Generally, radical right-wing populist parties have been rather careful to distance themselves from the extreme Right. Although in most cases they do aim at a fundamental transformation of the existing socioeconomic and sociopolitical system, they see and promote themselves as democratic alternatives to the prevailing system. For example, they are vigorously opposed to using violence as a means to achieve their objectives. Furthermore, despite a few notorious and at times rather deliberate slips of the tongue—most notably in the case of Jean-Marie Le Pen and Jörg Haider—the majority of radical right-wing populist parties has been relatively careful to avoid promoting any ideas that could be construed as outright racist.

To subsume a certain group of political parties under a common label evokes the impression that these parties are relatively akin to each other. Although radical right-wing populist parties share a number of characteristics that set them apart from other political party families, they also differ from each other in a number of important ways. Generally, one can distinguish two ideal types—national populism and neoliberal populism. What complicates any analysis of the radical populist Right even further is the fact that almost all radical right-wing populist parties have at one point or another adopted elements of both neoliberalism and populist nationalism into their programs. What ultimately determines whether a party should be characterized as a neoliberal populist party or a national populist party is the relative weight it attributes to the respective elements in its program. Generally, radical right-wing populist parties have been far from static in terms of their programmatic development. With a few notable exceptions, starting at the end of the 1980s, national populist elements have increasingly come to predominate over neoliberal ones. This reflected a larger recognition that the neoliberal policies of the 1980s may have managed drastically to reduce inflation but at the cost of mounting unemployment and accelerated social fragmentation and marginalization. Responding to the new opportunities engendered by growing public anxiety over economic globalization, a number of radical right-wing populist parties were quick to embrace a new, much more protectionist program.

This chapter attempts to provide a comprehensive analysis of the basic elements of the radical right-wing populist program and the shifts in emphasis of its two main components. The first part gives an account of the importance of neoliberal doctrines for the radical populist Right's political agenda. The second part presents an analysis of national populism and its adaptation to socioeconomic changes.

NEOLIBERAL AND LIBERTARIAN POPULISM

The rise of radical right-wing populism largely coincided with a significant shift in economic thinking in the advanced Western democracies from Keynesianism to what Alain Lipietz (1992, p. 30) has called "liberal-productivism." The liberal-productivist model emerged in the late 1970s in response to the failure of Western governments to restore economic and political stability following the oil shocks of 1973 and 1979. According to its proponents, two reasons accounted for this failure: the expansion of the state and the unreasonable demands of trade unions. By imposing a growing number of constraints on economic activities, the state and unions had hampered the free development of technology, starved firms of capital, and prevented necessary structural adjustments. In order to stop the deterioration of their competitive position, Western societies had to reverse course. Instead of continued welfare state expansion and state intervention in the economy, governments had "to withdraw from control of the economy, dismantle public ownership, cut public expenditure, revive private welfare, remove trade union privileges, and promote mobility of capital and labour" (Aimer, 1988, p. 1).

It was not until the rise of Thatcherism in Great Britain that the "neoliberal creed," as the radical departure from traditional economic thinking came to be known, became the dominant approach to solving the twin problems of the mid- and late-1970s—economic stagnation and inflation. By the early 1980s, not only center-right parties, but also left-wing parties like the French Socialists had adopted it to cure Western Europe's economies suffering from "Eurosclerosis." Among its most ardent proponents were some of the major parties on the radical populist Right.

SCANDINAVIA

The Progress parties in Denmark and Norway were among the first parties to advance a neoliberal program. This program reflected a distinctly productivist ideology, which promoted a Thatcherist vision of an "enterprise culture" that celebrates individualism, competition, efficiency, entrepreneurship, and selectivity (Worcester, 1989). The Danish Progress party made this quite clear when it characterized its main political objective as wanting "to raise the national income, i.e., production, above the current level of consumption."[1] Save for a few modifications, this vision still informed the Progress parties' programs in the late 1980s. Their emphasis on enterprise, and economic and government efficiency were also among the most striking factors distinguishing the Norwegian Progress Party from all other relevant Norwegian parties in the 1980s (see Strom and Leipart, 1989, p. 272). Their influence could also be strongly felt in the program of the Swedish New Democracy party in the early 1990s.

   Central to this vision are the classic liberal conception of individual freedom and a commitment to the family and private property as the foundations of society. The state and the bureaucracy are seen as the most serious potential threats to individuals and democracy (c.f., Fremskrittspartiet, 1989, pp. 3–4). It is thus hardly surprising that one of the most fundamental demands of all three parties has been a profound transformation of the existing welfare state. The Scandinavian welfare state is characterized by its extensive government involvement in delivering to the citizens services that are largely financed through general taxation. Citizens receive services free of charge or at low cost irrespective of previous employment, income, or contributions. No one is denied needed help because of occupational status, sex, age, or low income (Andersen, 1984, p. 120). However, the Nordic model is not without its problems. One of its main drawbacks is that it encourages behavior that ultimately undermines the system. Not only has each citizen an incentive to maximize his or her share of the benefits' pie, demand for expanded services tends to drive up costs that in turn increase the incentive for the individual citizen to escape paying the bill by evading taxes and participating in the underground economy. The result is a growing public debt and higher interest payments on public debt with a concomitant transfer of income from the poor to the rich (Andersen, 1984, pp. 124-129). Thus, the logic of the Nordic model tends to help those citizens who are aware of their rights and are well educated. "Any university graduate can pump more out of the social finances than most welfare recipients" (Andersen, 1984, p. 129).

   The ideological justification for the radical populist Right's attack on the welfare state stems largely from this analysis of the contradictions of the Nordic welfare model. Glistrup pointed to its inequality when he charged that while the Danish system had left wide loopholes for millionaires, the average wage-earner had to pay every single cent in taxes. Similarly the Norwegian Progress Party objected in its 1989-1993 program to "an economic policy of equalization, which for many people makes a work effort either unnecessary or punished through progressive taxation" (Fremskrittspartiet, 1989, p. 18). In order to redress this situation, the two Progress parties called for the eventual abolition of income taxes, and its substitution by a consumption tax, while New Democracy limited itself to calling for a drastic reduction of the tax burden from 57 to 47 percent of GNP within five years.

In addition, the parties asked the government to stop subsidizing industries and agriculture, arguing that subsidies had only led to an artificial leveling of incomes while protecting inefficient and lazy managers. Finally, the parties called for a drastic cutback in the number of public sector employees. Like drastically lowered taxes, cutbacks in the public sector would encourage production and growth in employment. Demand for more labor could then be met by former employees "from the least necessary public sector jobs and the least necessary university and equivalent studies."[2] In order to save taxes, the Danish Progress Party even initially proposed abolishing Denmark's defense forces (to be replaced by a recording with the message "We surrender" in Russian on an automatic answering machine). In addition, the party proposed to auction off the country's overseas possessions in Greenland and the Faeroe Islands to the highest bidder (Andersen, 1992, p. 196).

The ideas advanced by the Progress parties and New Democracy represent perhaps the most radical response to the transformation of Scandinavian society. Their advocacy of individualism and productivism represents a strong affirmation of existing societal trends rather than their rejection. The fact that the Progress parties managed to survive in the 1980s might at least in part be a reflection of broad changes in Scandinavian society. Thus the rise and establishment of the Progress parties coincided with a considerable change in public support for equality and freedom. Between 1981 and 1983 still one third of the Danish population considered equality or justice more important than individual freedom; by 1988 that number had declined to less than a quarter of the population. At the same time those who favored individual freedom increased from 50 to 66 percent (Brettschneider, Ahlstich, and Zügel, 1992, p. 545).

Their affirmation of individualism was also reflected in their stance on moral issues, which was a far cry from the authoritarian tendencies characteristic of right-wing parties (Andersen and Bjørklund, 1990, p. 207). Thus, despite strong support for the family, the Norwegian party refused to advocate a ban on abortion, giving its members instead the freedom "to vote according to their conscience" on the issue. Similarly, the party stressed its commitment to basic equality between men and women, arguing that competition and a free market were the best way to guarantee equality (Fremskrittspartiet, 1989, pp. 6, 17).

Although both Progress parties were firm believers in the forces of the free market, theirs was a radical, nonacademic, populist neoliberalism in favor of the lower strata (Andersen, 1992). Thus, despite favoring large scale privatization of hospitals, the Norwegian Progress Party repeatedly affirmed its conviction that the public had the responsibility to guarantee "that everyone should receive the necessary health services." It also supported "strong efforts to alleviate those who suffer in our society," however, with the important qualification "that those who need help, should be identified and individualized" (Fremskrittspartiet, 1989, pp. 17-18). Finally both Progress parties came out in support for higher pensions to secure everyone a reasonable standard of living (Andersen and Bjørklund, 1990, p. 204; Fremskrittspartiet, 1989, p.2; see also Strom and Leipart, 1989, p. 271).

AUSTRIA

Like the Scandinavian parties, the FPÖ owed its success in the late 1980s at least partly to the vigorous promotion of individualism and entrepreneurship. Under Haider's leadership, the FPÖ modernized its liberal image, turning it into what Andreas Mölzer, Haider's chief ideologue and strategist, called a "fundamental liberalism." Neither Haider nor Mölzer regarded the establishment of an individualized society as a political end in and of itself. Rather, they promoted neoliberal doctrines in order to erode the power basis of the established political parties and eventually put themselves in their place.

Haider made this quite clear when he accused the political establishment of having created a system characterized by nepotism, corruption, and the distribution of offices and other privileges according to party membership (see Haider, 1993, pp. 15-72). In Haider's view, this had led to a profound crisis between citizens and political institutions. Austria's citizens no longer believed that the established system was capable of responding to the tremendous challenges that were confronting the country: the country's integration into the European Community, the crisis of the future of the welfare state together with the cost explosion in public administration, and environmental problems. In the face of these challenges, both the distributive policies of the Socialists as well as "the interest group oriented politics of the lowest common denominator" that characterized the Austrian People's Party had reached a dead end. Yet despite their growing inability to respond to the challenges of a changing world, the established parties were unwilling to initiate the necessary reforms, which invariably would have reduced their power. As Haider noted, the "old parties don't want an effective deconcentration of power, and they really don't want genuine control in the democratic system; what they want instead is the total control over democracy and the public" (Haider cited in Mölzer, 1990, p. 115). In this situation, the FPÖ sought to curtail the power of the established parties and the bureaucracy by "introducing integrity and honesty" into politics and mobilizing more and more voters against the established system.[3]

In order to achieve this objective, the FPÖ initially propagated a radical neoliberal program. Central to the FPÖ's version of liberalism was the promotion of individual freedom and a strong emphasis on individual abilities and preferences. Andreas Mölzer characterized the FPÖ's conception of liberty as "fundamentally different" from the conception of *liberté* propagated by the French Revolution, which can be characterized by the notion that more freedom would invariably lead to more equality and more solidarity (see Heitmeyer, 1993, p. 4). Against that, the FPÖ extolled individual differences in abilities and preferences as a "field of tension conducive to cultural and social development" (Mölzer, 1990, p. 169; see also Haider, 1993, pp. 239-240). This conception of freedom was directed against the "leveling of differences" in the name of equality, while propagating an ethics of merit and elitism, particularly in the field of education (Mölzer, 1990, p. 171). Citizens should be educated to accept responsibility for themselves instead of expecting the community to take care of them (FPÖ, 1991, p. 35). Society should promote the development of individual initiative. More citizens should be encouraged to become entrepreneurs since "entrepreneurs make an essential contribution to the stability of the state."[4] In order to encourage entrepreneurial spirit and individual initiative, the FPÖ proposed a comprehensive program of economic decentralization, privatization, deregulation, tax reform, and incentives. These measures were supposed to benefit above all small and medium-sized enterprises, which the FPÖ considered to be the backbone of a future-oriented, competitive economy (FPÖ, 1991, p. 57).

As far as the state was concerned, its role should be limited to creating the conditions of social security necessary for the development of "individual initiative and life without existential misery" (Haider, 1993, pp. 150–188). This was a radical departure from the extensive provisions of the Austrian welfare state. One of Haider's most notorious interventions in the debate on the welfare state illustrates this point. In a debate on employment held in the Carinthian parliament in June of 1991, Haider asked that sanctions be imposed on unemployed persons who were able to work but unwilling to take a job that did not conform to their expectations. His party, he charged, could no longer support a system in which some citizens had to pay more and more taxes with their hard-earned money in order to allow others to have a good time in the "hammock of the welfare state" (cited in Stirnemann, 1992, p. 167). The debate ended in an *éclat* when in response to an intervention from the SPÖ that this would mean a return to the methods of the Third Reich Haider charged that the Third Reich had at least made a "proper employment policy."

The FPÖ's conceptualization of freedom and the role of the community represented a radical attempt to take advantage of the sociocultural transformation of society. It followed from its neoliberal program that despite its strong support for the family, the FPÖ not only refused to support a ban on abortion but expressly acknowledged that it was up to the woman to make the ultimate decision whether or not she was going to have an abortion (FPÖ, 1985).

Despite its generally neoliberal program, however, the FPÖ was quite ambiguous about international free trade. Although it had been a promoter of Austrian membership in the European Communities in the 1980s, in the early 1990s the party turned into the most ardent critic of the European Union and especially "the error of Maastricht" in Austria. For the FPÖ, Maastricht would, if realized, lead to a "super centralized state," a bureaucratized Moloch without democratic legitimation. Rather than representing a "Europe of the citizens," Maastricht represented a Europe that was directed against its citizens (Haider, 1993, pp. 272–273). Against that, the FPÖ proposed the creation of a confederation of states, consisting of a common security pact and a customs union, without, however, a common currency or common social policy (Haider, 1993, p. 283).

The party showed similar ambiguity toward the global market. Confronted with competition from low-wage countries in Eastern and Central Europe and the developing world, the party came out in support of limited and selective "protectionist measures for industry in the interest of the preservation of work places." Haider suggested that Austria develop an "ecological counter strategy against the free trade system" to protect the domestic economy against competitors from countries that disregarded human rights or gained a competitive advantage by exploiting the environment (Haider, 1993, p. 217).

SWITZERLAND

"Freedom—prosperity—joy of life!" No other party has brought the maxims of the new era as succinctly to the point, has celebrated the dawn of individualism and egoism as enthusiastically as the Swiss Automobile party. Appealing to the average Swiss citizens who "are capable of independent judgement," the party declared as its fundamental objectives "to preserve and create the highest possible level of individual freedom in all spheres of life," to revive the principles of the free market, and to restrict state intervention to a minimum (Autopartei, 1991, p. 1). Like the FPÖ, the Automobile party propagated a fundamental liberalism. Not surprisingly, this fundamental liberalism found its most pointed expression in the party's support of "free private transportation," which the party considered a fundamental element of a free society. In concrete terms this meant that the party called for a speedy expansion of the existing highway system, the construction of more parking spaces, as well as the abolition of "arbitrary speed limits and intentional traffic impediments."

Like the FPÖ, the Automobile party called for a cutback both in welfare expenditures and the public work force, arguing that the social safety net "must not become a hammock for those who don't want to make an effort" and work. It called for the abolition of direct taxes and their substitution with indirect taxes, the deregulation of the Swiss economy, the privatization of the state-run media, and the abolition of state subsidies for public transportation and agriculture. And like other radical right-wing populist parties, it stressed its support for small and medium-sized companies as the backbone of the Swiss economy.

With this radically liberal program the Automobile party made an explicit appeal to those voters in whose opinion the established center-right parties had sold out to the socialist Left and particularly to the Greens, which the Automobile party considered its most important opponent. In fact, no other radical right-wing populist party expressed as much open hostility toward the Greens as the Autopartei. At least in this instance, the rise of radical right-wing populism was a direct response to the emergence of the libertarian Left.

NORTHERN ITALY

The revival and strengthening of individual initiative, entrepreneurship, and free-market competition have also been one of the central concerns informing the Lega Nord's political interventions. Its neoliberal program is an intricate part of its larger regionalist and federalist aspirations. Despite the fact that, especially in its initial years, the party put a heavy emphasis on the defense of regional dialects, culture, and social and moral values, the protection of ethnocultural identities is not the primary motivation behind the Lega's call for regionalist autonomy. Rather, the objectives behind the Lega's demand for cultural autonomy are, foremost, "economic, financial, and ultimately organizational" (Poche, 1991/92, p. 75).

Underlying the Lega's political success has been their ability to convince northern voters that the centralization of political authority and economic resources in Rome has both disregarded and harmed northern regional interests and identity. Those primarily responsible for this development are the political class, comparable to the nomenklatura of Soviet-style systems. In his book *Che cosa vuole la Lega,* Giulio Savelli (1992, pp. 9-13) describes the Lega as an expression of growing resentment over the fact that in Italy a minority of the population, the *classe politica,* had appropriated more resources than it produced and destroyed the sources of prosperity. This situation had been perpetuated by an inefficient public administration largely dominated by southerners (p. 123).

For Bossi and the Lega this situation was bound to lead to a bitter political conflict between "the capital of parasitism and clientelism, which is Rome, and the capital of the economy, which is Milan" (Bossi with Vimercati, 1993, p. 170). Should the Christian Democrats have succeeded in preserving their power base in the south, these regions would have steadily drifted away from the north and thus from the rest of Europe. In his autobiography, Bossi predicted that the political and economic future of Italy would ultimately be determined in a confrontation between Christian Democrats and the Lega: "Soon only two representative forces will remain, the party of stagnation and conservation and the party of radical change. In the end we will be victorious, but the battle will be hard and uncertain" (Bossi with Vimercati, 1992, p. 120).

The Lega's political strategy and eventual success was predicated on its ability to convince northern voters to accept it as the advocate "of a productive and dynamic land" that was "endangered by the negligence and irrelevance of the central power" (Poche, 1991/92, p. 76). This meant that the party had to explain what accounted for the particular character of the northern regions. The Lega's answer was that if northern Italy was more affluent and prosperous than the rest of the country, this was largely due to the fact that before unification the region had been dominated by powers (especially Austria) that tended to stress efficiency and bureaucratic rationality and instilled a particular Calvinist-type work ethic in the region. In the party's view, northern Italy formed an intricate part of the advanced regions of Europe, whereas the south remained largely "without a modern economic culture" (Savelli, 1992, pp. 224–225). The hegemony of Rome and its spirit of clientelism and parasitism thus not only threatened to destroy northern Italy's particular cultural identity, but alienate it from the rest of Europe.

Umberto Bossi expressed these fears when he called for an end to the Italian mentality of *assistenzialismo.* This thinking prevented northern Italy from competing effectively with the countries of northern Europe and threatened to

reduce Italy to the status of a developing country (Bossi with Vimercati, 1993, p. 180). Only if northern Italy managed to preserve its cultural identity shaped by the Protestant work ethic, and at the same time managed to eradicate the spirit of *assistenzialismo* in the south, could it hope to prevent Italy from falling back into political and economic insignificance.[5]

In order to combat *assistenzialismo* and the power of the central state, the Lega adopted a radical version of economic liberalism, which promoted a rigorous respect for the rules of the market while rejecting any attempt on the part of the state to extend its sphere of influence. On the contrary, the state was to take on only those tasks that the market was unable to solve. Concretely this meant that the Lega advocated the reduction of some taxes and the abolition of others; the large-scale privatization of publicly held enterprises and parts of the public sector such as the media; a general deregulation of the private sector; and a restructuring of the remaining public services, including the introduction of a system of incentives and merits for public employees. Instead of a comprehensive welfare state, the Lega advocated what Bossi called a "cooperative liberalism." This meant that the Lega would not refuse to help those who were in difficulties, be it in Italy or elsewhere in the world. But the help would not consist of handouts, but of support for self-help.

Like other radical right-wing populist parties, the Lega promoted itself as the champion of small and medium-sized companies, artisans, professionals, and individual entrepreneurs, not the big corporations. The Lega explicitly acknowledged the role of the former as the productive backbone of the Italian economy and promised to remedy years of neglect by a central state, which had always favored big business (see Moioli, 1991, p. 164). This was in part a logical consequence of the party's promotion of economic and political decentralization. In part it followed from the Lega's expectations that as soon as the productive middle class was to gain access to capital necessary to finance the introduction of new technologies it would play a central role in the future development of advanced Western societies.

Economic motives, rather than the desire to preserve ethnocultural identities, were also behind the Lega's most controversial proposition—its call for the transformation of the country into three macroregions (north, center, south), joined together by shared values and cultural and socioeconomic characteristics. According to Bossi, these macroregions would then become the "basic elements of the new Europe" (Bossi with Vimercati, 1993, p. 10). In his most radical moments, Bossi even threatened to proclaim a *Repubblica del Nord* to be followed by the eventual secession from the rest of Italy. This led critics to charge that the Lega's main objective was less to put an end to the established political system than to put an end to Italy itself. In their view, the Lega's vocation was "not that of a federalist but that of a secessionist type. They promote a generic 'Europeanism' only to hide the fact that they prefer the Germans (and the Austrians) to the rest of the Italians."[6] In response to these charges, in late 1992, Bossi not only rejected the notion that the Lega was a secessionist or separatist movement, he also renounced (at least for the time being) the idea of a northern republic.[7] However, by mid-1993, the old ambiguities were revived. Once again Bossi threatened that should the south fail to follow the north and reject the old sociopolitical system within the next few years, the north would be forced to secede from the rest of the country. "And to secede will be the entire northern population: with a growing number of workers becoming unemployed, with factories being closed, forced to their knees by their competitors in the East, the fiscal pressure will no longer be tolerable. The integrity of the state will be questioned not for political reasons but for socioeconomic ones."[8] Thus, it was quite logical that at the Lega's party conference in December 1993 Bossi would advance the project of a reconstruction of Italy into a "free association" of three republics—Padania, Etruria, and a Republic of the South. And it was also quite logical that, confronted with vehement protests from various corners of the Italian political and intellectual establishment, Bossi would almost immediately moderate his tone claiming that the proposal had only been "a hypothesis, a provocation" designed to put the question of federalism back on the political agenda.[9]

The whole debate on federalism and the division of Italy into three regions or "republics" once again illustrates to what degree the Lega Nord's program has been determined and dominated by economic considerations. What largely explains the success of the Lega Nord in the affluent regions of northern Italy was a growing fear in the early 1990s that, confronted with new challenges posed by global economic changes and the acceleration of European integration, Italy might lose contact with its more advanced partners in Western Europe. Aldo Moltifiori, who had lived and worked for an extended period of time outside Italy before being elected mayor of Monza for the Lega Nord, expressed these sentiments perhaps most vividly when he said: "When I came back to Italy and saw my daughter's school, I realized that we were still more in the Third World than in Europe. If I joined the Lega, if I left my job to become the mayor of Monza, it is because I believe that the Lega is the last chance to stay in Europe or return to it" (quoted in Bocca, 1993, p. 254). Only against this background is it possible to understand the Lega's repeated affirmations that northern Italy was "ready to enter Europe in full title" now that it had laid its political fate into the hands of the Lega.[10] The Lega's neoliberal program, its celebration of the Protestant work ethic, entrepreneurship, and the productive middle class were central elements of a strategy designed to mobilize the population of northern Italy against the established system and for the safeguarding of the region's competitive position in the global market.

XENOPHOBIA AND RACISM

If in the early and mid-1980s radical right-wing populist parties were largely banking on the appeal of a radical neoliberal program, by the end of the 1980s a growing number had discovered the potential electoral appeal of a new issue—immigration. Particularly for the Scandinavian parties, this was an important development given the negative experiences the Danish party had made when it sought to mobilize xenophobia and latent racism in the late 1970s. In 1979, a local representative of the party attained notoriety when he wrote that immigrants were "multiplying like rats." However, the strategy backfired. "Although Mogens Glistrup to a large degree supported the attack on immigrants, this apparently only accelerated the declining popularity of the party" (Andersen, 1992, p. 198). However, immigration returned as a new issue in the late 1980s. Particularly, the success of the Front National showed that if exploited skillfully, growing public hostility toward immigrants and refugees could enhance electoral fortunes. Thus, when a member of the Danish Progress Party warned in 1987 before the election on a local radio station of the "terroristic hordes arriving from the Middle East and from Sri Lanka" who "were multiplying like rats," the party gained in electoral support (see Parlement Européen, 1991, p. 61). By the early 1990s, almost all radical right-wing populist parties had adopted antiimmigrant positions. The exception was the Lega Nord. Whereas its initial programs betrayed a strong sense of hostility first toward immigrants from southern Italy, then toward immigrants and refugees from developing countries, by the time of its success in the municipal elections of 1993 the party had virtually abandoned immigration as a political issue.

As the discussion in the previous chapter has shown, the question of immigration can hardly be reduced to a single issue. Generally, the public has blamed immigration for growing crime rates, the rise in unemployment, and the growing costs of the welfare state. On a more subtle level, immigration has been seen as a threat to national and cultural identity. Whereas radical right-wing populist parties have generally appealed to a number of these issues, neoliberal parties have put particular emphasis on the economic aspects of immigration, while occasionally reminding their voters that immigrants not only cause economic problems but also represent a threat to their hosts' culture and identity.

Both Glistrup and Hagen warned against the threat from an invasion of Muslims intent on destroying Danish and Norwegian culture. Particularly, Hagen gained much needed attention when, during the 1987 campaign for the local elections, he produced a letter that he had supposedly received from a Muslim immigrant. The letter's author threatened "that in due course Norway would become a Muslim country, the cross would be removed from the national flag and mosques would become as common in Norway as Christian churches had been so far" (Arter, 1992, p. 364). As one might have suspected, the letter turned out to be a forgery. Like in Norway, the Danish party adopted the immigration issue in the mid-1980s. When Mogens Glistrup returned to active politics in 1985, he made immigration the party's top political priority. However, by the late 1980s, the party increasingly disassociated itself from the more radical statements of some of its members.

When one of the party's members challenged the Danish lawmakers in a speech to the Danish parliament in the opening of the Parliament's 1990/91 session to make Denmark "a Muslim Free Zone," the party's chairperson and other members of the party disassociated themselves from that statement (Andersen, 1992, p. 198). This, however, did not mean that the party abandoned the question of immigration or refrained from overtly xenophobic statements altogether. Citing a long list of public concerns about immigration, the party introduced, for example, in October 1989, a proposal in parliament to tighten the existing laws on immigration. And in the 1990 electoral campaign, "when the party was keen to dissociate itself from Glistrup's style, Pia Kjærsgaard spoke of the immigrants as 'multiplying like rabbits' " (Andersen, 1992, p. 199).

Despite, on occasion, couching their opposition to immigration in cultural terms, neither the Progress parties nor New Democracy overly emphasized the cultural aspects of immigration. Instead they largely appealed to its economic aspects. When the Norwegian party adopted the immigration issue in the local elections of 1987, it deliberately couched it primarily in economic terms. The party's main argument was "that increased grants to refugees would mean worse conditions for 'our own' inhabitants, those of Norwegian birth" (Bjørklund, 1988, p. 217). The party's program for the 1989 election made a similar point. It stated that, considering its overall liberal economic philosophy, the party should support the free movement of goods, services, capital, and labor across borders. This presupposed, however, "that immigrants should not be allowed to benefit from welfare arrangements and other welfare arrangements which are contingent on long-term accumulation of rights through payments or through citizenship." Since Norway granted immigrants the same rights as Norwegian citizens, the party supported limiting immigration to short-term employment contracts, which excluded the right to bring family members. At the same time the party affirmed its commitment to Norway's traditional policy of receiving refugees as long as they returned to their home countries as soon as this was politically feasible (Fremskrittspartiet, 1989, p. 30).

A comparison between the positions of the Automobile party and New Democracy shows that radical right-wing populist parties hardly agree on what measures should be taken to discourage immigration. The Automobile party's program represents perhaps the most blatant appeal to the public's perception that immigration represents a growing financial burden on West European societies. The party repeatedly complained that foreign citizens from Switzerland's neighbors, Germany, France, or Austria, were denied work permits whereas "illegal, mostly unqualified immigrants from exotic countries" were allowed to enter the densely populated country.[11] Charging that the majority of refugees come to Switzerland for economic reasons, the Automobile party proposed drastic measures to stop the growing "flood" of refugees. Among other things, the party demanded that Switzerland cancel its adherence to the Geneva convention on refugees; that Switzerland stop all immigration as long as there were undecided asylum cases; that refugees who had entered the country illegally be immediately deported; and that asylum seekers be used for unpaid public works projects in order to cover the costs that they had caused.

By contrast, New Democracy's policy proposals were rather moderate. In its official program, the party called for a reorientation of the country's immigration policy by giving refugees temporary residence permits and allowing them to work temporarily. At the same time, the party called for the abolition of publicly organized and funded "native language instruction" (instruction in the immigrant's language). Instead, immigrants who wanted to stay in Sweden should be encouraged to integrate themselves into Swedish society. As Ian Wachtmeister made clear in an interview in 1993, the party's antiforeigner position was directed against "the flow of economic refugees who come here and want to live at the expense of Swedish society. It has not been very popular saying that. One is immediately branded a racist and immigrant hater, but we are not."[12]

If in Scandinavia and Switzerland the radical Right's case against immigration in the late 1980s was mainly directed against asylum seekers, in northern Italy the situation was somewhat more complicated. Since its foundation in the early 1980s, the Lega has been accused of promoting xenophobia and fostering racism toward immigrants (see Moioli, 1990). Initially, the Lega's hostility toward immigrants was directed almost exclusively against the large number of southern migrants, who had moved to the north during the years of the economic miracle to find jobs in factories and the public sector. The Lega charged the southerners of having brought with them clientelism and favoritism. This had led to the discrimination of the indigenous, north Italian population. In response, the Lega Lombarda demanded that jobs in the public administration and priority with regard to public housing be given to Lombards rather than new southern immigrants.

It was not until Bossi started to seek electoral support beyond the party's strongholds in the north that the party came to mute its attacks against the southern immigrant population. Instead, the party increasingly focused on the "invasion of negroes and Arabs" (Vimercati, 1990, p. 88). This was a response to the rapid increase in the number of legal and illegal immigrants from Africa and Asia, for which Italian society was largely unprepared. The Lega articulated wide-spread fears that the number of immigrants would continue to increase dramatically, that this would lead to unemployment and a decline in economic growth, and that the government was unwilling to solve the growing problems. In fact, the Lega accused the government of promoting immigration, since immigration allowed the political establishment to preserve their power. To transform Italy into a "multi-racial, multi-ethnic, and multi-religious country" modeled after the United States meant to keep Italy divided. For "excessive cultural differences, especially if expressed by skin color, are fatal for social peace. When streets and places are full of colored people," citizens no longer feel at home and lose their identity. For this reason "a multi-cultural society comes closer to hell than to paradise" (Bossi with Vimercati, 1992, p. 148). To forestall this outcome, the Lega proposed a drastic reduction in the number of immigrants. Only those foreigners who could prove before they even entered the country that they would have a place to work and live in Italy should be allowed to cross the border (Bossi with Vimercati, 1992, p. 146).

Despite the Lega's negative attitudes toward immigrants and the development of a multicultural society in Italy, the party increasingly abandoned past appeals to xenophobia. As early as in the 1992 election, the Lega made a determined effort to refute the charge that the party was running on a primarily xenophobic platform. A propaganda video designed to spread the Lega's message before the election contained a sequence that showed a number of African construction workers busily at work in Milan. The message was simple: the Lega had nothing against immigrants as long as they adopted the northern work ethic.[13] The Lega's conscious effort to disassociate itself from past xenophobic statements continued after the election. Whereas Umberto Bossi's first book, written before the 1992 election, included one whole chapter on immigration, his second book, written in early 1993, mentioned immigration only in passing. Although it is difficult to say to what degree xenophobic views were still held in private by party members and voters, by 1993, the party had clearly abandoned most of its past xenophobic rhetoric.[14]

The exception was growing hostility toward Muslims. According to the Lega, Muslims neither could nor wanted to be integrated into Italian society. Aldo Moltifiori, the Lega Nord mayor of Monza, made that quite clear when shortly after assuming office he said that foreigners could stay in Monza as long as their documents were in order. This, however, did not apply to Muslims. Neither he nor the Lega would allow that "the Koran destroys our culture."[15] In an interview with the newsweekly *Il Sabato,* Umberto Bossi confirmed this position. In his view, the world was divided in two camps: on the one side was culture and civilization represented by the West, on the other side was barbarism, represented by the Muslim world. Bossi went so far as to explicitly call for the use of Western force in order to contain the potential spread of Muslim influence in Africa. This left little doubt that the appeal to anti-Islamic sentiments had become a core element of the Lega's *weltanschauung* and its political program.

If the Lega gradually abandoned direct appeals to xenophobia, the FPÖ went the opposite course. Since Haider's assumption of the chairmanship of the party, the FPÖ has been accused of being a right-wing extremist party (Galanda, 1987; Fischer and Gstettner, 1990; Scharsach, 1992). These charges were largely based on Haider's consistent attempts to downplay the crimes committed by the National Socialist regime and to contribute to revisionist tendencies; on the FPÖ's advocacy of an ethnic and cultural conception of the nation; and from the party's propagation of a xenophobic program, which contributed significantly to the creation of a political climate hostile toward immigrants and refugees. Each one of these elements was part of a comprehensive strategy to fill the ideological void left by the erosion of traditional subcultures and to compensate for the loss of certainty resulting from social transformation (see Oswalt, 1989, p. 79). Andreas Mölzer made this quite clear when he characterized the party's ideology as a liberalism, which combined "individual readiness to work hard and the individual pursuit of self-realization with the need for national-cultural and regional rootedness" (Mölzer, 1990, pp. 18-19; see also Haider, 1993, pp. 86-106).

The FPÖ conceived of peoples as natural, organically grown communities, which share a common language, culture, and ethnic origins. Only those who recognized their ethnic belongingness were capable of contributing to the development of the cultural values and historical-cultural self-understanding of their ethnic community. This created particular problems in Austria. Because of Austria's association with the Germans, there were strong impediments preventing the Austrians from acknowledging their national roots. In the immediate postwar period, the Austrian elites had tried to create an Austrian national identity. "To an extent, this state-sponsored operation involved 'talking up' the Austrian consciousness, strengthening it claiming it was already there, and basing it on the empirically shaky proposition that Austrians under National Socialism had as a whole both been treated worse and behaved better than the Germans" (Knight, 1992, p. 287).

The FPÖ had always refused to recognize the existence of an Austrian nation. Although the party did not question Austria's existence as an independent state, it held that the Austrian people were part of a larger German cultural community (see Haider, 1993, pp. 109–110). These notions were particularly strong in Carinthia, where it fed on "the selfperception as a marshland situated at the borders of German-Austrian culture and called to resist a supposed Slav encroachment" (Knight, 1992, p. 288). Given his Carinthian background, it was hardly surprising that under Haider, German nationalist elements gained new grounds in the FPÖ (see Fischer and Gstettner, 1990). Haider was convinced that with the fall of Soviet-style socialist internationalism the future would belong to ethnic and cultural nationalism (Haider, 1992, pp. 53–54; Haider, 1993, pp. 107–125). He therefore explicitly sanctioned the revival of German nationalism in the party when he called the official attempts to create an Austrian national consciousness an "ideological miscarriage" (Mölzer, 1990, pp. 139–150).

The propagation of a German national identity explained Haider's numerous attempts to call into question that the Nazi regime should be judged by the crimes committed in the name of the German people and to rehabilitate former Nazis (Oswalt, 1989; Scharsach, 1992). However, realizing that this position was increasingly turning into a liability, Haider turned around and condemned National Socialism in his 1993 book, *Die Freiheit, die ich meine,* as the "most atrocious criminal regime" whose anti-Semitism and racism had led to mass extermination. Having been part of this regime the Austrians had to take responsibility for the crimes committed by it. At the same time, however, Haider called for an end to the "criminalization" of Austrian history, "as if the life of the war generation were a single rogues' gallery" (Haider, 1993, p. 116).

The FPÖ's position on national identity also explains the party's explicit hostility toward foreigners. Despite claiming in its 1985 program to appreciate the existence and achievements of ethnic minorities in Austria "as a valuable contribution to our common homeland," the party was strictly opposed to the transformation of Austria into a multicultural society. For Andreas Mölzer, multicultural societies would promote the leveling of ethnic differences, which could only end in "human suffering and massive economic loss rather than mutual cultural enrichment."[16]

In keeping with their ethnicly defined conception of the nation, the FPÖ was strongly opposed to the growing influx of immigrants and refugees in the late 1980s.[17] However, it was not until 1991 that the party turned the fight against immigration into a top political priority. Haider himself appealed to the Austrian population to raise their voice against the "unrestrained immigration movement. No people will tolerate for long to be degraded to the status of foreigners in their homeland." This, Haider charged, had nothing to do with xenophobia, but was "simply a sign of responsibility for the native population" (Haider, 1992, p. 55). In the face of a growing threat that it had helped invent, the FPÖ presented itself as the defender of the Austrian homeland against the threat of invasion from the East, which, as the party's pamphlets on immigration did not tire to point out, was turning into *the* political nightmare of the Austrian population.

Like other radical right-wing populist parties, the FPÖ strongly opposed "the utopia of a multicultural society" (Haider, 1993, p. 94). In Haider's view, its primary problem was that it encouraged newcomers to expect the indigenous population to adapt to the newcomers' customs and life-styles. This was particularly problematic in those cases, where the newcomers' customs and social norms were incompatible with those of the indigenous population. This was particularly the case with Muslim immigrants, because, as Haider put it, the "Islamic social order is opposed to our Western values" (Haider, 1993, pp. 92-93).

In order to prove their sense of responsibility for the native population, the party proposed a catalogue of measures designed to severely restrict the number and social rights of immigrants in Austria. They ranged from a complete stop to immigration until a solution had been found for the growing problem of illegal immigration and the lack of available housing, and until unemployment had not fallen below 5 percent; an increase in the police force in charge of foreigners and the creation of a special border guard; the limitation of the number of foreign students in elementary and vocational schools; rigorous measures against illegal employment and the abuse of social benefits; and the immediate expulsion of foreigners who had committed a crime. In addition, the FPÖ vigorously opposed giving foreign residents the right to vote in local elections or lowering the ten-year waiting period to attain Austrian citizenship. In order to allow the Austrian voters to express themselves on these issues, the FPÖ initiated a country-wide petition to have the party's proposals debated in parliament.[18] But faced with vehement opposition by Austria's major social, cultural, and political organizations, only 8 percent of eligible voters signed the petition.

The relative failure of the petition campaign seemed to be a first sign that Haider's opportunistic exploitation of pressing new issues was leaving the public increasingly uneasy. A minority within the party came to see the drastic turn to the right as further alienating the party from the mainstream of West European liberalism and bringing it closer to the position of the Front National or the Republikaner. The response was quick and decisive. Shortly after the closing of the petition drive Heide Schmidt, together with four members of the FPÖ's parliamentary group, left the party to found a genuinely liberal party modeled after the German FDP. However, despite the defection of its liberal wing, support for the FPÖ did not decline in opinion polls; it even appeared to gain the party new supporters. The mobilizing potential of xenophobia was clearly higher than the party's promotion of a fundamental liberalism.

The FPÖ's full embrace of an aggressive antiimmigrant position marked the recognition of the electoral potential of xenophobia. This was an experience that radical right-wing populist parties in France, Germany, and Belgium had already made in the mid-1980s. Particularly, the Front National owed its electoral success at least in part to its ability to mobilize public resentment against foreigners. Because of its electoral success, the Front National had become a model not only for the Republikaner in Germany and the Vlaams Blok in Belgium, but also for a host of right-wing extremist parties, which populated the fringes of West European politics.[19] Like the Front National, they embraced a national-populist agenda, whose central issue was the question of immigration.

THE FRONT NATIONAL

National populism was hardly a newcomer to French politics. Among its most important representatives in the past were Boulangism in the late 19th century, Pétainism in the 1940s, and Poujadism in the 1950s. Its main themes were the notion of decadence, caused by "deadly viruses" that contaminated French society and corrupted its people. These viruses were variously identified as the political class, Jews, or foreigners in general. In order to combat this deadly threat, France had to lay its destiny in the hands of a "savior who will regenerate the country, defend French identity, and make sure that national preference is respected" (Bréchon, 1993, p. 35).

While the Front National modernized the central elements of the national populist agenda, the party remained true to its basic analysis and objectives.

Unlike its predecessors, it sought to gain respectability by moderating its tone without, however, occasionally forgetting to use the well-tried tools of the extreme Right. Anti-Semitic statements—such as Le Pen's assertion that the gas chambers were "a mere detail of the history of the Second World War" in September 1987 or his allusion to the role the "Jewish International" had played in the creation of an "anti-national spirit" in August 1989—were both a ritual and part of a political strategy to probe the resilience of the party's supporters rather than directly aimed "at the Jewish community in present-day France" (McCarthy, 1993, p. 54).[20]

Like its predecessors, the Front National consistently affirmed its concern about France's decline and its desire to see French national greatness reestablished. In the party's view, moral and political problems rather than socioeconomic ones had caused France's decline (Taguieff, 1984, p. 116). In the face of a profound national crisis, the established parties (the "gang of four" of PS, RPR, UDF, and PCF) had proven incapable of responding to the exigencies of a swiftly and radically changing world. Dominated by a new class of administrators, technocrats, trade union functionaries, and media elites they had limited themselves to seeking socioeconomic solutions while pursuing a new political agenda centered around the promotion of human rights and antiracism, which opened the door even wider to third-world immigrations and thus only hastened the destruction of French national identity. As a result, France was "threatened in its very existence, its prosperity, its liberties."[21]

Against what it considered to be a mixture of social democracy and market liberalism of neo-Gaullists, center-liberals, and socialists the Front National promoted an exclusivist popular capitalism based on the notion that France is, and should be, above all for the French (Le Pen, 1985). With this program, the Front National managed to bring together the different strands of the traditional French extreme, radical, and conservative Right—the fascist and national revolutionaries' obsession with the decline of the West, the Poujadists' denouncement of "too much state and too high taxes," Catholic traditionalists' support of traditional values, and the conversion of parts of the new Right (particularly the so-called Club de l'Horloge) to the neoliberal ideas of Thatcherism and Reaganism (cf. Buzzi, 1991, pp. 36–40; Fysh and Wolfreys, 1992, p. 317).

This becomes particularly apparent with regard to the Front National's initial espousal of ultra-liberalist economic and social doctrines, which by the late 1980s were supported by a large majority of the party's cadres (see Ysmal, 1991, p. 192; Ignazi and Ysmal, 1992, p. 116). The party justified its conversion to neoliberalism by maintaining that there was a natural connection between property and rootedness, according to the formula: property = freedom =

responsibility = rootedness (*enracinement*). Only a free market rewarded individual initiative and effort, entrepreneurial spirit and imagination, while promoting responsibility and the willingness to take personal risks. Not only was economic liberalism supposed to guarantee material security, foster natural hierarchies by allowing those most capable to succeed, and thus combat the leveling tendencies of the welfare state, it was also supposed to encourage individual responsibility and enhance social peace (Le Pen, 1985, p. 62). Once individuals understood that they were responsible for damage caused to others, they would exercise self-restraint (Le Pen, 1989, p. 31). It is in this spirit that the Front National called for a France of "50 million proprietors" to be achieved by privatizing all public holdings and distributing their stocks free of charge among the French families according to the number of their children (Le Pen, 1985, pp. 65–67). Once a free market was established the state should restrict its duties to guaranteeing the security and defending the freedom of the individual citizens against internal and external enemies, and to dispensing justice. As Pierre Bréchon observed, this economic doctrine glorified "the ideal of an economic democracy of small proprietors" protected both against the threats from large enterprises and the tax-hungry state (Bréchon, 1993, p. 40).

Although in its basic elements the Front National's economic program resembled those advanced by the Progress parties or the FPÖ, its objectives were fundamentally different. Whereas the latter sought to enhance economic competitiveness or individual freedom vis-à-vis the state, the Front National subordinated purely economic goals to the safeguarding of French national identity. The party's reasoning was that only those rooted in a particular culture and community could be expected to show responsibility, respect for the national patrimony, and regard for the freedom of others. Those uprooted from their own culture and/or unwilling to identify themselves with French culture and values, in turn, could be expected to act irresponsibly and without regard for the law. For this reason market liberalism was incompatible with immigration, but also large, export-oriented companies, multinational corporations, and large global financial enterprises, which were only interested in getting "maximum benefits at any price. . . including opening the doors to third-world immigrants in order to exploit their labor force, to the detriment of the latter, of European interests, and future European politics" (Le Pen, 1989, pp. 30, 87).

Given this reasoning, it is hardly surprising that confronted with growing unemployment and a continued deterioration of France's position in the global economy the party gradually abandoned its neoliberal position to propagate a comprehensive policy of "national preference" (Lehideux, 1993, p. 37).[22] In the face of what the Front National saw as a disloyal competition from the newly industrialized countries and Anglo-Saxon and Japanese multinationals, and an increasingly frantic chase after productivity gains, France had to defend itself against the "effects of international economic war." In this situation, it was essential "to throw out the idyllic vision according to which global free trade (*le libre-échangisme mondial*) mean[t] prosperity. In reality, it [led] to an economic war without pity in which Europe and France, like their competitors, must use the arms of protectionism." What the country needed was a "pragmatic and offensive protection of the French economy and industry at the borders of the European market" (Front National, 1993, pp. 243–244). The regulation of competition, not the suppression of economic borders, had to become the main objective of international economic relations as a protection against "savage competition."[23]

The contours of the Front National's new policy were spelled out by Bruno Mégret in response to the economic proposals advanced by the Balladur government. Among others, Bruno Mégret called for the imposition of tariffs on all agricultural and industrial goods entering France from non-EC countries, based on the wage differentials between French and foreign labor; the suspension of France's participation in the GATT negotiations for two years to allow the outcome for its economy to be evaluated by an international court of arbitration; the suspension of the 1991 EC-Japanese accord on automobile imports; and the suspension of the Schengen agreement and the reintroduction of customs controls at the borders.[24]

But a return to a pragmatic economic nationalism was not enough to safeguard the viability of the French economy and French industry and combat rising unemployment. In order to halt unemployment, the party proposed a comprehensive policy package, which included, among other proposals, a drastic reduction of individual taxes and corporate expenditures on social benefits; a radical reduction in the size of the immigrant population; the fostering of vocational education and training programs; and the introduction of a "parental salary" to encourage women to leave the work force and return to their homes (Lehideux, 1993).

Given the party's overall concern with defending France's national identity, its shift from market liberalism to protectionism was hardly as radical a departure from established ideological positions as it might appear. Rather, protectionism brought the party's economic program in line with the central element of its ethno-nationalist agenda—the question of immigration. Le Pen himself emphasized the importance of this issue for the Front National when he wrote that the Front National was a "bio-political movement, a reaction of health against the threat of death contained in decadence, the subversion or invasion from the outside" (Le Pen, 1989, p. 108). This was an indication of the degree to which the Front National was obsessed by the question of immigration, where "immigration becomes a major symptom of decadence, because it represents the acceptance of biological, ideological, and cultural mixing, the renunciation of traditions and the qualities which are particular to ethnic origins, and the abdication of the West" (Honoré, 1985, p. 1868).

For Jean-Marie Le Pen and the Front National, immigration posed a deadly threat to French national identity. In their view, French identity had evolved during a thousand years of history during which it was transmitted from generation to generation. To belong to the French people meant above all being part of "a chain, a line," which connects the present to the past and to the future (Honoré, 1989, p. 1843; Le Pen, 1985, p. 128). Sharing in that heritage guaranteed exclusive rights to citizenship and preferential treatment with regard to jobs, housing, and social security and other benefits. Although the Front National did not exclude the possibility to acquire French citizenship, the party maintained that naturalization had to be more than a mere formality sanctioned by a bureaucratic act. Citizenship had to "be solicited and merited, if one is not born of French parents" (Front National, 1988, p. 81). Or, as the party put it, "être Français cela s'hérite ou cela se mérite."[25] Merit meant above all that a foreigner had to show his or her willingness to assimilate French culture, habits, and moral values. Obviously, or so Le Pen maintained, those geographically and culturally closer to the French people such as the Portuguese were more likely to be assimilated into French society (Le Pen, 1989, p. 29).

The Front National position on immigration derived mainly from Le Pen's well-known explanation of emotional affinities and attachment:

> I like my daughters better than my cousins, my cousins better than my neighbors; my neighbors better than strangers, and strangers better than enemies. As a result I prefer the French, that's my right. Then I prefer the Europeans, and then the Westerners, and then I like better than all other countries of the world those which are allies and those which like France. (cited in Honoré, 1985, p. 1853; Le Pen, 1989, p. 102)

Clearly, the group least liked by Le Pen and the Front National were North African Muslims who had settled in France. And this for two reasons: Because of their high birth rates, North Africans threatened to condemn the French to become a minority in their own country (Le Pen, 1985, pp. 112–114; Taguieff, 1984, p. 134);[26] and because they came from " 'closed' societies" they claimed their right to maintain their own culture against the process of assimilation, which was the rule in French society (Front National, 1988, p. 65). For both reasons, North African Muslims represented a deadly threat to France's cultural integrity and very survival as a Western nation: "as long as foreign communities settle for good on French soil without assimilating, national identity, civil peace, and national sovereignty are in peril" (Front National, 1993, p. 31). The root problem with foreigners of non-European origins settling in France was thus that they wanted to preserve their cultural identity, which necessarily endangered French cultural identity. Or, as Pierre-André Taguieff put it: "The foreigner is detestable only in that he is postulated as being inassimilable without provoking a destruction of community identity" (Taguieff, 1990, p. 120).

In this situation, France had to act quickly if it wanted to avert disaster. Already the concentration of muslim immigrants in urban ghettos threatened to transform whole communities into foreign cities characterized by "an asocial life-style like the one seen in Harlem or parts of Los Angeles." Already there existed "thousands of metastases" similar to those that threatened to lead to the outbursts of ethnic and social confrontation, which had destroyed Lebanon and were decimating ex-Yugoslavia. Already France experienced the emergence of "occupied zones, where the French citizens are deprived of a certain number of their essential rights connected to their freedom and security, something which cannot be tolerated."[27] Behind the Front National's rejection of multiculturalism there thus was the hidden assumption that when different populations come in contact with each other the result would inevitably be racial struggle (see Taguieff, 1990, p. 121). As Patrick McCarthy has noted, by portraying the French as victims, Le Pen not only usurped "the role played by the North African immigrant," but also redefined the immigrant "as oppressor" (McCarthy, 1993, p. 53).

In order to meet this threat the Front National put forward a comprehensive antiforeigner program, the central point of which was repatriation. Its core elements were spelled out in 50 points, proposed in November 1991 by Bruno Mégret, the director of Jean-Marie Le Pen's presidential campaign in 1988, and designed to create conditions conducive to settle the problem of immigration and to protect the national identity.[28] Prominently among these proposals were the repatriation of foreigners to their home countries; the expulsion of undocumented foreigners; the return of unemployed foreigners to their home countries and the detention of immigrants whose deportation was pending; the discouragement of new immigration by according priority to French citizens with regard to jobs, public housing, family allowances, and social security; the reform of the political asylum laws, and the reinforcement of existing border controls. Other measures included the proposal to establish health controls at the borders to prevent HIV infected persons from entering the country; to abrogate the law that gives citizenship to those born on French soil and replace it with the "right of blood"; and to impede the further construction of mosques and submit Islamic centers to strict regimentation.

If these measures were supposed to counter the cultural threat to French identity, others aimed at reversing the negative demographic trends of the French population and thus guaranteeing the survival of the French as a distinct people. In order to achieve these objectives, the Front National sought above all to reverse what the party considered the antifamily policies of the past decades, which discouraged marriage, weakened the family, and contributed to falling birth rates and thus the erosion of national identity. As early as in the mid-1980s, Le Pen had warned that only if France kept its population "young, energetic, and numerous" could it prevent the country from falling into the hands of foreigners. "It is for this reason that the state must have a natalist policy, because it cannot remain neutral in the face of the survival of the nation" (Le Pen, 1985, p. 129). It is for this reason that the party called for the repeal of France's liberal abortion laws, the abrogation of laws that penalized married couples financially or otherwise, and the introduction of subsidies for women (*revenue maternelle*) who chose to interrupt their career in order to raise children. The Front National was very careful, however, not to appear hostile to women's social or political gains. Although Le Pen did maintain that women had what he called "a fundamental mission both on the individual and collective level: to transmit life and educate the children," he also pointed out that it would be unrealistic to seek to prevent women from pursuing a career and thus deprive the community of their capacities (Le Pen, 1989, p. 18). Finally, the Front National called for the introduction of a "family vote," thereby giving families a supplementary vote for each minor. This would curb the danger of social and political standstill in a society that was increasingly dominated by the elderly who tended to prefer short-term solutions over medium- and long-term ones from which they were unlikely to benefit (Le Pen, 1989, p. 17).

THE REPUBLIKANER

Like the Front National, the German Republikaner promoted themselves as the defenders of national interests and national identity. In Germany in the 1980s the debate on national identity centered less around immigration than on the continued division of the country. The issue became particularly pressing at the end of the 1980s, when compared to the dramatic developments in Central and Eastern Europe, the German question remained an isolated rock in a sea of rapid change. Responding to growing public frustration over Germany's unresolved national question, the Republikaner attacked the established parties for ignoring German national interests. At the same time the party quickly seized the new political opportunities engendered by the massive influx of refugees in the late 1980s. After overcoming its programmatic and strategic paralysis in the face of unification, the party resumed its attacks against the established parties, this time for failing to respond to the problems created by unification. At the same time it pursued its radical xenophobic agenda.

In the years before unification the political intervention of the Republikaner had two objectives: The first was the restoration of national self-confidence, pride, and identity to the German people as a precondition for the restoration of national unity. The second was to prevent the threatening "foreignization" of Germany by putting a halt to the growing influx of immigrants and particularly refugees (see Leggewie, 1989, chapter 4). On both occasions the Republikaner charged the governing Christian Democrats with having betrayed basic conservative principles. Contrary to the principles they had espoused while in opposition, the Christian Democrats had failed to produce a genuine "spiritual-moral turnaround" with regard to domestic issues, while in foreign policy they had pursued the policies of their Social Democratic predecessors "with the result of a growing lack of orientation, emotionalization and ideologization of the citizens." Despite Germany's comparatively favorable economic and social position, its spiritual and political culture continued to degenerate while its will to restore national unity was vanishing. One of the main reasons for this development was, the Republikaner charged, that the "war propaganda of the victorious powers" had found entrance into German history books forcing young Germans "to believe their exaggerations and falsifications." As a result, it was still impossible to write an objective interpretation of history, which no longer reduced the whole of German history to Auschwitz. In response, the Republikaner called for an end to the stigmatization of the Germans, a process of "decriminalization" of German history, and as a result the restoration of self-confidence to the German people (Die Republikaner, 1987, p. 1; see also Schönhuber, 1987, chapter 6).

If the Republikaner could take credit for having put the question of national unification on the political agenda, the rapid pace toward unification in 1990 deprived them of their central issue. In fact, confronted with a quickening pace toward unification, the party appeared paralyzed. Although for a while the party sought to mobilize public opinion against the finalization of Germany's eastern border with Poland, these attempts were soon abandoned. Unification left the Republikaner with only one issue, the growing problem of foreign immigration. Charging the established political parties with having reconciled themselves to the prospects of a multicultural society, the Republikaner strictly rejected the notion that Germany was an immigration country. Germany, one of the most densely populated countries in the whole world, had to "remain the land of the Germans. Foreigners are guests." This excluded the right to permanent residence, unlimited labor contracts, family reunion, or social welfare claims. Neither did foreigners have the right to become German citizens, nor political refugees a right to asylum. The state could grant these rights, as long as Germany's capacity to receive them was not exhausted. In addition the program denied foreigns, including EC-nationals, the right to vote while demanding the immediate deportation of foreigners who had broken the law and of asylum seekers who had been denied the status of political refugees. Refugees should no longer get subsistence payments but assistance in kind for which they should perform community-oriented work (Die Republikaner, 1987, p. 9; 1990, pp. 17–18).

The party justified its frontal attack against Germany's immigration practice with the need to prevent abuse of the asylum law and to protect the security of German citizens. The real reason behind the party's hostility toward immigrants, however, lay in the party's folkish and ethnopluralist conception of identity and the importance it attributed to the ethnic homogeneity of German society. The party considered both Germany's identity and ethnic homogeneity seriously compromised by a crisis of meaning whose origins lay in the near exhaustion of the "moral defensive forces of our European culture" and which threatened to destroy Europe's cultural heritage. In the face of this danger Germany needed to reinforce its efforts to protect its cultural heritage by giving greater support to its traditions and customs while preventing the progressive "foreignization" of its language and culture (Die Republikaner, 1990, pp. 28–29). Fliers that, among other things, called upon women to reject the ideas of feminists were a clear indication of whom the Republikaner considered to be behind the destruction of Europe's cultural heritage. It was thus hardly surprising that the Republikaner called for a strict ban on abortion.

The exuberance following the fall of the Wall and the temporary economic boom following unification were hardly favorable to the party's gloomy message. This changed, however, when the prospect of high unemployment, higher taxes, and a lower standard of living, which marked the beginning of a new post-unification realism, led to massive public resentment. "Save the welfare state: expel false refugees! Eliminate unemployment: stop immigration! Fight against crime: deport foreign criminals!" These slogans summed up in large part how the Republikaner sought to regain lost political territory. They reflected renewed concerns in the German population about immigration, rising unemployment, and rising crime rates. At the same time the party sought to appeal to the protectionist nationalism of the "small people" threatened by the economic and social consequences of unification (Betz, 1990, p. 56). In particular, it accused big industry of promoting the global mobility of labor for the sake of higher profits. This invariably had to lead to the standardization of consumer products, the "life world," and ultimately the people, and thus would be highly detrimental to society. The "one world" of the economy would result in the "one world" of cultures, the leveling of differences and the *Gleichschaltung* of the people (Die Republikaner, 1992, p. 5).

These passages are a clear indication that despite the ups and downs of their electoral fortunes the party preserved its ideological and programmatic continuity. Its core lay in the confrontation between national identity and multiculturalism, which the Republikaner, like the Front National, considered a major threat to Western civilization. Like the Front National the Republikaner were most alarmist when it came to the growing presence and assertiveness of Muslims in Western Europe. Like the Front National, the Republikaner saw in the Muslim presence not only the most important sign of an expansion of multiculturalism, but above all the most imminent threat to European identity. Only against this background it is possible to take the party seriously when it warned that "Islam wants religious world domination" and therefore demanded that the European nations "meet the Muslim challenge" and "stop the advances of the aggressive and intolerant Islam in Germany and Europe!"[29]

The campaign for the local elections in Hesse saw a further expansion of the party's programmatic repertoire. Besides charging the established parties with having failed to confront the housing crisis, rising crime rates, and the refugee problem, the Republikaner also began to focus on political corruption and the threatening deconstruction of the social net.[30] With this strategy the Republikaner sought to benefit from both the dramatic increase in *Parteienverdrossenheit* and the growing problems of the established parties to deal with the economic consequences of unification. In an interview with the Italian newspaper *La Repubblica* (March 11, 1993, p.12) Franz Schönhuber explained the future programmatic direction of the party: "We want to say it the way it is: the golden years are over; we don't like big industry, and we don't want to be an American colony; our model is Bismarck, not the criminal Hitler." Blaming the established political parties for the growing economic problems, he compared the situation in Germany with that in Italy: "I no longer see a difference between the corrupt CDU/CSU and the mafia-penetrated DC. Perhaps in our country they are not mafiosi in the classical sense, but in a broad sense they are corrupt parties." Reiterating the party's disdain for big industry, he suggested that, confronted with the current economic crisis, the country had to modify its social-liberal market economy. It could no longer entrust itself to the free forces of the market; in some instances the state would have to intervene, especially in East Germany. In order to pay for the enormous costs of closing the gap between East and West, the rich, not the socially weakest, would have to bear the majority of the financial burden. And since the big enterprises had largely failed to do their part in the reconstruction of East Germany, the state should reorient its support toward the productive middle class by relieving it of some of the social and financial burden.

With this political program the Republikaner had established a clear identity. Appealing to wide-spread xenophobia, growing anti-big business and antiglobal market sentiments, and exploiting growing uncertainty and fears with regard to the future it conformed to the image of a populist advocate of the interests of the small people. As the election in Hesse showed, this program was attractive enough to gain the party about 10 percent support. One might speculate how much support the party would have been able to garner had it followed the example of the Lega Nord and mobilized growing West German resentments against East Germans. However, its commitment to ethnic nationalism disallowed such a strategy—at least for the time being.

THE VLAAMS BLOK

Like the Front National and the Republikaner, the Vlaams Blok owed much of its success to its national populist agenda. This agenda marked a departure from its original program, which in many ways resembled that of the Lega Nord. Initially, the party's program spoke out against high taxes and political corruption and for institutional reform and independence from Brussels. It was not until the early 1980s that the party began to complement its regionalist demands with appeals to xenophobia and, increasingly, overt racism. Imitating the formula of the Front National, the Vlaams Blok argued that the three main problems facing the country—immigration, insecurity, and unemployment—could only be solved by a program that gave absolute priority to the safeguarding of national identity.

This did not mean, however, that the party abandoned its nationalist pretensions. In fact, even while the party expanded its xenophobic agenda, Flemish independence remained its first political priority. Thus in its 1991 electoral program the party still called for a separate Flemish state with Brussels as its capital. National independence, however, was only meant to be a first step toward the eventual creation of a linguistic and cultural community with Holland and South Africa (Vlaams Blok, 1991, pp. 8–12, p. 27; Larsen, 1992, p. 8). The party justified the demand for national independence by appealing to various Flemish grievances. Similar to the Lega Nord's strategy to mobilize resentment against the fact that northern taxes were used to subsidize the south, the Vlaams Blok was quick to zero in on the huge financial transfer payments raised from Flemish taxpayers to pay for the growing social security needs of the Walloons and to cover the growing state deficit—money that could be put to much better use in Flanders. A second demand, however, indicated that economic considerations were not the only reasons for the Vlaams Blok's call for independence. According to its own statements, one of the party's central demands was an amnesty for all those persons who had been persecuted in the past for fighting for the cause of Flemish nationalism during the world wars. Since many of these persons presumably had collaborated with the Germans, the call for amnesty was also an attempt, similar to those by the FPÖ and the Republikaner, to put an end to the confrontation with the past, and remove a significant obstacle to the establishment of a strong, uninhibited national identity.

However, the party's programmatic development shows that by the end of the 1980s the party considered other threats to national identity to be far more serious than Flemish nationalism's unresolved past. Like the Front National, the Vlaams Blok charged that the threat to national identity was twofold. One stemmed from the growing number of legal and illegal immigrants; the other from the precipitous drop in the birthrate of the Flemish population. Its main slogan "Eigen volk eerst" (The own people first) and the title of the party's 1991 electoral program "Out of Self-Defense" summed up how the party sought to counter these threat. Self-defense meant above all a quick solution to the question of immigration.

The party accused the established parties, big companies, and the unions of having promoted the influx of immigrants and leaving it to the population to deal with the ethnic and cultural consequences of their policies. Despite mass unemployment and a massive deficit, the Belgian government continued with its policy of "positive discrimination," favoring immigrants with respect to jobs and social housing. As a result, Belgian cities were full of Turks, Moroccans, and other immigrants from developing countries. The consequences were nothing short of a disaster. Not only were these immigrants "uprooted and a permanent source of dissatisfaction and crime," they also changed whole areas to such a degree that in the long run nothing remained of their European or Flemish character.

Like other radical right-wing populist parties, the Vlaams Blok was particularly hostile to Muslims. As Filip Dewinter put it, Islam was "an anti-Western and intolerant religion," which refused to distinguish between political, cultural, and religious life (Dewinter, n.d., p. 8). Even more dangerous was the threat from Muslim fundamentalism. Uprootedness caused second and third generation immigrants to search for their cultural heritage and traditions. This made these people susceptible to religious fundamentalists, for whom the millions of North Africans in Europe represented an "Islamic fifth column" (Annemans and Dewinter, n.d., p. 18).

In its campaign against non-European, and especially Muslim, immigrants, the Vlaams Blok did not hesitate to appeal to overt racism. The party increasingly used cartoons to spread its message of fear and hatred. Motive and tenor were simplistic and predictable. The cartoons depicted streets populated by immigrants, whose features more often than not resembled the anti-Semitic stereotypes of Nazi propaganda. Churches were transformed into mosques. A native population, which was besieged by foreign cultures and threatened by foreign pickpockets and drug peddlers, was well on its way to becoming a minority in its own country. One drawing, attached to the party's dossier on foreigners (Annemans and Dewinter, n. d.), made the latter point in a particularly blatant way. It depicted two immigrants from North Africa and Turkey walking down the street in a neighborhood crowded with other immigrants. Looking up to a lonely elderly Belgian couple fearfully watching the scene below from a window, one immigrant says to the other: "Something must urgently be done about these foreigners!"

In order to reverse the trend toward a multicultural society in which a growing number of foreigners demanded to receive "a piece of the social pie" the Vlaams Blok launched a comprehensive antiforeigner package consisting of "70 solutions to the foreigner problem" (Dewinter, n.d.). Among these solutions were calls for an immediate stop to new immigration and the drastic reduction of the number of non-European residents; the immediate expulsion and return of illegal immigrants and foreigners who had committed a crime, and the return of unemployed foreigners after three months of unemployment; a stop to family reunification, the abolition of automatic citizenship for children born in Belgium to foreigners, and the reintroduction of the ius sanguis; and the introduction of separate social security systems for natives and foreigners, and drastic reductions in family allowances for immigrants to encourage them to return to their home countries. Although the party said it recognized in principle the right to asylum, it demanded a tightening of the asylum laws and the immediate return of refugees whose cases were rejected. Finally, in accordance with its anti-Muslim position, the party demanded a drastic reduction in the number of mosques, a ban on fundamentalist organizations, and the repeal of the recognition of Islamic religious services.

At the same time as it was stepping up its antiforeigner campaign, the Vlaams Blok promoted itself as the defender of traditional moral values and the family. In order to reverse the demographic decline, the party proposed a number of financial measures to encourage families to have children. The Vlaams Blok explicitly declared that its goal was a society that was once again open to families with more than two children. It was hardly surprising that the party was vehemently opposed to abortion. In its view, abortion was murder, which society and the authorities had the duty to persecute and punish. However, it was hardly traditional moral values that explained the party's strict opposition to abortion. Rather, its pronatalist proposals complemented their anti-immigrant position. Both were part of a political strategy whose main objective was the safeguarding and strengthening of Flemish identity. This also explains the party's relative paucity of economic ideas. Although in its 1991 program the party claimed to support a free market economy and made vague calls for the privatization of public services, its main emphasis was on supporting small and medium-sized companies and the Flemish farmers. Otherwise the party propagated a kind of corporatist capitalism rejecting both "class warfare and all forms of exploitation" and marketed it under the label of an "organic solidarism" as a third way between "individualized and egoistic liberalism" and repressive collectivism (Vlaams Blok, n. d., pp. 9–10).

By the early 1990s the Vlaams Blok was clearly the most blatantly xenophobic (if not overtly racist) among the major radical right-wing populist parties in Western Europe. Under Dewinter's leadership the party had attained a level of viciousness that surpassed even that of the Front National. However, this should not detract from the fact that by the early 1990s xenophobia and open hostility toward immigrants and refugees had become the hallmark of radical right-wing populism in Western Europe, with the notable exception (at least as far as overt expressions of xenophobia were concerned) of the Lega Nord.

What explains this shift from neoliberalism to xenophobia? Was this merely a response to the growing presence of immigrants and particularly refugees in Western Europe and growing public awareness of the immigrant issue? Or was it a reflection of more profound developments in the structure of advanced Western European societies? It is to these questions that we turn in the following chapter.

5

The Social Bases of
Political Resentment

As we have seen in the previous chapter, most radical right-wing populist parties rode to success in the 1980s on a platform that included strong elements of neo-liberalism. Not only genuinely right-libertarian parties like the Scandinavian Progress parties, the Swedish New Democracy party, or the Austrian Freedom Party, but also the French Front National and the Swiss Automobile Party appealed to individual initiative and entrepreneurial spirit while promoting privatization, deregulation, and generally free-market forces. Their programmatic proposals were primarily directed against the power of the central state and the established parties. What the different versions of this program had in common was their productivist bias. Like Margaret Thatcher in Great Britain, neoliberal populist parties promoted an enterprise culture, founded on the notion that the productive "be rewarded *through the market* for their contribution to production (or at least to the provision of profitable marketed goods and services)" whereas "the parasitic must suffer for their failure to contribute adequately (if at all) to the market (with little regard to the question of whether they are 'deserving' or otherwise)" (Jessop, Bonnet, Bromley, and Ling, 1984, p. 51). This productivist ideology allowed the populist Right not only to appeal to fundamentally bourgeois values, like individualism and free market liberalism, but also to more pragmatic interests, which generally can be assumed to transcend class lines, even if they might not necessarily be in the interest of all social strata (such as lower direct taxation, lower non-wage labor costs, no more subsidies for unproductive sectors, budget cuts).

Perhaps not surprisingly, with mounting economic problems and mass unemployment looming ever larger over a growing number of West European countries in the late 1980s, radical right-wing populist parties increasingly muted their commitment to individualism, entrepreneurship and a free-market spirit in favor of the new issues of xenophobia and ethnic exclusion. Some of the more successful parties, such as the Front National, the Vlaams Blok, the Republikaner, and to some extent the FPÖ intensified their campaign for the protection of national identity from foreign cultures or, as in the case of the Progress parties or the New Democracy party, at least for the protection of the material interests of the native population against new demands that were bound to arise from those lobbying in favor of immigrants and refugees. The most notable exception to this general trend was the Lega Nord, which increasingly moderated and finally almost completely muted its attacks on southern Italians and immigrants while intensifying its attacks against Rome and the established political parties in pronouncedly neoliberal terms.

The following discussion seeks to explain these shifts in the political agenda of radical right-wing populist parties. Were they merely a reflection of changing popular priorities or did they reflect more profound changes in the relations between radical right-wing populist parties and their constituency? The premise underlying our argument is that a party's choice of strategy depends above all on which social groups it seeks to attract. Which social groups it is able to attract, in turn, depends on two things: the extent to which its ideological positions and policy proposals correspond with the values and interests of these groups and the extent to which other parties are able and/or willing to adopt its program and make it their own. Both factors played a significant role in the strategic calculations of radical right-wing populist parties in the 1980s and early 1990s.

GENDER

One of the central findings of survey research on who supports radical right-wing populist parties is that these parties are gender-biased parties (see Table 5.1). As if following some unwritten law, radical right-wing populist parties have consistently attracted a considerably higher number of male than female voters. This is in sharp contrast to the supporters of the libertarian Left, who have increasingly been more numerous among women than among men. It is interesting to note that the gender gap in the radical right-wing populist vote has generally persisted regardless of a party's ideology or whether or not it had

Table 5.1

The Gender Basis of Radical Right-Wing Populist
and Left-Libertarian Parties (in %)

	Sweden ND (1991)	Italy LN (1992)	Aust. FPÖ (1990)	Switz. AP (1991)	France FN (1988)	Germany REP (1989)
Women	38	49	40	46	43	36
Men	62	51	60	54	57	64
	Greens	**Greens**	**Greens**	**Greens**	**Greens**	**Greens**
Women	69	n/a	58	54	n/a	53
Men	31	n/a	42	46	n/a	47

n/a = no gender figures available for Italian or French Green voters

established itself in the party system. The French case is a most telling example of the persistence of this gender gap. In 1984, when the Front National gained 11 percent of the overall vote, 13 percent of male, but only 9 percent of female voters gave their support to Jean-Marie Le Pen. By 1993 the difference between female and male support for the Front National had hardly changed. With 12.4 percent overall, the party received 15 percent of the male vote as compared to 10 percent of the female vote.

Despite the potentially profound implications of these findings, relatively few observers have ventured to explain what accounts for the relative reluctance on the part of women voters to support the radical populist Right. Some have pointed to the fact that women are generally less interested in politics than men and therefore more hesitant than male voters to support new political parties (Roth, 1989). They point to the fact that initially at least Greens, too, received more support from male than female voters; by the end of the 1980s, however, Greens were slightly overrepresented among women voters. In the 1984 election to the German *Bundestag*, for example, male voters accounted for more than 50 percent of the Green vote, whereas in 1990 the relationship was the exact reverse. However, even if this explanation appears to hold with regard to Green support, it consistently fails in the case of the radical Right. Even parties such as the Front National, which have been an established part of the political system as long as the German Greens have consistently attracted a higher percentage of support from male than from female voters.

Others have pointed to the fact that radical right-wing populist parties generally tend to promote values and concrete policy proposals that are intrinsically inimical to women's interests. Nonna Mayer, for example, has pointed to the Front National's hostile stance on abortion and its proposals aimed at discouraging women to enter the labor force, or sending those who are already working back behind the stove to explain the party's deficit among women (Mayer, 1991, p. 116). Although this might at least partially explain why parties like the Front National or the Republikaner have done relatively poorly among female voters, it does not explain women voters' reluctance to support neoliberal parties like the Progress parties or the FPÖ, which have relatively little to say about traditional moral values. Finally, one might propose that xenophobia and/or law-and-order issues simply do not appeal as much to women as they do to men. Empirical evidence, however, fails to support this proposition. Although women are significantly less willing than men to condone acts of violence against immigrants and refugees, they are hardly less hostile to immigrants or less supportive of law-and-order issues than men. In fact, available evidence points in the opposite direction. German women, for instance, who said they voted for the Republikaner in 1989 showed considerably more concern about crime and were considerably more likely to call for tougher measures to impede crime from spreading further than were male Republikaner voters. This is hardly surprising given the fact that women are generally more likely to be victimized. However, female Republikaner supporters were also considerably less likely to welcome German resettlers from Eastern Europe and East Germany or asylum seekers than their male counterparts (Molitor, 1992, p. 128).

A similar picture emerges from French surveys that have traced the level of support in the French population for the ideas advanced by Jean-Marie Le Pen. They show that as the Front National increasingly stressed law and order and sharpened its tone against immigrants, a growing number of women reported supporting the party's views. Thus, in late 1991, when the Front National proposed its comprehensive antiforeigner program, the approval rating among women was hardly different from that of men: 31 percent versus 33 percent (SOFRES, 1993, p. 65).

What then explains the gender differences in the support basis of radical right-wing populist parties? We would suggest that the answer has to be sought in a combination of explanations. These are related to gender differences in work force participation, women's position in the labor market, and women's greater likelihood to be religiously active. German and Austrian surveys suggest that a disproportionately large number of radical right-wing supporters are part of the working population. For example, in the 1992 election in Baden-Württemberg, 70 percent of Republikaner supporters said they were working (compared to 55 percent for the whole sample; see Forschungsgruppe Wahlen, 1992, p. 16). Similar results were obtained in the Viennese election in 1991 among FPÖ supporters. Since the proportion of women actively engaged in the work force is generally lower than that of men, it should come as no surprise that women are underrepresented among radical right-wing voters. Interestingly, in the Viennese election the proportion of working women voting FPÖ was only slightly lower than their representation in the overall population (22 percent to 25 percent overall) even while the proportion of women voting FPÖ was considerably below their average in the population (44 percent to 56 percent; see Plasser and Ulram, 1991c).

Secondly, as we have noted earlier, a large proportion of radical right-wing voters previously supported center-right parties. As a number of studies have shown, there still exists a strong relationship between religious practice and electoral preference. Generally, as religious practice increases, so does the voting preference for the traditional center-right. In 1990, for example, 61 percent of Austrian voters who reported going to church on a regular basis, said they voted for the ÖVP. Only 10 percent said they voted for the FPÖ (Plasser and Ulram, 1990, p. 9). These results agree with several other studies that found that the voters of radical right-wing populist parties were if anything less religiously attached than the voters of the established center-right parties (Lewis-Beck and Mitchell, 1993, p. 118; Roth, 1989, p. 14). Thus, a German study from 1989 found a disproportionate number of Republikaner supporters reporting rarely or never to attend church. Even in Catholic Bavaria support for the Republikaner was considerably lower among those who reported attending church often than among those who reported attending church only occasionally, rarely, or not at all (Kaase and Gibowski, 1990, p. 762). The differences between radical right-wing supporters and the rest of the population were particularly pronounced in the Italian case where still about half of the population reports attending church on a regular basis. Surveys showed that in 1992, Lega Nord supporters were significantly less likely to attend church regularly than the average Italian voter, or even supporters of the left-libertarian Greens (Klages and Neumiller, 1993, p. 16). Similar results were obtained by Luca Ricolfi in his study of the political orientations of young Lega Nord supporters. According to his data, only the ex-communist parties and the left-libertarian Radical Party had a higher proportion of secular supporters than the Lega Nord. From this Ricolfi concluded that the Lega if anything "purified" the social base of the Christian Democrats of its less religious components while leaving it with its most religiously devoted constituency (Ricolfi, 1993, pp. 136-138).

Generally, religious practice is correlated with gender and age. Women are more likely than men to go to church on a regular basis and the elderly more likely than the young. It should therefore come as no surprise if radical right-wing populist parties appear to be doing less well among women above a certain age than among other social groups. In fact, in the Viennese election, only 13 percent of the FPÖ's vote came from female pensioners, although they made up 20 percent of the whole population. Clearly, these are only very tentative approaches to what is certainly a complex and intriguing puzzle, which ultimately only more comparative research can solve.

AGE

A second characteristic that increasingly distinguishes the social base of radical right-wing populist parties from that of the established political parties is age. In most cases, radical right-wing populist parties have attracted a larger proportion of younger than of older voters. (The most significant exception has been the Danish Progress Party, which in the late 1980s and early 1990s received significant support from pensioners. See Andersen and Bjørklund, 1990, p. 204; Klages and Neumiller, 1993, p. 16). Their age profile thus resembles that of Green and other left-libertarian parties rather than that of the established parties. Interestingly enough, the appeal to younger voters has largely been independent of the parties' ideology and program. Vehemently xenophobic parties have been hardly less attractive to younger voters than their neoliberal counterparts (see Table 5.2 and 5.3). In the 1992 election in Baden-Württemberg, for example, the Republikaner received more than 16 percent of the vote from voters younger than 25, which was 70 percent higher than their overall proportion of the vote (11 percent). In the same year, more than 30 percent of voters under 24 reported voting for the Lega in Milan. This was twice the national average for this age group (Mannheimer, 1993, p. 92).

Not surprisingly, right-wing populist parties have been particularly attractive to younger male voters. In the 1993 French election, for example, young men aged 18 to 24 were almost twice as likely to vote Front National than young women (19 percent versus 10 percent; see *Liberation,* March 23, 1993, p. 6). In the 1989 Norwegian election a quarter of young men, but only 15 percent of young women voted for the Progress Party (Aardal, 1990, p. 156). At least with regard to the combination of age and gender, radical right-wing populist parties represent an almost exact mirror image of Green and other left-libertarian parties. In the state elections in Baden-Württember in 1992, for example, the Republikaner received 18.6 percent from young men in the 18–24 age group— proportionately about the same as the Greens. However, among women in the same age group, the Greens received almost twice as many votes (22 percent)

Table 5.2

Age Composition of New Democracy (1991) and Norwegian Progress Party (1989) Voters (in %)

	ND	All	PP	All
18–30	35	24	42	26
31–40	40	38	30	40
51+	26	37	28	34

ND/PP columns = voters for those parties

All = total Norwegian voters in each age group

Source: Taggart, 1992; Valen, Aardal, and Vogt, 1990, p. 108.

Table 5.3

Percentage of Electorate Voting for Front National (1993) and Republikaner (1992) by Age Distribution

Front National		REP	
18-24	15	18-24	16
25-34	14	25-34	13
34-49	11	35-44	11
50-64	13	45-59	12
65+	12	60+	7
Total	**13**	**Total**	**11**

Source: *Liberation,* March 23, 1993, p. 4; Forschungsgruppe Wahlen, 1992, p. 18.

as the Republikaner (13 percent). The situation was similar in the Swedish election in 1991. New Democracy received 13 percent of the male vote among 18- to 30-year-olds, but only half as much from women in the same age group. Against that the Greens received 3 percent of the vote from men, but 8 percent from women in that age group (Taggart, 1992, p. 15).

Generally, the fact that radical right-wing populist parties have drawn significant support from young voters should come as no surprise. As Mark Franklin and others have pointed out, young voters are generally more independent than any other age group from the established loyalties that in the past shaped and determined electoral preferences. As a result, younger voters can be expected to show less resistance to change than other age groups (Franklin, 1992, p. 395). Again, however, more research is necessary to explain these divergent voting patterns between young women and men. One possible explanation might be related to differences in work experience. Young women have generally been drawn to the expanding service-oriented jobs, which are domestically oriented and thus less likely to fall victim to rationalization than industrial jobs (Kitschelt, 1993, pp. 305, 307).[1] Particularly in the Scandinavian countries a large proportion of the female labor force is employed in socially oriented public-sector services (see Esping-Andersen, 1992; Svensson and Togeby, 1991, p. 154). These jobs generally involve considerable contact with marginalized groups such as immigrants and refugees. At the same time those holding these jobs are generally not likely to be threatened by competition from immigrants. Given the general hostility of radical right-wing populist parties toward the welfare state, the public sector, and immigrants and other marginalized groups, this might at least in part explain why young women are underrepresented among radical right-wing voters.

SECTOR EMPLOYMENT

If the radical populist Right's relative lack of success among female voters is somewhat puzzling, their relative lack of appeal to those employed in the public sector should hardly come as a surprise. Given their general preference for production over consumption, for lowering taxes and curtailing the power of the state, and their general hostility toward immigrants, radical right-wing parties could hardly expect to find much sympathy from those whose livelihood largely depends on the state and, as we have pointed out earlier, who tend to be among the groups most sympathetic to the material needs of immigrants and refugees. A number of election studies support this contention. The majority of these studies come from the Scandinavian countries, where the notion that public versus private employment status might be important determinants of electoral choice has received significantly more attention than in other Western European countries.

Available evidence from Denmark, Norway, and Sweden suggests that the private/public sector dichotomy is an important variable in explaining both the radical right-wing populist and left-libertarian vote. In Denmark, for example, support for the Progress Party in 1973 and 1975 was three times as high among those employed in the private sector than it was among those employed in the public sector. In 1973, when the Progress Party received roughly 16 percent of the vote, 22 percent of those employed in the private sector, but only 6 percent of those employed in the public sector declared they had voted for Glistrup's party (Andersen, 1982, p. 162; see also Hansen, 1982).

Norwegian electoral surveys from the late 1980s confirm the Danish findings. Both in the regional election of 1987, which marked the reemergence of the Progress Party as a significant force in Norwegian politics, and in the 1989 election to the *Storting* the Progress Party attained considerably higher results in the private than in the public sector. Thus, in 1989, 24 percent of the party's vote came from private-sector white collar employees (who comprised 19 percent of the sample), compared to a mere 9 percent from public-sector white collar employees (21 percent of the sample) (Valen, Aardal, and Vogt, 1989, p. 108; for 1987 see Bjørklund, 1988, pp. 225–226). Swedish studies of the 1991 election to the Swedish Rijksdag arrive at similar, if less pronounced, results for the New Democracy party (Taggart, 1992, p. 22; Gilljam and Holmberg, 1993, pp. 207-210).

In the absence of comparable data it is difficult to estimate to what extent private/public-sector employment influences the support of radical right-wing populist parties in other West European countries. German, French, and Austrian data suggest, however, that the differences persist, even if they might not be as pronounced as in the case of the Scandinavian parties. Thus one study on the German Republikaner found the percentage of public-sector employees reporting to support the Republikaner only slightly lower than the proportion of public-sector employees in the whole sample (29 percent as compared to 32 percent; Bauer and Schmitt, 1990, p. 20). However, Austrian and French surveys draw a somewhat more differentiated picture. Austrian surveys for the late 1980s and early 1990s imply that the FPÖ was somewhat less likely to appeal to civil servants (*Beamte*) than were the other parties. Thus, in the 1991 regional elections in Vienna, civil servants contributed only 5 percent to the total FPÖ vote (with civil servants comprising 7 percent of the sample; Plasser and Ulram, 1991). Finally, French electoral studies reveal that throughout the 1980s the Front National received considerably more support from private-sector employees than public-sector employees. Thus, in 1988, 16 percent of private-sector employees voted Front National, but only 12 percent of public-sector employees (Perrineau, 1990, p. 24; for 1984 see Le Gall, 1984, p. 47). And in 1989, only half as many private-sector employees voted for the party as did private-sector employees (7 to 14 percent; SOFRES, 1990, p. 180).

Available data on private/public sector political preferences raise an interesting question. Given the radical populist Right's relatively strong hostility toward the state, what accounts for the fact that a nonnegligible number of those employed by the state support the radical populist Right? In other words, what needs explanation might not be the fact that the FPÖ has done less well among civil servants than among other social groups, but that, for instance, in 1990 roughly one out of seven civil servants voted for Haider and his party. Or that in France, between 1986 and 1988, the number of public-sector employees voting for the Front National actually increased from 7 to 12 percent (Perrineau, 1988, p. 37). One possible explanation might be that radical right-wing populist parties appeal to particular segments of the public sector. Since right-wing populist parties stress insecurity as one of their major political issues, this might make them attractive to those employed in public sector services, to whom the preservation of internal and external security is entrusted, namely the police and the military. In his research on new social movement support in the Netherlands Hanspeter Kriesi found the members of what he called "the protective services" among the groups least likely to have taken part in these forms of unconventional politics (Kriesi, 1989, pp. 1097–1100).[2] Unfortunately, the lack of detailed data and the relatively small number of right-wing radical respondents in any survey make it virtually impossible to examine this proposition.[3]

CLASS

In order to gain more than marginal support at the polls every party has to appeal to a wide range of socially relevant groups. In this sense, every party pursues something of a catch-all strategy. For obvious reasons, we might expect this to be particularly true for the radical populist Right. After all, by their very nature radical right-wing populist parties should seek to appeal to "ordinary people" from all walks of life. However, political sociology shows that most parties are more successful among some groups than among others. Therefore, how a particular party should be classified depends largely on which social group dominates its social basis. As we have seen so far, two of the main characteristics of the social basis of radical right-wing populist parties is their overrepresentation among men and their predominance among those employed in the private sector. Given this strong showing in the private sector, we might expect the character of radical right-wing populism to be largely determined by which segment of the private sector dominates its social base.

In the 1970s and early 1980s most radical right-wing populist parties distinguished themselves by three factors: their strong showing among the self-employed, and their appeal to both manual workers and salaried white collar employees. With this social base, radical right-wing populist parties located themselves somewhere between the established center-right parties and the socialist Left. With the former they shared their appeal to the self-employed and white collar employees, with the latter their appeal to manual workers.

The Danish Progress Party is a case in point. Electoral studies reveal that its initial success was due in considerable part to its ability to mobilize self-employed voters. Both in 1975 and 1979 about 30 percent of that group supported Glistrup's party. This was about as much as the Liberals received from this social group. At the same time the party also received considerable support from both higher- and lower-level private sector employees (16 percent in each group in 1975 and 10 and 6 percent respectively in 1979; Andersen, 1982, pp. 161-162). Finally, the party also attracted a sizeable proportion of the blue-collar vote (15 percent in 1975, 13 percent in 1979). This was more than any center-right party could muster and about the same proportion as the libertarian Left. As Jørgen Goul Andersen has noted: "Whilst the Progress Party was not overrepresented among manual workers in the 1970s, the social composition was unique, for no other bourgeois party recruited a comparably large share of workers" (Andersen, 1992, p. 201).

As Table 5.4 shows, the party's social composition among the working population was about equally distributed among these three groups. This was also reflected in the educational profile of Progress Party voters. Generally, in the early 1970s, the party attracted about an even proportion of voters with lower, medium, and higher levels of education (see Table 5.5).

On a more superficial level, it might thus appear as if the Progress Party was a genuine catch-all-party. However, closer investigation shows that there was some logic to the party's seemingly disparate constituency. It seems that what attracted each one of these groups to the Progress Party was the party's neoliberal program. This was not only true for its supporters among the self-employed but also among its working-class supporters. Working-class support for the party came primarily from young male workers in the western part of the country (Andersen, 1980). In the 1960s, this part of the country saw the emergence of a decentralized industrial structure, characterized by small and medium-size companies employing "a combination of advanced technology and cheap, unskilled labour" and largely export-oriented (Christiansen, 1984, p. 16; Eysell and Henningsen, 1992, p. 7). As Niels Finn Christiansen has pointed out, blue-collar Progress party supporters were first generation workers from Denmark's traditional farmlands who "brought their agrarian work ethic with them into industry." Influenced by "the classical liberal ideology of the auton-omy of the individual and of the common interests between labour and capital" they were skeptical about trade-union organization and labor struggles. Instead they held "a modern producer ideology, whose corporatist features [were], however, of a markedly anti-statist hue" (Christiansen, 1984, p. 17). Hardly

Table 5.4

Class Composition of Those Supporting the Danish Progress Party (in %)

	1973	1977	1979	1988
Workers	33	34	38	50
Sample	37	35	36	36
Nonmanual wage earners	30	32	21	27
Sample	37	41	45	50
Self-employed	37	34	41	23
Sample	26	24	19	14

Source: Andersen and Bjørklund, 1990, p. 208.

Table 5.5

Support for the Danish Progress Party, by Education

(AS % OF OVERALL VOTE)

	1973	1977	1979	1988
Low	16	16	13	11
Medium	16	14	9	9
High	16	11	3	3

Source: Andersen, 1992, p. 201.

surprising, working-class support for the Progress Party correlated strongly with business size. The smaller a business the larger the proportion of blue-collar support for the Progress Party. In 1978, for example, 35 percent of working-class men employed in small private-sector enterprises (one to nine employees), but only 9 percent in large private-sector enterprises (500 employees and more) reported supporting the Progress Party (Andersen, 1980, p. 29; see also Hansen, 1982). Not surprisingly, the party gained few supporters from the "traditional stronghold of working-class culture in the Copenhagen area, despite high taxes, a high density of immigrants, etc." (Andersen, 1992, p. 202).

Given the rather idiosyncratic character of the Danish Progress Party's electoral base, how typical was this of radical right-wing populist parties in general? Empirical evidence shows that in the early stages of their rise to political prominence both the Front National and the FPÖ attracted constituencies similar to that of the Progress Party in the 1970s. In 1984, the Front National was supported most strongly by shopkeepers, artisans, farmers, and small-business owners, but also by upper and middle managers, executives, and those in liberal professions, while it was somewhat underrepresented among workers. In 1984, the Front National's electorate distinguished itself by what Nonna Mayer in her study on the Front National's implantation in Paris has called its "bourgeois character" (Mayer, 1989, p. 256). Or, as Gérard Le Gall has put it, its support was more pronounced in "*la France aisée*" than in "*la France populaire*" (Le Gall, 1984, p. 46). This was also reflected in the distribution of education attainments among Front National supporters. Whereas the party received only 8 percent from those with primary education, it received 12 percent from those with higher education (Mitra, 1988, pp. 54–56; Schain, 1987, p. 243).

Studies on the FPÖ's electorate in the late 1980s come to similar results. In 1986 the party received a disproportionate number of votes from the self-employed and professionals, from white collar employees, and skilled workers. This meant that as in the case of the Front National, voters with higher levels of education were overrepresented. The party received 14 percent from voters holding a university degree. Voters with not more than primary education, on the other hand, were considerably underrepresented. It received only 6 percent among voters whose level of education was not higher than compulsory education (Plasser and Ulram, 1989, p. 74). In the 1990 parliamentary election the FPÖ increased its support among skilled workers while retaining its support from professionals and the self-employed (Plasser and Ulram, 1990, p. 8). One study that divided the Austrian electoral map into different areas of electoral competition found the FPÖ to be particularly competitive among three groups: the upwardly mobile new middle classes (younger white-collar employees with above average level of education), the dynamic middle classes (younger self-employed or white-collar employees and civil servants, better educated), and populist blue-collar protest voters (unionized, skilled workers) (Plasser, Ulram, and Grausgruber, 1992, pp. 40–41).

Given the heterogeneous composition of their electorate, the parties' promotion of market liberalism and individualism finds a plausible explanation. Neoliberalism was part of a strategy to attract the better educated middle class disenchanted with the fact that the established center-right parties had abandoned traditional conservative positions and moved to the center. This was particularly pronounced in France, where in 1984, the traditional Right proposed a unified list for the European election headed by Simone Veil, whose strong interventions against racism and for the legalization of abortion were bound to alienate conservative quarters (Bréchon, 1993, p. 44). As Nonna Mayer points out, the mobilization in the better areas of Paris in favor of the Front National in 1984 reflected a radicalization of a part of the Right's electorate. Already exasperated by the Socialists' coming to power and unable to recognize themselves in the moderate list presented by Simone Veil, they seized the occasion to express their discontent in a relatively insignificant election (Mayer, 1987, p. 902).

This meant that once the established center-right parties adopted more conservative positions they had a good chance to recuperate those parts of their constituency who had joined the Front National. This is what seems to have happened in the mid-1980s. As Pascal Perrineau has shown, between 1984 and 1987 the Front National lost roughly 40 percent of its supporters among executives and the free professions, 20 percent among middle managers and employees (Perrineau, 1988, p. 25). Poll data confirm these findings. They show that it was among executives, free professionals, and middle managers that support for Le Pen's ideas declined most dramatically between 1984 and 1987. The decline of support among these groups appears to have been particularly pronounced in the fall of 1987, after Le Pen had made his infamous statement that the gas chambers were a mere detail in the history of World War II (see SOFRES, 1993, p. 65).

It is here that we find certain parallels with developments in the Danish Progress Party. Like the Front National in the mid-1980s, the Progress Party lost a considerable portion of its middle class support in the late 1970s. This coincided with a marked radicalization of the party's position compared to earlier elections. It culminated in 1979 when Mogens Glistrup launched his first attacks against foreigners. In response, half of all supporters with better than primary education abandoned the party. Those who remained loyal to the party had generally lower levels of education. Thus among those with only primary education the party lost only 20 percent. This turned the Progress Party into the party with the most poorly educated electorate of all major parties. This was particularly pronounced among young voters, whereas among the older voters, the differences in educational attainments between the Progress Party and the center-right parties were minimal (see Andersen, 1992, p. 201; Andersen and Glans, 1980, pp. 10–11).

The coming to power of a center-right coalition in 1982 under Poul Schlüter, which introduced a number of neoliberal policies, assured middle class voters that their interests would be heard. This benefitted particularly the

Conservative People's Party, which by 1984 appears to have absorbed a majority of former Glistrup supporters (Christiansen, 1984, p. 30; see also Andersen, 1982, p. 162).

As a result of the drain of better-educated middle class voters both the Front National and the Progress Party underwent a considerable proletarization of their social basis. This was particularly pronounced in the case of the Progress Party. In 1988, roughly half of all gainfully employed Progress Party voters were manual workers. This was about the same proportion as for the Social Democrats and more than twice as high as in the bourgeois parties. For all practical purposes, by 1988 the Progress Party had become a predominantly working-class party.

The shift in the social base of the Front National was similar, if less pronounced. Between 1984 and 1988, the Front National's appeal to working class voters increased significantly (Mayer, 1991, p. 116)—even if studies indicating that by 1987 working class voters had become the predominant social group among Front National supporters exaggerated the party's real strength among the working class (Grunberg, 1988, p. 5). Nonna Mayer, for example, in her study on the evolution of the Front National's vote in Paris found that those who voted Front National in 1986 included twice as many workers and three times as many unemployed than in 1984 (Mayer and Perrineau, 1992, p. 136). In view of these developments she agreed with Jérôme Jaffré that what stood behind the explosion of xenophobia characterized by the rise of the Front National was "the drama of unemployment and the consequences of the crisis which exacerbate[d] the reactions of a part of the popular electorate which [was] disoriented by the powerlessness of the political class, both on the Left and on the Right, to resolve their problems" (Mayer, 1987, p. 905).

The presidential elections of 1988 confirmed these trends. The Front National had a particularly strong showing among three groups—farmers, shopkeepers and small businessmen, and blue- collar workers. This meant that the Front National had successfully forged a broad electoral alliance between the different elements of *la France populaire*. As Pascal Perrineau put it, the Front National's results marked the synthesis between poujadism and urban blue-collar protest. In 1984, Le Pen "had appealed to the world of the small shops and the white collars. In 1986, he had kept the former, lost a number of the latter, and replaced them with enraged plebeians. In 1988, the political fusion of these two diverse clienteles [was] under way" (Perrineau, 1988, p. 36).

By 1993, this fusion appeared to be complete. The results of the elections to the National Assembly once again confirmed the proletarization of the Front National's electoral base (see Table 5.6). The party drew the fewest supporters

Table 5.6

Social Base of Front National Voters, 1993 (in %)

By Profession

Farmers	13
Artisans, Shopkeepers	18
Big Business	12
Liberal Professions	8
Employees	14
Skilled Workers	18
Unskilled Workers	17
Unemployed	17

By Length of Education

In School	11
14 years and less	14
15-16 years	16
17-18 years	16
19-21 years	11
22 years and more	8
Percentage of total population voting for FN	13

Source: *Libération,* March 23, 1993, p. 4.

among school teachers, professors, and the free professions and most among artisans and small shopkeepers (18 percent) and skilled and unskilled workers (18 and 17 percent respectively). It received disproportionate support from the unemployed and those voters who considered themselves to be socially disadvantaged (*défavorisés,* 20 percent) while attracting a disproportionately low number of voters with higher levels of education (8 percent; *Liberation,* March 23, 1993, p. 4).

The evidence provided so far suggests that there is good reason to believe that the growing emphasis radical right-wing populist parties put on immigration in the late 1980s was directly related to their growing appeal to less well educated working or lower middle-class voters. A brief survey of the social base of other parties that espoused a neoliberal philosophy in the 1980s supports this contention.

Table 5.7

Social Composition of Automobile Party Voters, 1991

	AP	Sample
By Occupation		
Self-Employed, Executives	36	23
Medium-Level Employees, Civil Servants	29	39
Lower-Level Employees, Civil Servants	7	13
Blue-Collar Workers	29	19
Farmers	0	6
By Education		
Low	12	13
Medium	76	62
High	12	25

Source: Longchamp and Hardmeier, 1992, p. 22.

The Swiss Automobile Party is a case in point. In 1991, the party distinguished itself by receiving disproportionate support from two social groups—executives and owners of small and medium-sized businesses on the one hand, blue-collar workers on the other (see Table 5.7). In fact, the proportion of blue-collar workers among AP voters was higher than among those of any other party; at the same time only the liberal FDP had a similarly high proportion of executives and self-employed among its voters (see Longchamp and Hardmeier, 1991). In addition, the party distinguished itself by the fact that the vast majority of its voters had attained a medium level of education. Those with higher levels of education, on the other hand, were significantly under-represented among the party's constituency.

The Automobile Party's profile in 1991 was remarkably similar to that of the New Democracy party in 1991 and, at least as the average level of education of its voters was concerned, the Norwegian Progress Party. Although New Democracy appealed to all social strata in Swedish society, it did particularly well among small businesses and blue-collar workers (Taggart, 1992; Gilljam and Holmberg, 1993, p. 200). The Norwegian Progress Party, on the other

Table 5.8

Social Composition of Norwegian Progress Party Voters, 1989

	PP	Sample
By Occupation		
Self-employed	9	8
Public White-collar Employees	9	21
Private White-collar Employees	25	19
Blue-collar Workers	39	32
Farmers, Fishermen	5	7
Students	8	6
Others	6	7
By Education		
low	20	24
medium	38	32
high/medium-high	30	24
high	12	20

Source: Valen, Aardal, and Vogt, 1990, p. 108.

hand, did particularly well among blue- and white-collar workers employed in the private sector (see Table 5.8). Both parties were significantly over-represented among voters with medium or medium-high (gymnasium I and II levels in the Norwegian case) levels of education and considerably un-derrepresented among voters with a high (university) level of education (see Taggart, 1992, p. 16). In addition, both the Progress Party and the New Democracy party were particularly successful among unemployed voters. More detailed evidence for the Progress Party suggests that this was particularly true for jobless voters from the second postwar generation (those born in the 1960s and coming of political age in the late 1970s and early 1980s) (Bjørklund, 1992). It was this generation that was particularly affected by the economic crisis of the late 1980s finding "itself confronted with a labour market which had a limited demand for labour just at the moment when this generation was finishing its years of schooling" (Bjørklund, 1992, p. 343).

Among the major parties that espoused a market-oriented program in the 1980s, the only party not to put increasing emphasis on immigration was the

Lega Nord. This might come as something of a surprise given the fact that the Lega appealed to a similar constituency as other radical right-wing populist parties. The Lega originated in relatively small, but well-off communities in Northern Italy with a high percentage of small businesses, artisans, and shopkeepers, an elevated number of workers rather than employees or executives, and a low number of immigrants (Natale, 1991, p. 92). The Lega thus emerged in the centers of what has come to be known as the "Third Italy." The Third Italy was the product of the great industrial transformation of the 1970s and 1980s in the center and north of Italy, which saw the emergence and expansion of a broad structure of small enterprises with extensive connections to local society on the periphery of the great metropolitan areas (Diamanti, 1993, pp. 116–117). In its initial phase the electoral base of the Lega Nord thus resembled that of the Danish Progress Party in the early 1970s. Like the latter, the supporters of the Lega shared both an entrepreneurial and productivist outlook and a profound aversion to the central state. This was compounded by the fact that in the 1980s growing international economic interdependence forced the Italian government to deal with the public debt through a substantial increase in taxes. As Ilvo Diamanti has argued, the expansion of the fiscal pressure affected particularly the small entrepreneurs and artisans of the Third Italy. They reacted with deep frustration, which was compounded by the fact that in the past they had been "spared" (Diamanti, 1993, p. 117).

In the parliamentary election of 1992, the social composition of the Lega Nord's electorate resembled that of the Automobile Party or the Norwegian Progress Party. Like the latter, the Lega appeared to do particularly well among small business owners, artisans, and shopkeepers and among workers and the unemployed (see Table 5.9). It did better among voters who had attained a medium level of education (and particularly well among those with lower medium education requiring eight years of school) than among those with either basic or higher education. Thus even the Lega Nord recruited a considerable proportion of its voters among "young, blue-collar workers with mid- to low-level educational qualifications" (Mannheimer, 1993, p. 92).

Despite appealing to an electorate that closely resembled that of the Swiss, Norwegian, or Swedish parties, the Lega Nord put great emphasis on confronting and trying to dispel the charges of racism during its campaign for the 1991 parliamentary elections and abandoned the question of immigration almost completely thereafter. The Lega Nord's programmatic shift away from xenophobia toward an almost exclusive emphasis on federalism can only be explained in the context of the rapid collapse of the established center-right parties and the Lega's concomitant rapid expansion throughout Northern Italy.

Table 5.9

Social Composition of Lega Nord Voters, 1991 (in %)

	LN	Sample
By Occupation		
Entrepreneurs, Professionals, Executives	6	5
Artisans	15	9
White-collar Employees	21	23
Workers, Unemployed	26	21
Housewives	14	14
Students	5	8
Pensioners	11	19
By Education		
low	19	25
medium-low	42	33
medium-high	35	34
high	4	8

Source: Mannheimer, 1992.

Unlike the Danish Progress Party in the 1970s and other radical right-wing political parties in the 1980s, the Lega Nord was presented with a chance to replace the established center-right party. Confronted with the collapse of the Christian Democrats in Lombardy and the Veneto in the early 1990s, the Lega Nord had the opportunity not only to become the dominant party on the center-right, but also a potential government party.[4] This meant that the Lega had to appeal to a broad and predominantly Catholic middle-class constituency. The promotion of xenophobia, particularly if presented in an explicit fashion, was more likely to scare away than attract these voters while opening the party to renewed charges of racism. It is for these reasons that Umberto Bossi appears to have decided to make the question of the restructuring of the Italian state along federal lines the central issue in the party's quest for political power in Northern Italy.

This was diametrically opposed to Jörg Haider's decision to exploit antiforeigner sentiments before the Viennese election. Both strategies can be explained by looking at the opportunity structure of the political market with which each party was faced in the early 1990s. As we have seen, in the 1980s, when the FPÖ marketed itself as a defender of individualism and the free market, a considerable proportion of its supporters belonged to the upwardly mobile strata of the middle and new middle class. It was not until the Viennese landslide election that the party adopted a pronouncedly xenophobic strategy. The reason for this programmatic shift presumably was that by the early 1990s the FPÖ had all but exhausted its possibilities to attract former center-right (ÖVP) voters. Any further expansion had to come at the expense of the SPÖ, which in the 1990 parliamentary election had only lost minimally compared to 1986. The results of the Viennese elections showed that the FPÖ's strategic move paid off. Forty percent of its total vote came from former SPÖ voters compared to a mere 15 percent from former ÖVP voters (Stirnemann, 1992, p. 152).

This outcome supports the general argument of this chapter. Although making gains among all occupational groups, the party did particularly well among blue-collar workers, and especially among skilled workers, 35 percent of whom voted for the FPÖ (see Plasser and Ulram, 1991c; Stirnemann, 1992, pp. 151–154). With this, the proportion of workers among FPÖ voters was almost as high as it was among SPÖ voters (21 percent and 23 percent respectively) and five times as high as it was among ÖVP voters. Ecological studies present a similar picture. The FPÖ became the second largest party in all working-class districts, while trailing both major parties in the distinctively middle-class districts. Finally, unlike in the past, the party was significantly underrepresented among voters with higher levels of education. Whereas the party received 23 percent of the overall vote, it received only 16 percent from voters with university education and 20 percent from voters with a university entrance degree (*Matura*).

The trend toward a proletarization of the party's electoral base continued in the state elections in the spring of 1994, where almost 25 percent of working class voters supported the FPÖ (Plasser and Ulram, 1994, p. 15).

Our analysis so far suggests that most radical right-wing populist parties, which at one point or another promoted free market policies, went through a significant process of proletarization during the late 1980s and early 1990s. This process went parallel with the deterioration of the socioeconomic prospects and expectations of a significant proportion of the population, which, at least in some cases, followed the adoption of free-market policies by the established parties. In response, the majority of radical right-wing populist parties increasingly stressed antiimmigration themes over their neoliberal propositions in an attempt to attract the potential victims of these policies. A comparison with national populist parties, which owed much of their electoral success in the late 1980s to the almost exclusive promotion of xenophobia, supports this proposition.

What distinguished both the Republikaner and the Vlaams Blok was their appeal to a disproportionate number of voters with lower levels of education and working class status. At the time of the European election in 1989, for example, the number of Republikaner supporters who had completed not more than compulsory education far exceeded those with higher or even university degrees. An Allensbach survey conducted between March and August 1989 found two thirds of Republikaner sympathizers to have completed not more than compulsory education (compared to 55 percent for the sample). This was considerably higher than among CDU/CSU supporters and even higher than among the supporters of the SPD (Noelle-Neumann, 1989). The same survey found considerably more working-class support for the Republikaner than for any other party. Support from skilled workers accounted for one third of the total Republikaner support, another fifth came from un- and semiskilled workers. This was significantly higher than the proportion of workers among SPD supporters (46 percent; Noelle-Neumann, 1989).

Dieter Roth's detailed comparison of the social base of the Republikaner support in the first six months of 1989 and 1990 provide a similar picture (see Table 5.10). According to these surveys much of the support for the Republikaner in 1990 came from younger men with basic education and a working-class background. This was confirmed in the results of the national election of 1990, where heavy losses reduced the Republikaner to nothing more than their core constituency. In this election, the party received relatively large support from two groups: young men, ages 18 to 24 (3.9 percent) and workers (3.6 percent) (Forschungsgruppe Wahlen, 1990, p. 31).

The lower-class character of the Republikaner vote was further confirmed by the results of the state election in Baden-Württemberg, where the Republikaner emerged with 10.9 percent of the vote as the third largest party in one of Germany's most affluent regions (see Feist, 1992; Schultze, 1992). The party's percentage among workers was almost twice as high as among the population at large and significantly higher than among SPD voters. Unlike in 1989, in 1992 the party attracted a higher percentage of un- and semiskilled workers than of skilled workers (see Table 5.11). Finally, the Republikaner attracted a disproportionately high number of unemployed voters (17 percent) (Forschungsgruppe Wahlen, 1992, p. 18). The reemergence of the Republikaner in 1992 was thus in large part accompanied by a further proletarization of the party's electoral base (see Roth, 1993, p. 6). This trend was confirmed by an Allensbach study conducted in early 1993, which found almost twice as many un- and semiskilled workers among Republikaner supporters as there were in

Table 5.10

Percentage of Population Favoring the Republikaner Party,
1989/1990, by Social Base

	1989	1990
By Occupation		
Un-/Semiskilled Workers	8.3	2.4
Skilled Workers	9.5	3.6
Lower and Middle-Level Employees and Civil Servants	5.6	1.2
Higher-Level Employees and Civil Servants	4.8	1.0
Self-Employed	6.6	1.5
Farmers	13.1	1.0
By Age and Education		
18–29 Low	9.3	4.7
Medium	6.5	1.7
High	1.2	1.1
30–39 Low	7.8	3.3
Medium	2.9	1.4
High	0.8	0.3
40–49 Low	7.3	1.7
Medium	4.2	0.6
High	1.0	0.4
50–59 Low	6.4	2.0
Medium	7.8	0.3
High	3.8	0.0
60+ Low	6.5	1.4
Medium	6.3	0.6
High	10.4	0.7
Percentage of Total Population Favoring Republikaner	5.8	1.5

Source: Roth, 1990, pp. 34-35.

Table 5.11

Social Composition of Republikaner Support,
Baden-Württemberg State Election, April 1992

	REP	Sample
Un-/Semiskilled Workers	22	12
Skilled Workers	21	12
Employees	32	35
Civil Servants	5	8
Farmers	2	2
Self-Employed	7	8

Totals do not add up to 100 as some respondents were either unemployed or did not give occupation.

Source: Forschungsgruppe Wahlen, 1992, p. 18.

the sample, whereas the proportion of skilled workers was only slightly higher (Noelle-Neumann, 1993).

In their study on the impact of structural change on milieus in Germany, Michael Vester and his collaborators came to similar conclusions. They found sympathies for the Republikaner to be particularly strong among two groups: older un- and semiskilled workers and employees whose parents had been workers or farmers and younger skilled workers or mid-level employees who had moved up from a working-class background (Vester et al., 1993, p. 49).

A number of ecological studies support the notion that support for the Republikaner is largely confined to the lower half of German society. One example is Eike Hennig's study of the rise of the Republikaner in Frankfurt in the European election of 1989 (Hennig, 1992). Hennig comes to the conclusion that the Republikaner did particularly well in those areas where a large number of the population has received only compulsory education, where there was a disproportionate number of workers and working-class Muslim immigrants predominantly employed in manufacturing, and which distinguished themselves by their low quality of housing (Hennig, 1992, pp. 150, 214). Hennig's findings correspond with those from other large cities. In Berlin, for example, in the elections to the city parliament in 1989, the Republikaner had their best results in areas characterized by low levels of education, high population density and thus limited living space, and high proportion of workers. The Republikaner were particularly strong in SPD strongholds where the CDU suffered heavy losses. A significant proportion of Republikaner voters were working-class voters who at one point in the past had abandoned the SPD either to vote for the CDU or abstain. By 1989, they had fallen out with the CDU as well. But instead of returning to the SPD they voted for the Republikaner.[5]

Ursula Feist's analysis of the success of the Republikaner in Baden-Württemberg in 1992 comes to similar conclusions. The Republikaner did particularly well in the "industrial belt" around Stuttgart, "once Germany's region of affluence and growth par excellence" and now among those most heavily affected by the crisis of German industry (Feist, 1992, p. 73).[6] The picture was not much different for Hamburg, where the radical Right (the Republikaner had to compete with the far-right German People's Party [DVU] for votes) gained 7.6 percent of the vote in the 1993 state election. According to the official analysis of Hamburg's statistical office, the radical Right made their biggest gains in traditional working-class areas, characterized by lower than average levels of education, high unemployment, and a lower than average standard of living. These were areas where the SPD had some of their best results in the 1970s and 1980s and where they were still relatively successful in 1993 (Statistisches Landesamt der Freien und Hansestadt Hamburg, 1993, p. 33).

These case studies suggest that, at least in the larger cities, the supporters of the German radical Right came from disadvantaged areas, which were particularly affected by the deterioration and restructuring of the German economy. This supports the contention that the voters of the Republikaner came predominantly from those strata that lacked the educational preconditions and occupational qualifications that would have allowed them to succeed, or at least find their way, in an increasingly complex world. These were the voters for whom the economy had less and less to offer in terms of good jobs and whose often existential problems the established parties had more and more neglected (Schutze, 1992, p. 887).

The social basis of the German Republikaner shows some close resemblance with that of the Vlaams Blok. As Marc Swyngedouw and others have shown, in its main bastion, Antwerp, the Vlaams Blok did particularly well in those areas characterized by lower standards of housing, few green spaces, a high rate of long-term unemployment, and the presence of immigrants, predominantly from North Africa (Swyngedouw, 1991, 1992). These were the areas where the Socialist Party had traditionally been the strongest (Commers, 1992).

Like the Republikaner in the early 1990s, the Vlaams Blok received a disproportionate share of the vote from voters with lower levels of education (compulsory education or vocational education and training, or secondary vocational or technical training), lower professional status, and a modest net family income. In 1991, 35 percent of Vlaams Blok voters reported not to have more than compulsory or vocational education and training; 40 percent reported a lower professional status (Swyngedouw and De Winter, 1991; Swyngedouw, 1992a). As a result, the social profile of the Vlaams Blok's electoral base resembled that of the Socialist Party more than that of any other party in Flanders (see Swyngedouw, Beerten, Billiet, and Carton, 1993).

WORKING-CLASS AUTHORITARIANISM OR VALUE CONFUSION?

Our analysis suggests that the social basis of radical-right wing populist parties has been far from static. Generally, radical right-wing populist parties have tried to pursue a catch-all strategy and draw voters from all social groups. However, the parties' ideologies and political programs invariably made them more attractive to some social groups than to others. Parties espousing a largely neoliberal, individualistic program gained sizeable support from among the better-educated middle class. If they attracted voters with working-class backgrounds, these were more often than not first-generation workers with strong individualistic tendencies, no ties, or only tenuous ties to the organized labor movement, and employed in small-sized companies characterized by traditional labor relations. Interestingly enough, these were the same kind of workers whom Thomas Childers had earlier found among Nazi supporters.

Evidence suggests that the support from better educated middle-class voters was rather tenuous. Particularly in those cases where the established center-right parties adopted a free market program and thus entered in direct competition with the radical Right, middle-class voters abandoned the latter as quickly as they had joined them. In response, radical right-wing populist parties generally moved further to the right, espousing a pronouncedly xenophobic political agenda in an attempt to appeal to lower-class voters. This led to a significant proletarization of the radical populist Right's electoral basis. By the end of the 1980s, the typical radical right-wing voter more often than not came from the lower classes, had only a low to moderate level of education, and tended to live in the disadvantaged areas of Western Europe's large and medium-sized cities. As a result, in the early 1990s, a number of radical right-wing populist parties resembled Socialist and Social Democratic parties more than any other of the established parties.

This also explains why some studies have found a relatively strong correlation between votes for radical right-wing populist parties and the presence of foreign worker populations (see, for example, Valen, 1990, p. 287; Perrineau, 1990, p. 21; Swyngedouw, 1991, p. 106; Lewis-Beck and Mitchell, 1993, p. 123). Foreign workers (such as North Africans in France, Turks in Germany) generally live in the same areas characterized by social housing and a generally lower standard of living as the lower class indigenous population. Immigrants are thus part of the broader social and economic context, which has given rise to radical right-wing support rather than its immediate cause (see Mayer, 1989).

Available evidence suggests that the transformation of the social profile of radical right-wing supporters has had significant implications for the parties' political agenda, and this not only with regard to immigration. In Denmark, for instance, the 1980s saw a dramatic change in Progress Party voters' attitudes toward the welfare state. Unlike in the 1970s, when Progress Party voters were the most vocal critics of the welfare state, by the end of the 1980s, Progress Party voters were far more inclined than the average supporter of the governing center-right parties to agree that cuts in the social budget had gone too far (Andersen, 1992, p. 200). In France, by the end of the 1980s, polls showed growing gaps between the party's free-market ideology and its supporters' attitudes toward social issues. Thus, in 1990, 88 percent of Front National cadres, but only 40 percent of its voters came out in support of privatizing public enterprises; 69 percent of cadres, but only 26 percent of voters supported raising the retirement age from 60 to 62; and 77 percent of cadres, but only 19 percent of voters supported limiting social security benefits in favor of the development of a voluntary insurance system (Ysmal, 1991, p. 191). Given the growing resistance of their supporters to the dismantling of the welfare state, it was hardly surprising if the radical Right moderated its market-oriented program.

With an increasing number of lower-class voters joining their ranks, the radical Right adopted an increasingly authoritarian agenda. Its most significant aspects are an open hostility to immigrants and refugees and an obsession with law and order. This only underscored the parties' right-wing character. There are, however, some major problems with an interpretation that reduces the radical right-wing populist agenda merely to authoritarianism. As we have seen, not all parties have taken an authoritarian position on major social issues. Neither the Swiss Automobile Party, nor the FPÖ, the Lega Nord, or the Scandinavian parties have adopted a restrictive line on abortion.

Even in the most extreme cases the value orientations of radical right-wing supporters have been far from uniform. In the case of the Front National, for example, as late as 1988, half of the party's supporters disagreed with the notion that reimbursements for abortions should be abolished (44 percent agreed compared to 32 percent for the whole population).[7] Similar ambiguities emerged from an analysis of the value orientations of Flemish voters in the 1991 election. It shows Vlaams Blok voters radically split on questions such as the right to security versus the right to privacy, public order versus free expression of opinion, and free entrepreneurship versus community control of enterprises. In each case there was a strong minority coming out most radically in favor of either position. This was in stark contrast to the question of immigration, where almost 90 percent of Vlaams Blok voters opted for the most restrictive choice (see Swyngedouw, 1993, pp. 110-111).[8] This suggests that while the influx of lower-class voters significantly expanded the proportion of xenophobes among radical right-wing supporters, it was far from fully eradicating support for the radical Right's promotion of individualism and free markets.

6

Political Conflict in the Age of Social Fragmentation

The emergence and rise of radical right-wing populist parties in the 1980s has been one of the most significant political events in the recent history of West European politics. Within a relatively short span of time, radical right-wing populist parties have consolidated substantial electoral gains and established themselves in the political system of a number of West European democracies. In a few instances they have become the dominant force in major cities (the Vlaams Blok in Antwerp) or whole regions (the Lega Nord in Northern Italy). Even if the radical Right has generally been shunned by the political establishment, they have nevertheless not been without influence on some of the policies advanced by the traditional parties (the most significant instance has been the French center-right's adoption of a number of the Front National's demands with regard to immigration after the 1993 parliamentary election).

The rise of radical right-wing populist parties has coincided with a marked increase in public disaffection and disenchantment with the established political parties, the political class, and the political system in general. At no other point of time in postwar West European history has the level of political distrust and cynicism been so profound, pronounced, and widespread as in the 1980s.

Throughout Western Europe voters appear to have grown tired of the same old faces, which guided their destinies for most of the postwar period. As a result, by the end of the 1980s, electoral politics was at least as much driven by sentiments of resentment toward the political parties and politics as a process in general as it was driven by a clear-headed and rational choice between different political alternatives. Given the profound public disaffection with the established political parties, it might hardly come as a surprise that a substantial number of West European voters have decided to cast their votes for new parties on the radical Right, rather than for the established political parties.

Our analysis, however, suggests that more than anything else political distrust gave rise to a political climate propitious to new political forces capable and willing to exploit it as a salient political issue. There can be little doubt that public political distrust and resentment opened up opportunities and prepared the ground for the radical Right's politics, which was largely geared toward exploiting popular resentment and thus played an important role in the rise of the radical Right. However, the link between disenchantment and right-wing radical electoral gains should not be overstated. The more profound reasons for the success of radical right-wing populist parties appear to lie deeper.

In a recent article on the situation of immigrants in his country, the Italian sociologist, U. Melotti, has characterized the recent period as "the ultimate act of a drama: the formation and extension of the capitalist system to a global scale, with all its contradictions. Beyond that it represents the first chapter in a new stage in history. This stage is characterized by the transformation of the world into a new configuration of multiracial, multiethnic, multicultural, multi-linguistic, and multireligious social formations. These new social formations are divided by increasing diversity, and yet also more and more interdependent, and thus at least tendentially united in their destiny" (Melotti, 1990, p. 27). As the analysis put forward in this book suggests, the West European public's response to this dual challenge has been at the least, highly ambivalent, if they have not rejected it altogether. It is within this context that the emergence and rise of the radical populist Right attain their sociopolitical significance as the reflection and expression of profound and widespread anxieties in the face of a radically changing world.

THE RADICAL RIGHT'S RESPONSE

The emergence and rise of radical right-wing populist parties in the 1980s was a direct response to the transition from industrial welfare capitalism to postindustrial individualized capitalism. Confronted with a growing failure by the state to govern the economy in the face of global competition the radical Right proposed a neoliberal economic program, which was intensely hostile to the comprehensive nature of the social democratic welfare state while extolling the virtues of economic deregulation, privatization, and individual entrepreneurship. With this program, the radical Right fully accepted the postindustrial logic of individualization, according to which more freedom leads to less equality and more competition, more competition to less solidarity and less societal integration, which in turn lead to an ever more relentless pursuit of one's individual interests (see Heitmeyer, 1993, p. 4). What Luca Ricolfi has noted with regard to the Lega Nord can be extended to the whole spectrum of neoliberal right-wing radicalism: "Its rejection of social policy is a consequence of its faith in the market; its lack of trust in the state a consequence of its belief in civil society" (Ricolfi, 1993, p. 145).

This also explains the relative tolerance of several radical right-wing populist parties and their supporters for behavior that deviates from the traditional norms. It grows out of the notion that individuals have the right to govern themselves, as long as their behavior does not infringe on the rights of others. This explains, for example, the low level of hostility of young Lega Nord supporters toward alcoholics and substance dependents (Ricolfi, 1993, p. 141). It might also explain the New Democracy party voters' relatively liberal attitudes on abortion, pornography, and especially on alcohol consumption, or the fact that in the late 1980s the supporters of the Norwegian Progress Party were more liberal on the question of abortion or the "free distribution of pornography" than the average Norwegian voter (Andersen and Bjørklund, 1990, p. 207; Gilljam and Holmberg, 1993, p. 149).

With regard to their economic policies most radical right-wing populist parties have been close to the positions advanced by Margaret Thatcher. Like Thatcherism in Great Britain, radical right-wing neoliberalism on the continent has promoted a productivist enterprise culture aimed at improving national competitiveness. Like Thatcherism, the radical Right have appealed to the knowledge accumulated by ordinary people, a popular pragmatism that "put the family, respectability, hard work, 'practicality,' and order first" (During, 1993, p. 14). Like Thatcherism they have offered an exclusionary ideology as a compensation for the anxieties inevitably created by the new insecurities generated by the globalization of the market place. Simon During's analysis of the rationale behind the political strategy employed by Thatcherism also applies to a large degree to our analysis of the radical populist Right:

> The more the market is freed from state intervention and trade and finance
> cross national boundaries, the more the nation will be exposed to foreign

influences and the greater the gap between rich and poor. Thatcherism's appeal to popular values can be seen as an attempt to overcome this tension. In particular, the new Right gives the family extraordinary value and aura just because a society organized by market forces is one in which economic life expectations are particularly insecure (as well as one in which, for some, the rewards are large and life exciting). In the same way, a homogeneous image of national culture is celebrated and enforced to counter the danger posed by the increasingly global nature of economic exchanges and widening national, economic divisions. The new Right image of a monoculture and hard-working family life, organized through traditional gender roles, requires a devaluation not just of other nations and their cultural identities, but of "enemies within": those who are "other" racially, sexually, intellectually. (During, 1993, p. 14)

As we have seen, if there is something that unites the different forms of radical right-wing populism in Western Europe, it is their pronounced hostility toward immigrants and refugees. The notable exception has been the Lega Nord, which after initially exploiting widespread animosities toward southern Italians and non-European immigrants increasingly dropped xenophobia as a mobilizing tool in order to gain political respectability. For all other parties, hostility toward immigrants and refugees has proved to be an issue that appeals to a far greater portion of the population than that which would generally consider voting for them. Thus, more than twice as high a percentage of the French population agreed in 1991 with the Front National's extremist position on immigration than generally voted for the party in regional or national elections. This suggests that xenophobia has become the most significant response in Western Europe toward the second major challenge associated with the transition to postindustrial individualized capitalism, namely the coming of a multiethnic and multicultural world.

Manfred Kuechler has proposed to divide the sentiments of indigenous populations toward foreigners into three analytically distinct categories: racism, xenophobia, and self-defense (Kuechler, 1993, p. 1). In its strictest sense, racism is the belief that history represents a struggle between races rather than classes or nations. More broadly defined, racism is the belief in the superiority of one's own racial or ethnic group. In its extreme form, racism "calls for the annihilation of other racial or ethnic groups (like the Nazis' genocide of Jews and Gypsies); in less extreme forms it denies other racial or ethnic groups equal rights and opportunities regardless of their willingness to assimilate and to acculturate or of merit." By contrast, xenophobia (or what might perhaps be more adequately called heterophobia) refers to the fear of the other, namely, to practices, customs, and behavior foreign to one's own culture. As Pierre-André Taguieff has noted, xenophobia derives from "mixophobia": "The foreigner is detestable only in that he is postulated as being inassimilable without provoking a destruction of community identity" (Taguieff, 1990, p. 120). This tends to provoke defense mechanisms, which range from avoidance of those considered as "others," their exclusion and/or segregation in ghettos to verbal and physical attacks on them and their property. Finally, self-defense refers to a "pattern where there is openness to foreigners, but where the adjustability of the native system has been stretched to the limits, where the native identity and/or legitimate interests of the natives are threatened."

If we accept these criteria as useful distinctions we can say that what comes closest to describing the response of West European populations to the influx of migrants and refugees is a mixture of xenophobia and self-defense. In the semiotics of postindustrial societies, migrants represent for many West Europeans the carriers of an alien culture, customs, and way of life and thus represent a threat to their own culture, customs, and way of life. Migrants also represent cheap, easily exploitable labor, and thus a threat to job security. In addition, they are claimants on public services, resources, and benefits and thus one more threat to the welfare state. Potentially, newcomers are also drug dealers and pickpockets and are involved in other forms of criminal behavior and thus a threat to physical security. On a more profound level, immigrants and refugees represent the embodiment both of a rapidly changing world and of the nation-state's growing impotence when confronted with it. For this reason, they have become the most prominent object of the politics of resentment in the 1980s and the politics of gloom in the early 1990s.

During the past several years the various perceptions of threat emanating from immigrants and refugees have come together in the image of the Muslims. As French observers noted in 1990, reviewing the attitudes of their compatriots toward foreigners: "Islam has replaced Communism as the threat to Western Europe" (SOFRES, 1990, p. 239). The fact that even the Lega Nord felt free to express openly their hostility toward Islam and Muslims without fearing negative repercussions for their electoral fortunes provides perhaps the most telling evidence for the extent to which hostility toward Islam and Muslims has become acceptable in Western Europe.

Radical right-wing populist parties have been astute in exploiting growing popular hostility toward immigrants and refugees. On the most mundane level, the radical populist Right has promoted what Scandinavian observers have aptly called a form of "welfare state chauvinism"—the notion that welfare services should be restricted to the native population (Andersen and Bjørklund, 1990, pp. 212, 214). This has become even more pronounced with the influx of lower-class voters into the ranks of the radical populist Right who are mainly concerned about maintaining their standard of living.

These demands for restricting welfare benefits to the indigenous population resonate not only with the radical Right's general hostility to the expanded social objectives of the social democratic welfare state (such as guaranteeing otherwise marginalized groups full citizen rights) and their demands to restrict benefits to the truly needy. They also resonate with popular anxieties regarding the continued viability of the welfare state as an institution that guarantees continued well-being for the majority of the population. A state that is no longer in a position to provide for the least fortunate among its inhabitants might no longer be in a position to provide all of its citizens with the standard of living to which they grew accustomed. In this sense immigrants might be seen as the most significant challenge to the core assumptions of modern West European welfare states. By eliminating the rights of nonnatives to receive benefits, the majority not only eliminates competition for increasingly scarce public resources, it also eliminates the most visible signs of the welfare state's decreasing viability in the vain hope that this will somehow save it from exhaustion.

POSTINDUSTRIAL INDIVIDUALIZED CAPITALISM AND POLITICAL CONFLICT

With their mixture of market liberalism and welfare state chauvinism, radical right-wing populist parties have attracted a significant portion of the West European electorate. The social base of this electorate is far from homogeneous and has undergone significant changes over time. However, a few characteristics do stand out. Generally, radical right-wing populist parties have been particularly attractive to younger men in their twenties and early thirties. They have been more successful among secular voters than among voters still strongly attached to traditional religious milieus. Their support lies more in the private than in the public sector. And they have been more successful both among a petite bourgeoisie of small entrepreneurs, shopkeepers, artisans, and other self-employed voters and among working-class voters than among new-middle-class voters.

Given the relative heterogeneity of the radical Right's programs and electoral basis, and the country-specific characteristics and idiosyncrasies of individual cases, anyone seeking a single comprehensive explanatory scheme for the rise and success of the radical Right is bound to be disappointed. There is much to be said for the notion that the "failure of left- and right-wing governments successfully to address the problems of long-term mass-unemployment, a crisis in the housing market arising from penury or deterioration of the existing stock, and rising crime rates, have contributed to the revival of the far Right, which has tended to blame all three on immigration" (Mény 1993, p. 63; see also von Beyme, 1988, pp. 10–11). However, this statement is as true as it is mundane since it fails to explicitly state under what conditions these objective social conditions get translated into votes for the far Right.

Theoretical explanations that see in the rise of the radical Right above all a materialist and authoritarian response to the postmaterialist revolution of the last decades are on equally shaky ground (see, for instance, Inglehart, 1990; Flanagan, 1987; Minkenberg and Inglehart, 1989; Minkenberg, 1992). On this view, the radical Right represents the "populist-extremist version of a neoconservative reaction against a fundamental change in culture and values" in advanced Western democracies, a "new coalition of forces which see their common enemy in the post-materialist oriented strata of the New Left, and their new political agenda" (Minkenberg, 1992, pp. 56, 58). Although these authors recognize the general importance of authoritarian orientations in the appeal of the radical Right, they overstate this aspect of radical right-wing politics while ignoring the profound ambiguities of at least some of the positions found on the radical Right.

Thus, as we have seen, even the supporters of the Vlaams Blok, which is by far the most xenophobic if not openly racist of all radical right-wing populist parties, have been deeply divided over a number of value choices. And this is not only with regard to typically left-libertarian positions like free speech. When asked to choose between quality of life or maintaining high economic growth, for example, Vlaams Blok supporters in 1991 were closer than the supporters of any other party to the position taken by the supporters of the Flemish Greens (Agalev), the great majority of whom opted for the postmaterialist quality of life choice (Swyngedouw, 1993, p. 100).[1] Secondly, although some parties have promoted themselves as the direct opponents of the libertarian Left (the most blatant example being the Automobile Party), others have drawn quite different conclusions. Thus, Andreas Mölzer has not hesitated to argue that both the FPÖ and the Austrian Greens (as well as the Front National and the German Greens) represented "citizen emancipation movements" against an ossified political system (Mölzer, 1990, p. 16).

Given these ambiguities in the value orientations of radical right-wing populist parties and their supporters, the charge that the radical Right is merely a reaction to the new values promoted by the libertarian Left loses much of its persuasive edge. Clearly, radical right-wing supporters are far more ambivalent with regard to a range of basic social values than theory would concede. Furthermore, by restricting themselves to interpreting the rise and success of the radical Right merely to culture and values, the authors ignore the possibility that the transformation of the political space of advanced Western democracies might be directly related to the broader sociostructural changes generated by the shift to postindustrial individualized capitalism.[2]

The most socially significant aspect of this shift has been an acceleration in the process of social fragmentation and individualization in the form of an erosion of traditional social bonds, subcultures, and milieus, which are increasingly being replaced by a culture based on informal networks and individual self-promotion. Radical right-wing populist parties have increasingly recruited their supporters among those social groups most negatively affected by these developments. What distinguishes these groups is their relative lack of sufficient amounts of "cultural and social capital" in the form of educational qualifications and titles, social relations, and contacts and networks (see Eder, 1993, chapter 4; Vester 1993).

Given the rapid pace of technological innovation and modernization, education has become a central determinant of social position. In individualized postindustrial societies education determines access to the job market, level of income, and social mobility more than any other single factor. In addition, education "is connected to other individual personal characteristics and abilities and thus an indicator of how persons are able to respond to their social situation, how they can shape their life and life world" (Geißler, 1992, p. 93). Individualized postindustrial societies have opened up new opportunities for social mobility while at the same time closing others. Thus, it is becoming increasingly clear that the expansion of mass education has not only opened up new opportunities for upward social mobility, but also raised the "entrance price" to the job market. As a result of the growing influx of new better-trained generations into the labor market, entrance requirements have been raised for a growing number of jobs. Jobs that once required a high school degree, now often require a college degree; jobs that once required a college degree, now often require a master's degree, and so on. This has led to a "devaluation" of educational titles (Geißler, 1990, p. 92). This process has been exacerbated by the introduction of new technologies and new production and management concepts as well as by the pressures of international competition. This affects not only "young school leavers who have been trained for disappearing industries" but also older workers employed in enterprises no longer competitive in the global market whose accumulated knowledge and experience are threatened to become obsolete (Swyngedouw, 1992, p. 68; Vester, 1993, p. 16).

The result of these developments has been a segmentation of society into those who possess the necessary education and social contacts to survive in a rapidly changing world and a minority that is increasingly falling behind. According to a recent study on structural change and lifestyles in Germany, in 1991, roughly a quarter of the (German) population could be classified as underprivileged

(*Deklassierte*). The majority of them were blue-collar workers, lower-level employees, pensioners, and jobless persons (Vester et al., 1993, p. 49).

Particularly in the large cities, the socioeconomic and sociocultural segmentation of advanced West European societies is reflected in geographic segmentation. One example is Frankfurt. As Hans-Gerd Jaschke has observed, during the past decades Frankfurt has split into two radically different cities: "that of the banks, of culture, and the middle classes and that of the crowded living conditions, the limited life chances, and of those who are threatened by poverty." There is the Frankfurt of the new elites and "the 'creative' whose frame of reference are 'life-style' and design, high tech and high culture; and there is the Frankfurt of those tormented by social status anxieties who feel threatened by foreigners" (Jaschke, 1992, p. 99).

This picture fits in well with the notion of urban anomy, which Pascal Perrineau has introduced into the debate on the rise of the Front National (Perrineau, 1988; Mayer and Perrineau, 1989, pp. 344–345). On this view, economic restructuring, the decomposition of organically grown social networks, and the disintegration of the traditional political infrastructure in many major cities has led to a loss of social stability and political orientation. The recent literature on the radical populist Right abounds of examples how the resulting feelings of anxiety and social isolation, political exasperation and powerlessness, loss of purpose in life, and insecurity and abandonment have paved the way for radical right-wing populist parties (see, for example, Jaschke, 1992; Swyngedouw, 1992; Commers, 1993).[3] It is thus hardly surprising that the radical Right has done particularly well in the anonymous housing projects on the periphery of Western Europe's metropolitan areas whose inhabitants are driven by fears of encirclement and invasion by immigrants and by growing resentment over the fact that they have been abandoned by the rest of society and that they lack the material means to escape from the ghettos of old and new poverty.[4]

Empirical evidence suggests, however, that the link between lack of cultural and social capital, social disintegration, and feelings of social anxiety and relative deprivation and support for the radical Right might not be quite as direct as one might expect. In 1993, for example, Republikaner supporters reported neither higher unemployment rates than the average German citizen nor were they more likely to fear that they might become unemployed within the next six months (Noelle-Neumann, 1993). In a similar vein, Michael Lewis-Beck and Glenn Mitchell found only a relatively weak correlation between unemployment (on the departmental level) and votes for the National Front in the 1986 parliamentary election (Lewis-Beck and Mitchell, 1993, p. 123). If direct measures of social deprivation fail to explain support for the radical Right, we have to look for indirect links between the amount of cultural capital a person possesses and political orientations and behavior.

It has been suggested that the increase in jobs calling for better education, increased skill levels, and higher qualifications tends to lead to more professional autonomy and formal egalitarianism on the workplace. Professional autonomy and formal egalitarianism, in turn, are potentially important determinants of social and political values and preferences. Commenting on the findings of sociopsychological studies, Jerald Hage and Charles H. Powers conclude that "people in jobs characterized by considerable autonomy come to value personal initiative, while people in jobs that are narrowly constrained or closely supervised come to value conformity and external authority" (Hage and Powers, 1992, p. 65). Those better educated are generally more likely to have the capacity to think independently. In addition, they are also more likely "to question the received interpretations of the world" and eschew the largely hierarchically structured, elite-directed politics of the traditional parties in favor of libertarian values such as "tolerance for individual creative self-fulfillment and cultural variety of life styles" and participatory forms of democracy (Offe, 1987, p. 89). On the contrary, those performing narrowly defined and closely supervised tasks (characteristic of traditional Fordist mass production or the new McDonaldized services) are likely to favor more authoritarian politics, in form and content, such as "hierarchical command structures, paternalist authority and social homogeneity" (Kitschelt, 1993, p. 303).

In the past, socialist and communist parties both catered to these authoritarian orientations and moderated them by providing a fairly paternalistic organizational structure while inculcating their supporters with a commitment to egalitarian values. Social individualization and fragmentation have led to the erosion of traditional working-class movements and organizations, networks, and party affiliations, and with it the collapse of traditional social solidarity.[5] As Oystein Gaasholt and Lise Togeby have argued for the Danish case, the erosion of traditional socialist networks and affiliations has led to the breakdown in the internal coherence and consistency of left-wing belief systems, which included commitment to universal welfare and civil liberties to all and therefore required their holders to reject attitudes (such as hostility toward foreigners) that violated the logic of tolerance.

> Workers and other groups at the lower end of the social stratification system in Denmark are. . . increasingly being de-mobilized, abandoning their traditionally close attachment to political movements, organizations, and parties in favor of individual, unorganized excursions into the right zone of the ideological landscape. These excursions take place in a spirit

of populist disaffection, providing considerable support for parties of the far right, but without translating into participation in organized political life. In this landscape people of modest individual resources are permitted to give expression to their fragmented views and emotions without being required to arrange them in a logically coherent system of thought. (Gaasholt and Togeby, 1992, p. 11)

This might also explain the prevalence of individualistic and neoliberal orientations among lower-class voters. They represent a revival of social Darwinist views in response to both the breakdown of social solidarity and the general closing of opportunities for social mobility (see Möller, 1993, pp. 6–7). A recent German study found, for example, that a considerable portion among those whom the study defined as underprivileged held belief systems characterized as a "pronounced economic individualism, according to which everyone should be only concerned with their personal advantage and show no compassion with those who are weaker" (Vester et al., 1993, pp. 351). This might also explain why in the late 1980s young unemployed Norwegians were increasingly attracted to the neoliberal program of the Progress Party despite the fact that the Progress Party advocated restricting financial benefits to the unemployed. Whereas the older generation associated the expansive state with recovery from the Great Depression and full employment, the younger generation identified it as the main obstacle to full employment (Bjørklund, 1992, pp. 348–349). Individualist and neoliberal orientations thus not only appeal to emerging groups that accept the market as the ultimate arbiter over individual life chances and whose relatively high amount of cultural capital allows them to play the game of individual effort, self-promotion, and self-advertisement, but also to those on the lower end of the social ladder, who see their chances of social mobility blocked by political parties, unions, and the state, which protect the entrenched interests of established and organized groups (not to mention the vast patronage systems that political parties have established and that guarantee them influence in personnel decisions) while preventing outsiders from marketing themselves on a competitive basis.[6]

This discussion suggests that the underlying causes for the rise and success of radical right-wing populist parties during the 1980s and early 1990s are considerably more complex than existing theoretical approaches would lead us to believe. Additional in-depth research is needed to arrive at a more detailed analysis of the various factors that link sociocultural changes to political orientations, which favor the radical populist Right. As Michael Vester and others in Germany have shown, in the future we might have to pay more attention to new social categories such as life style and milieu (see Vester, 1993). In addition, we need to expand the range of existing social variables in comparative surveys to include questions that tap various aspects of sector employment, exposure to new technologies, or living circumstances. Ultimately, only research that takes into account the growing fragmentation of social reality will allow us to draw inferences as to its implications for political preferences and orientations.

RADICAL RIGHT-WING POPULIST PARTIES AND THE LIBERTARIAN LEFT

One research project that might fulfill the criterion above would be to compare the emergence and rise of radical right-wing populist parties to those of Green and other left-libertarian parties. As we have seen, it has been argued that the emergence of the radical populist Right represented a reaction to the postmaterialist agenda of the libertarian Left. Although our discussion suggests that the links are more complex than this theory proposes, this should not detract from the possibility that the two party families are somehow related.

As a number of studies have shown, Green and other left-libertarian parties are largely organized and supported by young, highly educated professionals and students. A sizeable proportion of left-libertarian activists and supporters tend to be employed in the public education, health care, and cultural service sectors of the economy, or in culture- and/or human-oriented services in the private sector, or tend to study subjects oriented toward these occupations (see Kitschelt, 1990). Because of their high levels of education, the supporters of left-libertarian parties tend to have a greater propensity to emphasize individual freedom, personal development, and individual self-realization as important goals (Schulze, 1993, pp. 312-321). They distinguish themselves by their pronounced interest in politics and the extent to which they are politically mobilized and interested in active political participation. As a result, left-libertarian voters have tended to be more likely to participate in new social movements than the voters of the established political parties (Chandler and Siaroff, 1986; Veen, 1989; Bennulf and Holmberg, 1990; Kitschelt, 1990). Left-libertarian parties thus represent and reflect the values, political goals, and the life-style of a core segment of the postindustrial work force, which has been variously defined as 'symbolic specialists' or 'new cultural intermediaries' (Featherstone, 1991).

The social background and value preferences of left-libertarian party supporters are closely reflected in the political identity of these parties. As Herbert Kitschelt has persuasively argued, Green and other left-libertarian parties are Left insofar as they share "with traditional socialism a distrust of the marketplace, of private investment, and of the achievement ethic, and a commitment to egalitarian redistribution." They are libertarian insofar as they "reject the authority of private and public bureaucracies to regulate individual and collective conduct." Against those who insist "on the discipline of the market or on various hierarchical authorities as the final arbiter of social organization" they call for "participatory decentralized decision making" respecting the autonomy of individuals and groups "to define their economic, political, and cultural institutions unencumbered by market or bureaucratic dictates" (Kitschelt, 1990, p. 180; 1992, p. 13). As a result, left-libertarians have tended to support the expansion of welfare state benefits via community-sponsored services; the political inclusion of social, ethnic, and cultural minorities and marginalized groups; and the creation and extension of institutional arrangements, which allow the ordinary citizens to participate in political discussion and decision-making processes.[7]

This brief overview suggests that Green and other left-libertarian parties are in a number of important aspects the direct opposite of the radical populist Right. This is particularly the case in terms of their social background, the amount of cultural capital at their disposition, their attitudes toward the market as instrument of social organization and ultimate determinant factor in the allocation of life chances, and their pronounced support for and active engagement in various forms of unconventional political behavior. What they have in common is a general emphasis on libertarian values and their rejection of established authorities. This should, however, not detract from the fact that these attitudes derive from fundamentally different motivations. However it is with regard to immigrants and the prospects of a multicultural future that the two party families are most fundamentally opposed to each other. If radical right-wing populist parties have emerged as the most adamant opponents to both further immigration and the transformation of Western Europe into a multicultural society, Greens and other left-libertarian parties have been the most fervent advocates and proponents of both. Among the major Green parties, the Austrian, Belgian, German, and Swiss Greens have called for making it easier for immigrants to settle in Western Europe and become citizens of their adopted country and to extend full social and political rights (including the right to vote in major elections) to foreign residents. In addition, the Greens have strongly advocated the development of a multicultural society. As the German Greens write in their electoral program for the 1990 parliamentary election:

> The Greens are for a multicultural society, where cultural variety is accepted and able to develop. The coexistence of different cultures entails

conflict and friction as well as the chance for mutual education. The precondition is that in the Federal Republic all immigrants and refugees have the right to cultural selfdetermination and can live with us as equals.[8]

Surveys designed to measure attitudes toward immigration and multi-culturalism in Western Europe invariably show that the supporters of Green and other left-libertarian parties are generally the least prejudiced with regard to foreigners and the most supportive of extending full citizen rights to them of all relevant political groups (among the exceptions are the Radical Liberals in Denmark who have tended to be even more liberal with regard to immigrants than the libertarian Left; see Andersen and Bjørklund, 1990, p. 211). They also impressively show that the supporters of radical right-wing populist parties, at least as this aspect of the political discourse and struggle is concerned, place themselves invariably on the opposite end of the attitudinal spectrum, repre-senting something like mirror images of each other (see Table 6.1).[9] Given the fact that both are responses to the same underlying developments grounded in distinct social groupings, it might not be exaggerated to claim that what we are witnessing here is the emergence of a powerful new line of sociopolitical and sociocultural conflict. Superficially it might seem that this struggle is primarily over economic issues, driven by relative deprivation and socioeconomic despair. However, underneath these economically inspired fears and resentments lie more profound questions about individual and national identity.

THE FUTURE OF RADICAL RING-WING POPULISM

The future of radical right-wing populism will ultimately depend on the degree to which it manages to translate the question of national identity into a coherent political program. Given the logic and dynamics of electoral competition and the recent evolution of the radical Right's electoral base, one might expect that—at least in the intermediate future—radical right-wing populist parties will only survive as a viable political factor if they embrace a national populist agenda. (This might even apply for the Lega Nord, if changes in the electoral law and its inability in finding allies prevent it from translating support in the polls into political offices, and the political center manages to reconstitute itself.) The core elements of such a national populist ideological program have already emerged in the current debate on the future of Western Europe. They are ethnopluralism and protectionism.

As we have already seen, national populist parties have justified their hostility toward immigrants and refugees on economic as well as cultural grounds. The cultural justification is grounded in a line of argumentation that represents a rather insidious reconstruction of traditional racism along new lines. Its core is the notion of ethnopluralism, which was one of the key concepts developed by the intellectual New Right (and here particularly the French *nouvelle droit*) in the 1970s and 1980s. The New Right appropriated one of the core ideological concepts of the 1970s and 1980s, the notion of "difference," and reversed its meaning (see Guillaumin, 1992, pp. 19-21). Whereas the progressive Left had advocated the right to difference as a central precondition for the creation of a pluri-cultural society, the New Right transformed it into the "claim that true racism is the attempt to impose a unique and general model as the best, which implies the elimination of differences." Consequently, true anti-racism is founded on the absolute respect of differences between ethnically and culturally heterogeneous collectives (Taguieff, 1990, p. 111). This line of argumentation has then been used to legitimize calls for the preservation of national culture and national identities as a precondition for the preservation of differences.

Ethnopluralism stands behind the revival of the form of ethnic nationalism that has sprung up throughout Europe "supplanting the nationalism based on a nation-state that is increasingly losing its political and economic powers" (Swyngedouw, 1992, p. 71). Its ideological advantage is that it escapes the established criteria of racism. Unlike traditional racism, ethnopluralism focuses not on the question of racial or ethnic superiority, but on the question of the threatened loss of identity. As Jean-Marie Le Pen has written: "Peoples cannot be summarily qualified as superior or inferior, they are different, and one must keep in mind these physical or cultural differences" (quoted in Taguieff, 1990, pp. 116). It is on this basis that Le Pen and others have proclaimed their respect for foreign cultures and identities—as long as their carriers remain in their own countries (Le Pen: "I love North Africans, but their place is in the Maghreb." Schönhuber: "I love Turks, but it's in Turkey that I love them most."[10]). This has allowed the radical Right to promote themselves as protectors not only of West European culture and identity but also of the identity and culture of the immigrant populations. On this view the integration of foreigners from different cultures can only lead to mutual impoverishment and thus to a situation in which both the foreign and the indigenous communities gradually lose their basic values, which define their individual character (see Guillaumin, 1992, p. 20).

Ethnopluralist discourse thus shifts the core of the debate on multicultural-ism away from the right of minorities to maintain their differences within a national society vis-à-vis the indigenous majority to the right of all cultural entities to preserve their culture and identity within a global society. The central argument is that multiculturalism can only exist if there are distinct cultures.

Since immigration must inevitably lead to a leveling of differences and thus the destruction of individual cultures, it is inherently inimical to multiculturalism defined in this way. It is this reasoning that underlies the New Right's attacks against American society (prevalent, as we have shown below, in the discourse on multiculturalism of parties as different as the Front National and the Lega Nord) whose notion of the melting pot is seen as the worst instance of a leveled society, faceless and anonymous, which inevitably must end in societal chaos and ultimately ethnic and cultural self-destruction. From this it follows that the Americanization of European society cannot but lead to "monstrous urban agglomerations" characterized by alienation and uprooting where the "forced coexistence of different, if not incompatible, races and cultures will invariably provoke revolts and social turbulence" (Bossi and Vimercati, 1992, p. 203). It is against this phantasm of a "multicultural European unity society in which the different European cultures get absorbed" that the radical Right promotes its notion of a "Europe of diversity," which allows each country to preserve its cultural identity, traditions, and history.[11] The other side of diversity is, of course, the eradication of Europe's minority communities via a slow process of restricting and ultimately denying them access to basic citizen rights and their forced repatriation.

The electoral appeal of radical right-wing parties that promote a pronouncedly national populist agenda is an indication that these notions resonate at least to a certain degree among the indigenous West European population. However, given the extent of the socioeconomic challenge confronting Western Europe today, a political strategy built on the protection of national identity can hardly limit itself to ethnic and cultural protectionism. The survival of the radical Right as a viable political alternative to the established parties will ultimately depend on its ability to develop an alternative economic program that responds to the economic interests as well as the fears and anxieties of its constituency.

In the introduction to this book we have argued that the rise of the radical populist Right in the 1980s and early 1990s was a response to a combination of far-reaching economic, social, and cultural developments, which have dominated the past several years. Among these developments have been the emergence of a global economy characterized by interdependent markets, high capital mobility, and increased global competition; the emergence and rapid diffusion of new information and information-controlled production technologies; and the expansion of knowledge-based and human-oriented jobs in the service sector. Each of these developments has had a particularly strong impact on society and politics in Western Europe.

Western Europe's economic success in the postwar period was largely built on a degree of societal consensus and collective responsibility that distinguished continental Western European capitalism from its capitalist competitors elsewhere (see Albert, 1991). This consensus was built on two central components that characterized the postwar settlement in Western Europe—namely the commitments to full employment and to the creation and expansion of the welfare state.

The global socioeconomic and sociocultural transformation, which has by now reached Western Europe, presents a fundamental challenge to these commitments. Technological innovation has not only increased demand for highly skilled labor, it has also been a major contributing factor in the rise of mass unemployment. Confronted with dramatic productivity increases among their competitors abroad, companies have been under enormous pressure to "downsize" their work force. It increasingly appears that in the perceptions of many West Europeans the result of these developments has been the dawning of what French and German observers have characterized as a "*civilisation du chômage*," a civilization of unemployment. The German publicist Claus Koch has defined it as "a social condition in which full employment is no longer possible and therefore must be abandoned as a norm for economic policy and science" (Koch, 1993, p. 934). This, Koch and others suggest, has far-reaching implications for Western Europe's welfare states.

Whereas in the past the state was primarily concerned with the accumulation of national wealth and its equitable redistribution, under conditions of rising mass unemployment the state is called to use all its forces for the creation of jobs. However, as Fritz Scharpf has pointed out, economic globalization has increasingly deprived states of the major policy options of the past. The growing fiscal crisis threatening most West European states precludes the employment of traditional Keynesian stimulus mechanisms; the threat on the part of employers to dislocate their operations to the new markets in Central Europe and East and Southeast Asia precludes the option to increase the tax burden borne by capital (Scharpf, 1993, p. 544). It should therefore come as no surprise that most states adopted a new macroeconomic policy set in the late 1970s and 1980s, which allowed them to restrict themselves to guaranteeing price stability and a stable exchange rate while at the same time absolving them from responsibility for the drastic increase in the level of unemployment (see Notermans, 1993, pp. 137-139). The result is bound to add to the crisis of the welfare state. Neither benefit systems nor work-creation schemes were ever intended to cope with a persistent reduction in the amount of available jobs and its inevitable consequences of mass unemployment, affecting as much as 15 percent of the working population. "The costs involved, in both financial and human terms, are simply too great."[12]

For West European observers this experience suggests that technological innovation and economic globalization question the fundamental tenets of the

European welfare state by exposing the weakness of the state, which is no longer capable of banishing the risk of unemployment.[13] Once global financial markets are in a position to eliminate enterprises and destroy whole industrial sectors, the "sudden termination of the working life must be experienced by many, just like in pre-welfare state times, as an accident, and thus individualized." The civilization of unemployment is thus "a European phenomenon, refers to the political societies of the European welfare states" (Koch, 1993, pp. 935–936).

More than that, the rise of mass unemployment denotes a fundamental crisis of the continental European economic model (or what Michel Albert has referred to as the "Rhine model" of capitalism). It was only a short time ago that its admirers heralded it as a "unique, and highly successful, synthesis of capitalism and social democracy" whose "sense of balance and proportion" was no less impressive "than the efficacy of its economic performance" while claiming that its "solid grounding in social solidarity will remain a source of competitive advantage through its emphasis on continuous development of labour skills and technology" (Albert, 1993, pp. 125–126; Hodges and Woolcock, 1993, p. 329). The rapid spread of new technologies and the opening up of global markets have called most of this into question. West Europeans are only now starting to realize that in a global market revolutionized by increasingly rapid communication and transportation, work will go to those most productive. And those, as a growing number of studies have shown, do not live in the high-wage countries of Western Europe (see Botho, 1993).[14]

In response, Western European observers have suggested that in order to halt the erosion of Western Europe's competitive position in the global market, Western Europeans must be prepared to accept significant changes in the system to which they have become accustomed and to revise their expectations about the future. Among the measures deemed necessary to increase productivity and with it Western Europe's competitiveness are the readjustment of wages so as to correspond to actual productivity, heightened flexibility of the work force, and cuts in social provisions (see Lauk, 1993; Chesnais, 1993, p. 120). If carried through, these measures would mean nothing less than the corrosion of the West European model in a process of gradual "Americanization."

Given these prospects, the temptation to resort to trade barriers to protect Western Europe's economy against cheap imports from emerging producers in the developing world and thus to decouple Western Europe from the global market is bound to increase. Ross Perot's relatively successful campaign to bring together a vastly disparate group of NAFTA opponents in the United States has shown to what degree protectionist sentiments can mobilize economic anxieties and resentments.[15] In Western Europe, it is particularly in France that attacks against the global free market have struck a responsive chord. As Suzanne Berger has remarked, the "understanding of the economy is undergoing a fundamental shift across all groups in French society as the conviction spreads that the troubles of the economy begin at the borders and that solutions lie in a new protectionism. The loss of faith in government's ability to halt the hemorrhage of jobs through intervention in the domestic economy seems to be compensated by the belief that the openness of the European Community to the rest of the world is responsible for the rise in unemployment and that closing down access to French and European markets would slow or reverse this tendency" (Berger, 1993, p. 1).

Perhaps no one in France has argued that point more forcefully than the French-British businessman James Goldsmith. In his book *Le piège* Goldsmith claims that given the existing wage disparities between advanced industrial societies and developing countries, and the advances in capital and technological mobility, whatever choice Western industries pursue, they will invariably lead to more unemployment. This is the case if industries decide to transfer their production to developing countries and then import their cheap products in Europe, and it is the case if they specialize by concentrating on high-tech products requiring relatively little human labor. "Only these activities allow a high-wage country to obtain a comparative advantage" (Goldsmith, 1993, p. 59). Faced with these realities Western Europe can only survive if it abandons the traditional principles guiding international economic relations, such as the law of comparative advantage, and adopts an alternative strategy: to guarantee a free internal market where goods, services and capital can circulate without restrictions while protecting its borders and territory against its competitors in the United States, Japan, and the developing world, where labor costs are a fraction of what they are in Western Europe (Goldsmith, 1993, pp. 31, 34, 68–69).

Despite the potential political appeal of these ideas, the established political parties in Western Europe have been loath to adopt them. The reason is that these ideas appeal primarily to the actual and potential victims of economic globalization, still a relatively small proportion of the population, which the established political parties, in the 1980s, had generally written off in their pursuit of the "modernized new middle classes." It is for exactly this reason that the questions of global competition, economic dislocation, and their repercussions for Western Europe's labor force open up new opportunities for the radical Right. Economic protectionism not only complements the radical Right's promotion of cultural protectionism. In the form advocated by Goldsmith and others it also goes with the radical Right's general support for the market—as long as the market is limited to the confines of Western Europe.

In addition, economic protectionism complements the radical Right's generally very restrictive position on foreign aid to developing countries as well as

Table 6.1

Attitudes toward Immigrants and Foreign Residents (in %)

Foreigners' way of life can enrich our way of life (Germany, 1989):

	Greens	REP	All
strongly agree	39	0	9
strongly disagree	3	38	15

Do not mind there being many foreigners in Germany(1993):

	Greens	REP	All
	75	13	45

Find it good that in Germany foreigners subjected to political persecution have the right to asylum (Germany, 1993):

	Greens	REP	All
	89	49	72

Find having Turks as neighbors is (Austria, 1992):

	Greens	FPÖ	All
pleasant	29	0	13
unpleasant	12	52	25
don't care	57	36	55

Find having Jews as neighbors is (Austria, 1992):

	Greens	FPÖ	All
pleasant	33	0	18
unpleasant	5	39	13
don't care	57	48	63

The FPÖ's demand that foreigners should not be given the right to vote (Austria, 1992):

	Greens	FPÖ	All
opposed	43	6	25

Financial support to immigrants should be increased to allow them to maintain their customs (Norway, 1988):

	Socialist Left	Progress Party	All
agree	50	8	24

During difficult times jobs should go to Norwegians first:

agree	23	70	49

Immigrants should have the same rights as Belgians (1993):

	AGALEV	Vlaams Blok	All
agree	67	6	30
should have fewer	19	93	56

Sources: ipos, 1993, pp. 78–83; Emnid/Spiegel poll, March 1989; Institut für Konfliktforschung, "Xenophobie und Antisemitismus," 1992; SWS-poll, no. 288, 1992; Swyngedouw, 1993, p. 110.

their position on European cooperation and integration. While the majority of radical right-wing populist parties have supported European integration in one way or another (one exception was the Swiss Automobile Party), their conception of a future Europe is radically different from that of the established parties. They range from a Europe of fatherlands (Front National, Vlaams Blok) to regionalist ideas (Lega Nord, FPÖ). What all of them have in common is a strong focus on the protection of Europe's identity as a major objective of European integration.

Finally, if these ideas respond to the interests of any distinct social group, it is to the interests of the predominant groups among the radical Right's constituency—blue-collar workers, artisans, and entrepreneurs running small and medium-sized businesses. For these reasons, the recent adoption of protectionist platforms by the Front National and the FPÖ is perhaps the most significant development on the radical Right (see chapter 4).

Given the not unlikely prospects of steadily rising mass unemployment, and with it the expansion of the marginalized segments of the labor force; the likely prospects of new distributional conflicts, as workers employed in the prospering sectors of internationally competitive regions see their interests increasingly clashing with those of the growing number of marginalized groups in the declining sectors of the domestic economy; and the almost certain prospects of continued and growing political volatility caused by a combination of partisan dealignment, public political disaffection, and a fundamental lack of ideas on the part of the political class as to new strategies to lead Western Europe out of its socioeconomic predicament, there are no good reasons to expect that the radical populist Right will disappear from the political scene in the foreseeable future. On the contrary, if radical right-wing populist parties should manage to promote themselves successfully as the advocates of a cultural and economic "fortress Europe" protecting Western Europe's cultural identity and economic prosperity against the rest of the world, they might well succeed in securing a permanent niche in Western Europe's emerging political market.

NOTES

Chapter One

1. "Information Document on *The Danish Progress Party (Fremskridtspartiet),*" pp. 2–3.
2. Renzo Redivo, "Stivale delle dieci Leghe," *Panorama,* October 11, 1992, pp. 40–43.
3. Denis Mack Smith in an interview with Enzo Golino, *L'Espresso,* November 1, 1992, p. 30.
4. This was the result of a new electoral law. According to it only those candidates who won an absolute majority in the first round were elected as mayors. If no candidate could muster an absolute majority, the winner would be determined by a run-off election between the two candidates who had won the most votes in the first round. This system encouraged parties to form electoral alliances.
5. See *La Repubblica,* March 30, 1994, p. 16.
6. See Beppe Errani, "Bossi: 'Adesso apro l'asta per il governo,' " *Il Resto del Carlino,* March 30, 1994, p. 4.
7. On the decline of Front National support after the 1993 election see Olivier Biffaud, "L'adhésion aux idées du Front national est en recul dans la société," *Le Monde,* February 4, 1993, pp. 1, 8.
8. See Philippe Brewaeys, "De Clan Dewinter," *Knack,* June 3, 1992, p. 80.
9. *Blick,* March 16, 1988, p. 1.
10. See the interview with Giuliano Bignasca under the telling title "Lega ticinese: che terroni i lumbard," *Corriere della sera,* October 22, 1992, p. 9.
11. Jeremy Rifkin, "A Risk: High-Tech Elites Ruling a Jobless Nation," *International Herald Tribune,* February 26, 1993, p. 5; Reginald Dale, "Toward a World Without Jobs?" *International Herald Tribune,* May 18, 1993, p. 11.

Chapter Two

1. Alan Cowell, "Europeans Fear That Leaders Are Not Equal to Their Task," The *New York Times*, August 11, 1993, p. 1.
2. "Information Document," p. 5.
3. See the survey article on the Swedish economy in *The Economist*, March 3, 1990; also Hermann Orth, "Orientierungshilfen kommen aus Kopenhagen und Bonn," *Das Parlament*, January 22, 1993, p. 13.
4. *Panorama*, January 12, 1992, p. 46; Diamanti, 1993, p. 102.
5. *Panorama*, October 11, 1992, p. 60; *Corriere della sera*, July 15, 1993, p. 6.
6. Gian Antonio Stella, "'Noi paghiamo le tasse, ma in cambio?'," *Corriere della sera*, March 27, 1992, p. 2.
7. Vittorio Testa, "Il piacere di bastonare Roma," *La Repubblica*, October 1, 1992, p. 8; Dido Sacchettoni, "Brescia, un safari per Bossi," *Il Messagero*, March 26, 1992, p. 4.
8. Fessel+GfK, "Gesellschaftspolitischer Monitor," 1992.
9. In October 1990, 75 percent of FPÖ supporters (69 percent of ÖVP supporters and 59 percent of SPÖ supporters) considered the fight against corruption extremely important. *SWS-Rundschau* 30 (4) 1990, p. 569.
10. *Libération*, March 23, 1993, p. 6.
11. EMNID, March 1989; Wildenmann, 1989, p. 48.
12. EMNID, March 1989.
13. "Germany: Is Reunification Failing?" *Business Week*, November 15, 1993, p. 49.
14. "Abstieg in die zweite Liga," *Der Spiegel*, no. 19, 1993, pp. 138-147.
15. Rick Atkinson, "Germany's Economic Engine Breaks Down," The *Washington Post*, November 16, 1993, p. A32.
16. *Financial Times*, November 9, 1993, pp. 1, 4.
17. EMNID-Spiegel poll, March 1989.
18. Richard von Weizsäcker quoted in Brandon Mitchener, "Lean Years for Germany: As Leaders Warn of Structural Flaws, Public Prefers to Ignore the Crisis," *International Herald Tribune*, May 26, 1993, p. 1.
19. EMNID, March 1989.
20. EMNID, March 1989.

Chapter Three

1. *Nouvelle Observateur*, November 13-19, 1990, p. 6; Forschungsgruppe Wahlen, "Politbarometer 11/91," no page.
2. See the interview with Charles Pasqua, *Le Monde*, July 2, 1993, pp. 1, 13. On the practical consequences of this policy see Alan Riding, "France to Deport More Immigrants," The *New York Times*, January 7, 1993, p. A5.
3. Emnid poll, August/September 1991.
4. Forschungsgruppe Wahlen, "Politbarometer 11/91."
5. See J. M. Mushaben, "Behind the German Neo-Nazi Phenomenon." The *Christian Science Monitor*, November 18, 1991, p. 19.
6. EMNID-Spiegel poll, March, 1988, February 1989.
7. Institut für Demoskopie Allensbach, *allensbacher berichte* no. 22, 1991.
8. EMNID-Spiegel poll, November/December 1991.
9. ISPES, 1991, p. 453; Central Bureau of Statistics, "Attitudes towards Immigrants," 1988; EMNID-Spiegel poll, 1989.
10. In 1990, 58 percent of the Austrian population agreed completely or in part with the statement that "the Austrian economy could not function without foreign labor" (Plasser and Ulram, 1991, p. 321). For similar views in France, see Schain, 1990, p. 261.
11. *"rk-spezial"*, no. 8, 1990, p. 8.
12. IFOP-L'Express poll, *L'Express*, September 16, 1993, p. 31.
13. *"rk-spezial"*, no.8, 1992, pp. 7-8.
14. IFOP-L'Express poll, *L'Express*, September 16, 1993, p. 31.
15. Norbert Kostede, "Der Ausländer als Verbrecher," *Die Zeit*, June 19, 1992, p. 8.
16. Ibid.
17. Wassermann, 1992, p. 15. This article is particularly noteworthy. It appeared in *Aus Politik und Zeitgeschichte*, a supplement to the weekly paper *Das Parlament*, which is published by the Federal Office for Political Education and read widely among teachers.
18. For an illustration of the latter problem see Glotz, 1989, pp. 63–64. Peter Glotz, a prominent SPD politician, tells the story of a woman who voted for the Republikaner in 1989 after having voted SPD "for many years." The reason: In her city-owned house lived a young couple with a child and another one under way. When a larger apartment became available in the house, the young couple applied for it, but the city computer assigned it to a Turkish family with four children. Since they did not have enough "points" (symbol of Social Democratic neutrality and fairness) to compete with the Turkish

family, the Germans had to move out to find a larger apartment in the free housing market. The result is a growing feeling of "foreignization." As one resident of the neighborhood put it to Glotz: "Nine out of ten apartments go to foreign families and no-one can do anything about it. The foreigners simply have the higher number of points, they have more children. The Germans in the area feel that they get pushed against the wall."

19. Observa poll, 1985.
20. GfK poll, August 1993.
21. EMNID-Spiegel poll, November/December 1991.
22. EMNID-Spiegel poll, March 1989.
23. Wolfgang Koch, "Segen für die Rentenversicherung," *Das Parlament,* January 8–15, 1992, p. 10.
24. Tom Weingärtner, "Ausländer schaffen Wohlstand"; Lothar Klein, "Sie backen am Kuchen kräftig mit," *Das Parlament,* January 8–15, 1992, pp. 6, 10.
25. Wolfgang Koch, "Segen für die Rentenversicherung," *Das Parlament,* January 8-15, 1992, p. 10.
26. GfK survey, October 1991.
27. *Europeo,* November 20, 1992, p. 129.
28. GfK poll, May 1992.
29. Observa poll, August 1985.
30. GfK/Observa poll, March 1991.
31. Sabino Acquaviva, "Generare: follia o saggezza?" *Educazione al sesso,* lession XI, weekly supplement to *Medicina e salute,* p. 166, *Corriere della sera,* June 7, 1993. For similar trends in France see Safran, 1991.
32. Observa poll, August 1985.
33. "Multikulturelle Gesellschaft," *Allensbacher Berichte,* no. 9, 1992.
34. In 1991, 10 percent agreed completely with that statement, another 14 percent at least in part. See EMNID-Spiegel poll, November/December 1991, Table 35.
35. Ursula Feist, "Wählerpotential der neuen Rechtsparteien," infas, Bonn-Bad Godesberg, April 1993.
36. IFOP-L'Express poll, *L'Express,* September 16, 1993, p. 31.
37. "Extremisten werden sozial geächtet," *Allensbacher Berichte,* no. 1, 1993, Table 1.
38. A 1992 study of Italians' attitudes toward different groups in society comes to similar conclusions (see Dini, 1992, pp. 130, 132).
39. EMNID-Spiegel poll, August/September 1991.
40. See, for example, the account by the Moroccan journalist Tahar Ben Jelloun, "Meglio turchi che tedeschi dell'Est," *Corriere della sera,* August 9, 1992, p. 7.
41. EMNID-Spiegel poll, March 1989.
42. GfK poll, August 1993. As might be expected, Progress Party voters were particularly hostile toward non-Europeans. When asked, in 1991, which

groups should be allowed to enter Denmark in the context of family reunion, 51 percent chose "none" in the case of Eastern Europeans, 77 percent with Arabs, 79 percent with Asians, and 72 percent with Africans. GfK poll, October 1991.

Chapter Four

1. "Fremskridtspartiet," in *Danish Political Parties in Their Own Words*, The Royal Danish Ministry of Foreign Affairs, December, 1990.
2. Ibid.
3. *Blaue Markierungen. Schwerpunkte Freiheitlicher Erneuerungspolitik für Österreich*, Vienna, 1990, pp. 3–5; see also the party's self-characterization in *The Nationalrat Election in Austria*, Austria Documentation, Vienna: Federal Press Service, 1990, p. 14.
4. *Blaue Markierungen*, p. 20.
5. Interview with Umberto Bossi, *Oggi*, December 21, 1992, p. 71.
6. "Nord e sud, chi ha rotto l'Italia . . . ," *La Repubblica*, October 6, 1992, p. 4.
7. Interview with Francesco Speroni, *Corriere della sera*, December 30, 1992, p. 2; also, interview with Umberto Bossi, *Oggi*, December 1992, p. 69 and *Panorama*, May 9, 1993, pp. 60–61.
8. Interview with Umberto Bossi, *Panorama*, May 9, 1993, p. 61.
9. *La Repubblica*, December 16, 1993, p. 7.
10. Interview with Gianfranco Miglio, *Epoca*, November 11, 1992, p. 125.
11. *Tacho*, no. 42, 1991, p. 4.
12. Bengt Ericson, "Jag kan tänka mig en fusion med KDS," *Veckans Affärer*, March 24, 1993, p. 27.
13. *Tutto quello che avreste voluto sapere sulla Lega e che non vi hanno mai raccontato*, video, 1992.
14. Thus, one might suggest that by 1992 regio-nationalist sentiments were so deeply engrained among segments of the north Italian population that the Lega no longer saw the need to mobilize them.
15. *Epoca*, June 29, 1993, p. 19; *Corriere della sera*, May 10, 1993, p. 3.
16. Andreas Mölzer, "Tragödie der Multikultur," *Neue Freie Zeitung*, May 13, 1992, p. 7.
17. See FPÖ, *Heimatsuche*, Vienna, 1991.
18. See FPÖ, *Österreich zuerst. Volksbegehren: 12 gute Gründe Punkt für Punkt*, Vienna, 1992.

19. Among the most notable of these parties were, in Germany the DVU (German People's Union), the Belgian Front National, the Dutch Center Democrats (CD), Center Party (CD '86), and Netherlands Bloc.

20. Colette Ysmal's study of Front National cadres shows, however, that at least among the party faithful anti-Semitic sentiments were very prevalent. Thus, in 1990, 88 percent of party delegates agreed that Jews had too much power in France (Ysmal, 1991, p. 193).

21. *Le Front national c'est vous!* supplement to *La Lettre de Jean-Marie Le Pen,* no. 128, January 1–5, 1990, p. 4.

22. On the rationale behind this shift to the left see Jean-François Kahn, "Des vérités qui font mal," *L'évenement du jeudi,* March 12, 1992, p. 39.

23. *La lettre de Jean-Marie Le Pen,* no. 175, April/May 1993, p. 14.

24. *Le Figaro,* May 13, 1993, p. 2.

25. "Pourquoi feraient-ils demain ce qu'ils n'ont pas su faire hier?" Front National election pamphlet, 1988.

26. The fear of invasion has pervaded much of Front National rhetoric. See among others Le Pen's intervention in February 1983 on Antenne 2 where he warned of a threatening dual hegemony stemming, on the one hand, from the Soviet Union, on the other from the "demographic explosion of the Third World and, in particular, in the Islamic-Arabic world, which is currently penetrating our country and, progressively, colonizing it." Le Pen continued: "The Front National prides itself in having been the first formation during the past ten years to have warned the French of this mortal danger, evidently felt much more in the lower class areas than in the bourgeois ones" (quoted in Taguieff, 1984, p. 134).

27. Jean-Marie Le Pen, quoted in *Le Monde,* May 4, 1993, p. 8.

28. Front National, "Immigration: 50 mesures concretes—Les Français ont la parole," flier, 1992.

29. Die Republikaner, "Deutsche Bürger wehrt Euch!" leaflet, 1992; Die Republikaner, 1992, p. 19; interview with Franz Schönhuber, *Die Zeit,* June 26, 1992, p. 56.

30. Die Republikaner, "4 Gründe am 7. März wählen zu gehen," leaflet, Frankfurt, 1993.

Chapter Five

1. In Germany, in the late 1980s, more than 50 percent of 25 to 34-year-old gainfully employed women worked in these and similar occupations (Vester et al., 1993, p. 296).

2. A recent study on the impact of the labor-market sector on ideological orientation in the United States and Sweden, by Erik Olin Wright and Donmoon Cho, supports this argument. Wright and Cho divide state employment into state apparatuses constituting the political superstructure of capitalism and state services embodying elements of a decommodified postcapitalist form of social production. They find that in Sweden there are sharp differences within the state between the political superstructural and service middle class with regard to their political orientations. Generally, the Swedish service middle class is considerably more anticapitalist and prostatist than the political superstructural middle class (Wright and Cho, 1992, p. 185).

3. Nonna Mayer and Pascal Perrineau provide some evidence for this proposition. They report that in one district in Grenoble, where the Front National regularly achieved its best results, there is a police garrison, which furnishes about one third of the registered voters in the district (Mayer and Perrineau, 1989, p. 344).

4. The culminating point of this strategy was Bossi's promotion of the Lega as the cornerstone of a new liberal-democratic center. See *La Repubblica*, December 12/13, 1993, p. 2.

5. Schmollinger, 1989, p. 319; see also "Materialien zur Wahlanalyse: Die Republikaner," Pressemitteilung für die LPD am 6. 2. 1989, Statistisches Landesamt Berlin, February 1989. For similar results for Munich see Kreiling, 1989, pp. 362, 269; for Hannover see Vester et al., 1993, p. 179. Their analysis was confirmed by the state elections in early 1994 in Lower Saxony, where the Republikaner managed to quadruple their support in Hannover, surpassing the crucial 5 percent mark. See Hans-Peter Sattler, "Schönhubers Beutezug an der Leine," *Rheinischer Merkur*, March 18, 1994, p. 2.

6. Baden-Württemberg is a prime example for the connection between deteriorating life chances and support for the radical Right. In the 1980s still Germany's technological showcase, by 1992 the *Land* had turned into one of Germany's worst crisis regions—the result of a combination of state-sponsored technocratic hubris and failed investments in the wrong technologies. By the end of 1993, Baden-Württemberg had the highest increase in unemployment among all *Länder*. Youth was particularly affected. In the Stuttgart region, for instance, none of the medium-sized and large enterprises was able to provide jobs for all of the apprentices they had trained. The average rate was 30 percent, "that means that 70 percent of trained apprentices were unemployed and out on the street after their exams" (Schröter, 1994, p. 10).

7. *Le Point*, April 30, 1988, pp. 40–41. About the same proportion of Front National supporters had judged the liberalization of abortion as progress in surveys conducted between late 1983 and early 1984 (see Schain, 1987, p. 248).

8. For instance, with regard to the choice between public order and free expression of opinion, on a scale from 0 (public order) to 10 (free expression of opinion), 23 percent chose the most radical option regarding public order (0 and 1), whereas 33 percent chose the most radical option on free expression of opinion (9 and 10). Only in regard to immigration, 89 percent chose choices 9 and 10 (restrict rights of immigrants).

Chapter Six

1. Not surprisingly, given the ideological evolution of the Lega Nord, Ilvo Diamanti even found postmaterialists with high tolerance toward immigrants among Lega Lombarda supporters (Diamanti, 1991, p. 169)
2. This, of course, is also a charge that has been brought against "neoconservative" theorists such as Daniel Bell and his interpretation of the "cultural contradiction of capitalism" (see Habermas, 1982).
3. An excellent example is Gilbert Rochu's analysis of the socioeconomic and sociocultural changes in Marignane, where the Front National gained 49.5 percent of the vote in the second round of the 1993 parliamentary election. Michel Rochu, "Marignane, anatomie d'un fief du Front national," *Le monde diplomatique,* August 1993, pp. 26-27.
4. On this point see, for instance, Marc Ambroise-Rendu, "Le 'mal des banlieus' s'étend," *Le Monde,* August 18, 1991, p. 20.
5. For an exemplary case study see Dietmar Loch's analysis of the rise of the Front National in Marseilles (Loch, 1991, chapter 4).
6. This, of course, is a central argument in the debate about the 13th generation in the United States (see Howe and Strauss, 1993). Interestingly enough, it also seems to have played a role behind the electoral success of Vladimir Zhirinovsky in the recent Russian election. According to one report, Zhirinovsky appealed, among others, to better-educated younger voters from big cities, "a young opposition, young men demonstrating their youth, energy and resolution" who were drawn by Zhirinovsky's "television propaganda and the sense of action and force." Steven Erlanger, "Who Voted for Rightist in Russia? Mostly Nervous Young Men, a Poll Shows," The *New York Times,* December 30, 1993, p. A10.
7. Marc Swyngedouw provides persuasive evidence for these propositions (Swyndegouw, 1993, pp. 98–100). In his analysis of the 1991 election in Belgium he finds the supporters of the Flemish Greens (AGALEV) to come out most forcefully in favor of free expression of opinion (versus support for

public order), community control of enterprises (versus entrepreneurial freedom), quality of life (versus economic growth), the environment (versus jobs), and equal rights for immigrants (versus less rights for immigrants). The English edition of AGALEV's program provides a comprehensive, self-referential exposition of AGALEV's political universe. In the section "Social Affairs" the party writes: "We want to pay special attention to prevention, (re)integration of marginal groups, and participation of all those concerned. Welfare services must be taken as close to the citizens as possible. We as Greens must have confidence in the fundamental strength of the individual to take his or her situation in hand and to improve it.... AGALEV asks for a complete emancipation policy for both men and women. . . . The right to fulltime and equal work for both sexes should be guaranteed. Through the reduction of working time, together with a universal income, the Greens want to reach a more balanced distribution of professional and house work, and at the same time a more human existence for both men and women." AGALEV, *May We Present AGALEV,* Brussels, 1991, p. 14.

8. Die Grünen, *Das Programm zur 1. gesamtdeutschen Wahl 1990,* Bonn, 1990, p. 38. See also Die Grüne Alternative, *Leitlinien grüner Politik,* Impuls Grün, no. 7/8, 1990, pp. 59–62; AGALEV, *EEN groene kijk op samen leven,* Brussels, 1991, pp. 18–20; Grüne Partei der Schweiz, "Ursachen und nicht Menschen bekämpfen," Bern, 1989.

9. Mikael Gilljam and Sören Holmberg provide a graphic illustration of the opposite location of the two parties on this new politics axis in their analysis of the 1991 Swedish election. See Gilljam and Holmberg, 1993, p. 19.

10. Quoted in Taguieff, 1990, p. 119, and *Le Nouvel Observateur,* December 30, 1993, p. 33.

11. FPÖ, "Österreich zuerst. Unser Weg nach Europa," Beschlusspapier des ausserordentlichen Bundesparteitages der Freiheitlichen Partei Österreichs, *Schnell-Info,* 9/93, no page.

12. Daniel Goeudevert, "Unemployment: Toward Solidarity and a Novel View of Work," *International Herald Tribune,* April 27, 1993, p. 4.

13. For a particularly pronounced expression of this view see the contributions in *Les frontières de l'économie globale,* Le Monde diplomatique, Manière de voir, no. 18, May 1993.

14. See, for example, "Europe's Economy: What Must Be Done?" *Business Week,* February 15, 1993, pp. 22–26.

15. There are a number of interesting parallels between the Perot phenomenon in the United States and radical right-wing populism in Western Europe. As a *Los Angeles Times* poll from June 1993 shows, Perot supporters (16 percent of the sample) were the most distrustful of the political system (40 percent said

they hardly ever thought they could trust the government in Washington to do what was right, compared to 31 percent for the whole sample); the most pessimistic about the future (67 percent thought the next generation of Americans would live worse than the present generation, compared to 51 percent for the whole sample); the most opposed to the free-trade agreement between the United States and Mexico (37 percent strongly opposed it, compared to 23 percent for the sample); and most in favor of restricting foreign imports in order to protect jobs and domestic industries (71 percent compared to 68 percent for the whole sample). See *Los Angeles Times Poll,* Study #317, National Politics, June 1993, pp. 9, 14.

BIBLIOGRAPHY

Aardal, B. (1990). "The Norwegian Parliamentary Election of 1989," *Electoral Studies* 9 (2) 151–158.

Abramson, P. R. and Aldrich, J. H. (1982). "The Decline of Electoral Participation in America," *American Political Science Review* 76 (September) 502–521.

Ackaert, J., de Winter, L., Aish, A.-M., and Frognier, A.-P. (1991). "L'Abstentionisme électoral et vote blanc et nul en Belgique," *Res Publica* 34 (2) 209–226.

Albert, M. (1993). *Capitalism Against Capitalism* (London: Whurr Publishers).

Aimer, P. (1988). "The Rise of Neo-Liberalism and Right Wing Protest Parties in Scandinavia and New Zealand: The Progress Parties and the New Zealand Party," *Political Science* 40 (December) 1–15.

Andersen, B. R. (1984). "Rationality and Irrationality of the Nordic Welfare State," *Daedalus* 113 (Winter) 109–139.

Andersen, J. G. (1993). "Udviklingen i den politiske tillid 1991-1993," Institut for Statskundskab, Aarhus Universitet.

———— (1992). "Denmark: The Progress Party—Populist Neo-Liberalism and Welfare State Chauvinism," pp. 193–205 in P. Hainsworth (ed) *The Extreme Right in Europe and the USA* (New York: St. Martin's Press).

———— (1992a). *Politisk mistillid i Danmark*, Institut for Statskundskab, Aarhus Universitet.

———— (1982). "Electoral Trends in Denmark in the 1980s," *Scandinavian Political Studies* 9 (2) 157–174.

———— (1980). "Partipolitiske skillelinier i arbejderklassen," Institut for Statskundskab, Aarhus Universitet.

———— and Bjørklund, T. (1990). "Structural Changes and New Cleavages: the Progress Parties in Denmark and Norway," *Acta Sociologica* 33 (3) 195–217.

———— and Glans, I. (1980). "Sociale klasser og partivalg ved folketingsvalgene 1977 og 1979," Institut for Statskundskab, Aarhus Universitet.

Annemans, G. and Dewinter, F. (n. d.). *Dossier vreemdelingen, deel 1: gastarbeid,* Merksem.

Arter, D. (1992). "Black Faces in the Blond Crowd: Populist Racialism in Scandinavia," *Parliamentary Affairs* 45 (3) 357-372.

Assheuer, T. and Sarkowicz, H. (1992). *Rechtsradikalismus in Deutschland,* 2nd ed. (Munich: Beck).

Autopartei—die Freiheitlichen (1991). *Parteiprogramm,* Egerkingen.

Bauer, P. and Schmitt, H. (1990). *Die Republikaner,* Zentrum für Umfrageanalysen und Studien (ZEUS), University of Mannheim, Mannheim.

Beck, U. (1987). "Beyond Status and Class: Will There Be an Individualized Class Society?" pp. 340–355 in V. Meja, D. Misgeld, N. Stehr (eds) *Modern German Sociology* (New York: Columbia University Press).

———— (1986). *Risikogesellschaft* (Frankfurt: Suhrkamp).

Bennulf, M. and Holmberg, S. (1990). "The Green Breakthrough in Sweden," *Scandinavian Political Studies* 13 (2) 169–176.

Berger, S. (1993). "The Coming Protectionism or, Why France, a Country with a Trade Surplus, Sees Foreign Trade as the Source of Rising Unemployment," paper prepared for the conference on "The New France in a New Europe," Center for German and European Studies, Georgetown University, Washington, D.C.

Bester, H. (1990). "Hindernisse für Vollbeschäftigung," pp. 160–178 in *Wirtschaftspolitik* (Bonn: Bundeszentrale für politische Bildung).

Betz, H.-G. (1992). "Postmodernism and the New Middle Class," *Theory, Culture & Society* 9 (2) 93–105.

———— (1990). "Politics of Resentment: Right-Wing Radicalism in West Germany," *Comparative Politics* 23 (October) 45–60.

———— (1990a). "Post-Modern Anti-Modernism: The West German Republikaner," *Politics and Society in Germany, Austria and Switzerland* 2 (Summer) 1–22.

Biedenkopf, K. (1990). "The Federal Republic of Germany: Old Structures and New Challenges," pp. 79–99 in D. P. Calleo and C. Morgenstern (eds) *Recasting Europe's Economies* (Lanham/New York/London: University Press of America).

Biermann, R. (1992). "Migration aus Osteuropa und dem Magreb," *Aus Politik und Zeitgeschichte* B 9/92 (February) 29–36.

Biorcio, R. (1991/92). "The Rebirth of Populism in Italy and France," *Telos* 90 (Winter) 43–56.

Birsl, U. (1992). "Frauen und Rechtsextremismus," *Aus Politik und Zeitgeschichte* B3-4/92 (January) 22–30.

Bischoff, D. and Teubner W. (1991). *Zwischen Einbürgerung und Rückkehr* (Berlin: Hitit Verlag).

Bjørklund, T. (1992) "Unemployment and Party Choice in Norway," *Scandinavian Political Studies* 15 (4) 329–352.

———— (1988). "The 1987 Norwegian Local Elections: A Protest Election with a Swing to the Right," *Scandinavian Political Studies* 11 (3) 211–234.

Blanchet, D. and Marchand, O. (1991). "Au-delà de l'an 2000, s'adapter à une pénurie de main-d'oeuvre," *Economie et statistique* 243 (May) 61–68.

Blondel, J. (1974). *The Government of France*, 4th ed. (New York: Thomas Y. Crowell Company).

Bocca, G. (1993). *Metropolis: Milano nella tempesta italiana* (Milan: Mondadori).

Boltho, A. (1993). "Western Europe's Economic Stagnation," *New Left Review* 201 (September/October) 60–75.

Boneng, L., Horak, R. and Lasek, W. (1985). "Bewusstseinswandel in der Jugend: Sub-, Gegenkulturen, Alternativbewegung und Rechtsextremismus in Österreich," *Österreichische Zeitschrift für Politikwissenschaft* 14 (4) 381–401.

Boos-Nünning, U. (1990). "Einwanderung ohne Einwanderungsentscheidung: Ausländische Familien in der Bundesrepublik Deutschland," *Aus Politik und Zeitgeschichte* B23-24 (June), 16–25.

Borre, O. (1987). "Some Results from the Danish 1987 Election," *Scandinavian Political Studies* 10 (4) 345–355.

———— (1980). "The Social Bases of Danish Electoral Behaviour," pp. 241–282 in R. Rose (ed) *Electoral Participation: A Comparative Analysis* (Beverly Hills: SAGE).

———— (1977). "Recent Trends in Danish Voting Behavior," pp. 3–37 in K. H. Cerny (ed) *Scandinavia at the Polls* (Washington, DC: American Enterprise Institute for Public Research).

———— (1974). "Denmark's Protest Election of December 1973" *Scandinavian Political Studies* 9, pp. 197–204.

Bossi, U. with Vimercati, D. (1993). *La rivoluzione. La Lega: storia e idee* (Milan: Sperling & Kupfer).

———— (1992). *Vento dal nord* (Milan: Sperling & Kupfer).

Brand, K.-H. (1990) "Cyclical Aspects of New Social Movements: Waves of Cultural Criticism and Mobilization Cycles of New Middle-Class Radicalism," pp. 23–42 in R. Dalton and M. Kuechler (eds) *Challenging the Political Order* (New York: Oxford University Press).

Bréchon, P. (1993). *La France aux urnes* (Paris: La documentation Française).

———— (1990) "L'abstentionisme électoral en France depuis 1988" *Regards sur l'actualité* 164 (September/October) 11–20.

———— and Mitra, S. (1992) "The National Front in France: The Emergence of an Extreme Right Protest Movement," *Comparative Politics* 25 (1) 63–82.

Brettschneider, F., Ahlstich, K., and Zügel, B. (1992). "Materialien zu Gesellschaft, Wirtschaft und Politik in den Mitgliedstaaten der Europäischen Gemeinschaft," pp. 433–625 in O. W. Gabriel (ed) *Die EG-Staaten im Vergleich* (Bonn: Bundeszentrale für politische Bildung).

Bubendorfer, H. A. (1988). "'Zwischen alternativ und etabliert.' Jugend und Parteiensystem in Österreich 1960 bis 1986. Eine empirische Bestandsaufnahme," pp. 331–349 in A. Pelinka and F. Plasser (eds) *Das österreichische*

Parteiensystem Studien zur Politik und Verwaltung 22 (Vienna, Cologna, Graz: Böklan).

Bundesamt für Ausländerfragen (1991). *Die Ausländer in der Schweiz—Bestandsergebnisse* Statistischer Bericht 2, Bern.

Bundesamt für Flüchtlinge (1992). *Asylstatistik 1991,* Bern.

Bundesministerium für Wirtschaft (1993). *Zukunftssicherung des Standortes Deutschland,* Bonn.

Busch, B. (1990). "Mauerbau und Rassismus rund um die 'Festung Europa': Österreichs Fremdenpolitik im ausländerfeindlichen Harmonisierungstrend," pp. 50–67 in G. Fischer and P. Gstettner (eds) *"Am Kärtner Wesen könnte diese Republik genesen"* (Klagenfurt: Drava).

Buzzi, P. (1991). "Le Front national entre national-populisme et extrémisme de droite," *regards sur l'actualité* 169 (March) 31–43.

Camus, J.-Y. (1989). "Origine et formation du Front national," pp. 17–36 in N. Mayer and P. Perrineau (eds) *Le Front national à découvert* (Paris: Presses de la Fondation nationale des sciences politiques).

Caracosta, L., Fleurbaey, M., and Leroy, C. (1991). "Competitivité, croissance et employ: la France de l'an 2000 en perspective," *Economie et statistique* 243 (May) 69–87.

Castells, M. (1993). "The Informational Economy in the New International Division of Labor," pp. 15–44 in M. Carnoy, M. Castells, S. S. Cohen and F. H. Cardoso, *The New Global Economy in the Information Age* (University Park: The Pennsylvania State University Press).

Cavalli, A. and de Lillo, A. (eds) (1993). *Giovani anni 90* (Bologna: Il Mulino).

Cavazza, F. L. (1992). "The Italian Paradox: An Exit from Communism," *Daedalus* 121 (Spring) 217–249.

Chandler, W. M. and Siaroff, A. (1986). "Postindustrial Politics in Germany and The Origins of the Greens," *Comparative Politics* 18 (April) 303–325.

Charlot, M. (1986). "L'émergence du Front national," *Revue française de science politique* 36 (February) 31–45.

Chesnais, J.-C. (1993). "Mediterranean Imbalances and the Future of International Migrations in Europe," *SAIS Review* 13 (Fall) 103–120.

Childers, T. (1983). *The Nazi Voter* (Chapel Hill: University of North Carolina Press).

——— (1980). "National Socialism and the New Middle Class," pp. 19–33 in R. Mann (ed) *Die Nationalsozialisten: Analysen faschistischer Bewegungen.* Historisch-sozialwissenschaftliche Forschungen 9 (Stuttgart: Klett-Cotta).

——— (1976). "The Social Bases of the National Socialist Vote," *Journal of Contemporary History* 11, pp. 17–42.

Christiansen, N. F. (1984). "Denmark: End of the Idyll," *New Left Review* 144 (March/April) 5–32.

Cohn-Bendit, D. and Schmid, T. (1992). *Heimat Babylon* (Hamburg: Hoffmann und Campe).

Coleman, D. A. (1992). "Does Europe Need Immigrants? Population and Work Force Projections," *International Migration Review* 26 (Summer) 413–461.

Commers, Ronald (1992). "Antwerpen: Eine europäische Stadt driftet nach rechts," pp. 135–143 in C. Butterwegge and S. Jäger (eds) *Rassismus in Europa* (Cologne: Bund-Verlag).

Cook, S., Pakulski, J., and Waters, M. (1992). *Postmodernization: Change in Advanced Society* (London, Newbury Park, New Delhi: SAGE).

Dalton, R. (1984). "Cognitive Mobilization and Partisan Dealignment in Advanced Industrial Democracies," *Journal of Politics* 46 (1) 264–284.

Darnstädt, T. and Spötl, G. (1993). "Streunende Hunde im Staat: Die liberale Demokratie am Wendepunkt," *Der Spiegel*, March 29, pp. 142–159.

Daten und Fakten zur Ausländersituation (1992). Mitteilungen der Beauftragten der Bundesregierung für die Belange der Ausländer, Bonn.

Desplanques, G. and Tabard, N. (1991). "La localisation de la population étrangère," *Economie et statistique* 242 (April) 51–61.

Dewinter, F. (n. d.). *Immigratie: De oplossingen*, Brussels.

Diamanti, I. (1993). *La Lega: Geografia, storia e sociologia di un nuovo soggetto politico* (Rome: Donzelli editore).

———— (1992). "La mia patria è il Veneto. I valori e la potesta politica delle Leghe," *Polis* 6 (August) 225–255.

———— (1991). "Una tipologia dei simpatizzanti della Lega," pp. 159–190 in R. Mannheimer (ed) *La Lega Lombarda* (Milan: Feltrinelli).

Dietrich, P. (1993). *Abschlußbericht zur Feldstudie "Jugendszene und Jugendgewalt im Land Brandenburg"*, Institut für Familien- und Kindheitsforschung an der Universität Potsdam, Potsdam.

Dini, M. (1992). "Più che l'ebreo è l'errante che irrita gli italiani," *Europeo*, November 20, pp. 128–135.

DOXA (1991). "Gli stranieri in Italia—Risultati di tre sodaggi: del maggio '91, del novembre '89 e del luglio '87," *Bolletino della DOXA* 45, no. 9-10-11.

Dupoirier, É. (1994). "Les Français à l'épreuve de la crise," pp. 55–75 in SOFRES *L'état de l'opinion 1994* (Paris: Seuil).

During, S. (1993). "Introduction," pp. 1–25 in S. During (ed) *The Cultural Studies Reader* (London/New York: Routledge).

Dyson, K. (1989). "Economic Policy," pp. 148–167 in G. Smith, W. E. Paterson, P. H. Merkl (eds) *Developments in German Politics* (Durham: Duke University Press).

Eatwell, R. (1992). "Why Has the Extreme Right Failed in Britain," pp. 175–192 in P. Hainsworth (ed) *The Extreme Right in Europe and the USA* (London: Pinter Publishers).

———— (1982). "Poujadism and Neo-Poujadism: From Revolt to Reconciliation," pp. 70–93 in P. G. Cerny (ed) *Social Movements and Protest in France* (New York: St. Martin's Press).

Eder, K. (1993). *The New Politics of Class* (London/Newbury Park/New Delhi: SAGE).

Eichwalder, R. (1991). "Lebensbedingungen ausländischer Staatsbürger in Österreich," *Statistische Nachrichten* 46 (2) 164–174.

Erichsen, R. (1988). "Zurückkehren oder bleiben? Zur wirtschaftlichen Situation von Ausländern in der Bundesrepublik Deutschland," *Aus Politik und Zeitgeschichte* B24/88 (June) 14–25.

Esping-Andersen, G. (1992). "Postindustrial Cleavage Structures: A Comparison of Evolving Patterns of Social Strategification in Germany, Sweden, and the United States," pp. 147–168 in F. Fox Piven (ed) *Labor Parties in Postindustrial Societies* (New York: Oxford University Press).

———— (1990). *The Three Worlds of Welfare Capitalism* (Princeton: Princeton University Press).

Eysell, M. and Hennigsen, B. (1992). "Dänemark: Politik, Wirtschaft und Gesellschaft diesseits and jenseits von Maastricht," *Aus Politik und Zeitgeschichte* B43/92 (October) 3–11.

Fagerberg, J., Cappelen, A., Mjoset, L., and Skarstein, R. (1990). "The Decline of Social-Democratic State Capitalism in Norway," *New Left Review* 181 (May/June) 60–94.

Falter, J. W. (1990). "The First German Volkspartei: The Social Foundations of the NSDAP," pp. 53–81 in K. Rohe (ed) *Elections, Parties and Political Traditions* (New York/Oxford/Munich: Berg).

———— (1988). "Wahlen und Wählerverhalten unter besonderer Berücksichtigung des Aufstiegs der NSDAP nach 1928," pp. 484–504 in K. D. Bracher, M. Funke, and H.-A. Jacobsen (eds) *Die Weimarer Republik,* 2nd. ed. (Bonn: Bundeszentrale für politische Bildung).

———— (1986). "Unemployment and the Radicalisation of the German Electorate 1928-1933: An Aggregate Data Analysis with Special Emphasis on the Rise of National Socialism," pp. 187–208 in P. D. Stachura (ed) *Unemployment and the Great Depression in Weimar Germany* (London: Macmillan).

———— (1984). "Die Wähler der NSDAP 1928-1933: Sozialstruktur und parteipolitische Herkunft," pp. 47–59 in W. Michalka (ed) *Die nationalsozialistische Machtergreifung 1933* (Paderborn, Munich, Vienna, Zurich: Schönigh).

Featherstone, M. (1991). *Consumer Culture & Postmodernism* (London/Newbury Park/New Delhi: SAGE).

Feist, U. (1993). "Wählerpotential der neuen Rechtsparteien," pp. 177–183 in Friedrich Naumann Stiftung Dokumentation, *Rechtsextremismus und Gewalt* (Sankt Augustin: COMDOK).

———— (1992). "Rechtsruck in Baden-Württemberg und Schleswig-Holstein," pp. 69–76 in K. Starzacher, K. Schacht, B. Friedrich, and T. Leif (eds) *Protestwähler und Wahlverweigerer* (Cologne: Bund-Verlag).

Fischer, G. and Gstettner, P. (eds) (1990). *"Am Kärntner Wesen könnte diese Republik genesen"* (Klagenfurt: Drava).

Flanagan, S. (1987). "Value Change in Industrial Societies," *American Political Science Review* 81 (4) 1303–1319.

Fondazione Agnelli (1990). *Il futuro degli italiani* (Turin: Fondazione Agnelli).

Forschungsgruppe Wahlen (1992). *Wahlen in Baden-Württemberg,* Berichte der Forschungsgruppe Wahlen e. V., no. 67, Mannheim.

———— (1990). *Bundestagswahl 1990: Eine Analyse der ersten gesamtdeutschen Bundestagswahl am 2. Dezember 1990,* Berichte der Forschungsgruppe Wahlen e. V., no. 61, Mannheim.

FPÖ (1991). *Programm für Wien 1991* (Vienna: Landesgruppe Wien).

———— (1985). *Österreich politisch erneuern: Programm der Freiheitlichen Partei Österreichs,* Vienna.

Franke, H. and Buttler, F. (1991). *Arbeitswelt 2000* (Frankfurt: Fischer).

Franklin, M. (1992). "The Decline in Cleavage Politics," pp. 383–405 in M. Franklin, T. Mackie, H. Valen et al. *Electoral Change: Responses to Evolving Social and Attitudinal Structures in Western Countries* (Cambridge: Cambridge University Press).

Fremskrittspartiet (1989). "Political Program of The Progress Party (Norway)," Oslo.

Frey, L. (1988). *La Disoccupazione in Italia: Il punto di vista delgi economisti.* Quaderni di Economia del Lavoro 136 (Milan: FrancoAngeli).

Fritzmaurice, J. (1992). "The Extreme Right in Belgium: Recent Developments," *Parliamentary Affairs* 45 (3) 300–308.

Front National (1993). *300 Mesures pour la renaissance de la France* (Paris: Editions Nationales).

———— (1988). *Passeport pour la victoire,* supplement to *La Lettre de Jean-Marie Le Pen,* no. 70, March 15, 1988.

Fuchs, D., Gerhards, J., and Roller, E. (1993) "Wir und die anderen," *Kölner Zeitschrift für Soziologie und Sozialpsychologie* 45 (2) 238–253.

Fysh, P. and Wolfreys, J. (1992). "Le Pen, the National Front and the Extreme Right in France," *Parliamentary Affairs* 45 (3) 309–326.

Gaasholt, Ø. and Togeby, L. (1992). "Interethnic Tolerance, Education, and Political Orientation: Evidence from Denmark," paper presented at the Fifteenth Annual Scientific Meeting of the International Society of Political Psychology, San Francisco.

Gabriel, O. W. (1993). "Institutionenvertrauen im vereinigten Deutschland," *Aus Politik und Zeitgeschichte* B43/93 (October) 3–12.

Gaspard, F. (1990). "L'évolution du F.N. à Dreux et dans les environs (1978-1989)," *Revue politique et parlamentaire* 945 (January/February) 62–69.

Gehmacher, E., Birk, F., and Ogris, G. (1987). "Das Wahljahr 1986: Welche Theorien stimmen?" *Journal für Sozialforschung* 27 (2) 155–171.

Geißler, R. (1992). *Die Sozialstruktur Deutschlands* (Opladen: Westdeutscher Verlag).

—— (1990). "Schichten in der postindustriellen Gesellschaft," pp. 81–102 in P. A. Berger and S. Hradil (eds) *Lebenslagen, Lebensläufe, Lebensstile*, Soziale Welt, Sonderband 7 (Göttingen: Schwartz).

Gilljam, M. and Holmberg, S. (1993) *Väljarna inför 90-talet* (Stockholm: Norstedts Juridik).

Glotz, P. (1989). *Die deutsche Rechte* (Stuttgart: Deutsche Verlags-Anstalt).

Gluchowski, P. and Zelle, C. (1992). "Demokratisierung in Ostdeutschland," pp. 231–274 in P. Gerlich, F. Plasser, and P. Ulram (eds) *Regimewechsel: Demokratisierung und politische Kultur in Ost-Mitteleuropa* (Vienna/Cologne/Graz: Böhlau).

Goldsmith, J. (1993). *Le piège* (Paris: Fixot).

Grunberg, G. (1988). "Recent Developments in French Electoral Sociology" *Electoral Studies* 7 (1) 3–14.

Güllner, M. (1993). "Parteien und Wahlen—'Volkes Stimme'? Empirische Analyse einer Entfremdung," pp. 33–51 in J. Buchholz (ed) *Parteien in der Kritik* (Bonn: Bouvier).

Guillaumain, C. (1992) "Une société en ordre. De quelques-unes des formes de l'idéologie raciste," *Sociologie et sociétés* 24 (Fall) 13–23.

Habermas, J. (1982). "Die Kulturkritik der Neokonservativen in den USA und in der Bundesrepublik," *Merkur* 36 (November) 1047–1061.

Habich, R. and Krause, P. (1992). "Niedrigeinkommen und Armut," pp. 482–495 in Statistisches Bundesamt (ed) *Datenreport 1992* (Bonn: Bundeszentrale für politische Bildung).

Hage, J. and Powers, C. H. (1992). *Postindustrial Lives: Roles and Relationships in the 21st Century* (Newbury Park: SAGE).

Haider, J. (1993). *Die Freiheit, die ich meine* (Frankfurt/Berlin: Ullstein).

—— (1992). *Wiener Erklärung* (Vienna: Freiheitliches Bildungswerk/Politische Akademie der FPÖ).

Hammar, T. (1989). "Comparing European and North American International Migration," *International Migration Review* 23 (3) 631–637.

Hansen, E. J. (1982). "The Progress Party in Denmark is a Class Party—But Which Class?" *Acta Sociologica* 25 (2) 167–176.

Harmel, R. and Svåsand, L. (1990). "The Impacts of New Political Parties: The Cases of the Danish and Norwegian Progress Parties," paper prepared for delivery at the 1990 Annual Meeeting of the American Political Science Association, San Francisco.

——— (1989). "From Protest to Party: Progress on the Right in Denmark and Norway," paper prepared for delivery at the 1989 Annual Meeting of the American Political Science Association, Atlanta.

Harvey, D. (1989). *The Condition of Postmodernity* (Oxford: Basil Blackwell).

Haut Conseil à l'Intégration (1993). *L'intégration à la française* (Paris: Éditions 10/18).

Heise, M. (1993). "Die deutsche Wirtschaft im international en Standortwettbewerb," *Wirtschaftsdienst* 73 (July) 248–355.

Heitmeyer, W. (1993). "Gesellschaftliche Desintegrationsprozesse als Ursachen von fremdenfeindlicher Gewalt und politischer Paralysierung," *Aus Politik und Zeitgeschichte* B2-3/93 (January) 3–13.

——— (1989). *Rechtsextremistische Orientierungen bei Jugendlichen*, 3rd. updated ed. (Weinheim/Munich: Juventa)

Hennig, E. (1991). *Die Republikaner im Schatten Deutschlands* (Frankfurt: Suhrkamp).

Hernes, G. (1991). "The Dilemmas of Social Democracies: The Case of Norway and Sweden," *Acta Sociologica* 34 (4) 239–260.

Hinrichs, K. (1988). "Vollbeschäftigung in Schweden: Zu den kulturellen Grundlagen und den Grenzen erfolgreicher Arbeitsmarkt- und Beschäftigungspolitik," *Politische Vierteljahresschrift* 29 (4) 569–590.

Hodges, M. and Woolcock, S. (1993). "Atlantic Capitalism versus Rhine Capitalism in the European Community," *West European Politics* 16 (July) 329–344.

Höhne, R. (1990). "Die Renaissance des Rechtsextremismus in Frankreich," *Politische Vierteljahresschrift* 31 (1) 79–96.

Hof, B. (1991). *Für mehr Verantwortung—Langzeitarbeitslosigkeit und Soziale Marktwirtschaft*, Beiträge zur Wirtschafts- und Sozialpolitik 193 (Cologne: Deutscher Instituts-Verlag).

——— (1991a). "Arbeitskräftebedarf der Wirtschaft, Arbeitsmarktchancen für Zuwanderer," mimeo, Bonn.

——— (1990). *Gesamtdeutsche Perspektiven zur Entwicklung von Bevölkerung und Arbeitskräfteangebot* (Cologne: Deutscher Instituts Verlag).

Hoffmann-Martinot, V, (1993). "Frankreichs Parteiensystem nach den Parlaments-wahlen," *Aus Politik und Zeitgeschichte* B32/93 (August) 10–16.

Hollifield, J. F. (1991). "Immigration and Modernization," pp. 113–150 in J. F. Hollifield and G. Ross (eds) *Searching for the New France* (New York/London: Routledge).

Holmberg, S. and Gilljam, M. (1987). *Val och väljare i Sverige* (Stockholm: Bonnier-Fakta Bokförlag AB).

Honoré, J.-P. (1985). "Jean-Marie Le Pen et le Front national," *Les Temps modernes* 465 (April) 1843–1871.

Hoskin, M. (1991). *New Immigrants and Democratic Society: Minority Integration in Western Societies* (New York/Westport/London: Praeger).

Howe, N. and Strauss, B. (1993). *13th Gen: Abort, Retry, Ignore, Fail?* (New York: Vintage).

Hradil, S. (1992). "Die 'objektive' und die 'subjektive' Modernisierung," *Aus Politik und Zeitgeschichte* B29-30 (July) 3–14.

——— (1990). "Postmoderne Sozialstruktur? Zur empirischen Relevanz einer 'modernen' Theorie sozialen Wandels," pp. 125–150 in P. A. Berger and S. Hradil (eds) *Lebenslagen, Lebensläufe, Lebensstile,* Soziale Welt, Sonderband 7 (Göttingen: Schwartz).

——— (1990a). "Epochaler Umbruch oder ganz normaler Wandel? Wie weit reichen die neueren Veränderungen der Sozialstruktur in der Bundesrepublik," pp. 73–100 in Bundeszentrale für politische Bildung (ed) *Umbrüche in der Industriegesellschaft* (Bonn: Bundeszentrale für politische Bildung).

Hübner, E. and Rohlfs H.-H. (1992). *Jahrbuch der Bundesrepublik Deutschland* (Munich: Beck).

Humbertjean, M. (1985). "Les français et les immigrés," pp. 75–88 in SOFRES, *Opinion public 1985* (Paris: Gallimard).

Husbands, C. (1992). "Belgium: Flemish Legions on the March," pp. 126–150 in P. Hainsworth (ed) *The Extreme Right in Europe and the USA* (New York: St. Martin's Press).

——— (1988). "The Dynamics of Racial Exclusion and Expulsion: Racist Politics in Western Europe," *European Journal of Political Research* 16 (November) 701–720.

Hutcheon, L. (1988). *A Poetics of Postmodernism* (New York: Routledge).

Ignazi, P. (1989). "Un nouvel acteur politique," pp. 63–80 in N. Mayer and P. Perrineau (eds) *Le Front national à découvert* (Paris: Presses de la Fondation nationale des sciences politiques).

——— and Ysmal, C. (1992). "New and Old Extreme Right Parties," *European Journal of Political Research* 22 (July) 101–121.

Inglehart, R. (1990). *Culture Shift in Advanced Industrial Society* (Princeton: Princeton University Press).

ipos (1993). *Einstellungen zu aktuellen Fragen der Innenpolitik 1993* (Mannheim: *institut für praxisorientierte sozialforschung*)

——— (1992). *Einstellungen zu aktuellen Fragen der Innenpolitik 1992* (Mannheim: institut für praxisorientierte sozialforschung).

——— (1990). *Einstellungen zu aktuellen Fragen der Innenpolitik 1990 in Deutschland* (Mannheim: institut für praxisorientierte sozialforschung).

ISPES (1991). *Rapporto Italia '91* (Rome: Vallecchi Editore).

——— (1991a). *L'atteggiamento degli italiani nei confronti dell'immigrazione extracomunitaria* (Rome: Istituto di Studi Politici Economici e Sociali).

Jackman, R. W. (1987). "Political Institutions and Voter Turnout in the Industrial Democracies," *American Political Science Review* 81 (June) 405–423.

Jäger, S. and Wichert, F. (1993). " 'Wir können uns hier nicht alles aufladen.' Flucht und Einwanderung im deutschen Alltagsdiskurs," pp. 96–110 in C. Budderwegge and S. Jäger (eds) *Europa gegen den Rest der Welt* (Cologne: Bund-Verlag).

Jahn, D. (1992). "Schweden: Kontinuität und Wandel einer postindustriellen Gesellschaft," *Aus Politik und Zeitgeschichte* B43 (October) 22–35.

———— (1992a). "Die Wahl zum schwedischen Reichstag 1991. Das Ende des schwedischen Modells?" *Zeitschrift für Parlamentsfragen* 2 (1) 83–94.

Jaschke, H.-G. (1992). "Nicht-demokratische politische Partizipation in der sozial polarisierten Stadt," pp. 94–112 in K. Starzacher, K. Schacht, B. Friedrich, and T. Leif (eds) *Protestwähler und Wahlverweigerer* (Cologne: Bund-Verlag).

Jenson, J. and Mahon, R.(1993). "Representing Solidarity: Class, Gender and the Crisis in Social-Democratic Sweden," *New Left Review* 201 (September/October) 76-100.

Jessop, B., Bonnet, K., Bromley, S., and Ling, T. (1984) "Authoritarian Populism, Two Nations, and Thatcherism," *New Left Review* 147 (September/October) 32–60.

Jonzon, B. and Wise, L. R. (1989). "Getting Young People to Work: An Evaluation of Swedish Youth Employment Policy," *International Labour Review* 128 (3) 337–355.

Kaase, M. (1984). "The Challenge of the 'Participatory Revolution' in Pluralist Democracies," *International Political Science Review* 5 (3) 299–318.

———— and Gibowski, W. G. (1990). "Die Ausgangslage für die Bundestagswahl am 2. Dezember 1990—Entwicklungen und Meinungsklima seit 1987," pp. 735–785 in M. Kaase and H.-D. Klingemann (eds) *Wahlen und Wähler* (Opladen: Westdeutscher Verlag).

Katzenbach, E. (1992). "Thesen zur deutschen Wirtschaftspolitik," *Wirtschaftsdienst* 72 (May) 239–246.

Kellner, H. and Heuberger, F. (1988). "Zur Rationalität der 'Postmoderne' und ihrer Träger," in *Soziale Welt* Sonderband 6: Kultur und Alltag, pp. 325–337.

Kern, H. and Schumann, M. (1989). "New Concepts of Production in West German Plants," pp. 87–100 in P. Katzenstein (ed) *Industry and Politics in West Germany* (Ithaca: Cornell University Press).

Kesselman, M. (1992). "France," pp. 131–231 in M. Kesselman and J. Krieger *European Politics in Transition*, 2nd ed. (Lexington/Toronto: DC Heath).

Kimmel, A. (1991). "Innenpolitische Entwicklungen und Probleme in Frankreich," *Aus Politik und Zeitgeschichte* B47-48/91 (November) 3–15.

Kitschelt, H. (1993). "Class Structure and Social Democratic Party Strategy," *British Journal of Political Science* 23 (July) 299–337.

———— (1992). "The Formation of Party Systems in East Central Europe," *Politics & Society* 20 (1) 7–50.

———— (1990). "New Social Movements and the Decline of the Party Organization," pp. 179–208 in R. J. Dalton and M. Kuechler (ed) *Challenging the Political Order* (New York: Oxford University Press).

Klages, E. and Neumiller, J. (1993). "Extremist Parties Within a New Politics Perspective," paper presented at the 1993 Annual Meeting of the American Political Science Association, Washington, DC.

Knight, R. (1992). "Haider, the Freedom Party and the Extreme Right in Austria," *Parliamentary Affairs* 45 (3) 285–299.

Knight, U. and Kowalsky, W. (1991). *Deutschland nur den Deutschen?* (Erlangen, Bonn, Vienna: Straube).

Koch, C. (1993). "Zivilisation der Arbeitslosigkeit oder Vor dem Ende des Nationalstaats?" *Merkur* 47 (November) 927–939.

Köcher, R. (1992). *Demokratie braucht Unerbittlichkeit,* Institut für Demoskopie Allensbach, Allensbach.

Krause, P. (1992). "Einkommensarmut in der Bundesrepublik Deutschland," *Aus Politik und Zeitgeschichte* B49/92 (November) 3–17.

Kreiling, H.-W. (1989). "Die Europawahl am 18. Juni in München" *Münchner Statistik* (June) 341–371.

Kriesi, H. (1989). "New Social Movements and the New Class in the Netherlands," *American Journal of Sociology* 94 (March) 1078–1116.

Kuechler, M. (1993). "The Germans and the 'Others': Racism, Xenophobia, or Self-Defense?" paper presented at the 1993 Annual Meeting of the American Political Science Association, Washington, D.C.

———— (1982). "Staats-, Parteien- oder Politikverdrossenheit," pp. 39–54 in J. Raschke (ed) *Bürger und Parteien* (Opladen: Westdeutscher Verlag).

Kühl, J. (1993). "Arbeitslosigkeit in der vereinigten Bundesrepublik Deutschland," *Aus Politik und Zeitgeschichte* B35/93 (August) 3–15.

Kuhnle, S. (1992). "Norwegen," *Aus Politik und Zeitgeschichte* B43/92 (October) 12–21.

————, Strom, K., and Svåsand, L. (1986). "The Norwegian Conservative Party: Setback in an Era of Strength," *West European Politics* 9 (3) 448–469.

Lacroix, T. (1990). "Le marché du travail dans les années 80," pp. 36–49 in *Données Sociales 1990* (Paris: INSEE).

Lafferty, W. M. (1990). "The Political Transformation of a Social Democratic State: As the World Moves in, Norway Moves Right," *West European Politics* 13 (January) 79–100.

────── and Knutsen, O. (1984). "Leftist and Rightist Ideology in a Social Democratic State: An Analysis of Norway in the Midst of the Conservative Resurgence," *British Journal of Political Science* 14 (July) 345–367.

Larsen, F. (1992). "En Belgique, l'extrême droite s'installe dans les coulisses du pouvoir," *Le monde diplomatique* 39 (February) 8–9.

Lauk, K. J. (1994). "Germany at the Crossroads: On the Efficiency of the German Economy," *Daedalus* 123 (Winter) 57–83.

Layton-Henry, Z. (1990). "Race and Immigration," pp. 162–181 in D. W. Urwin and W. E. Paterson (eds) *Politics in Western Europe Today* (New York and London: Longman).

Lebon, A. (1992). "Des chiffres et des hommes," *Revue française des affaires sociales* 46 (December) pp. 15–27.

────── (1990). *Regards sur l'immigration et la présence étrangère en France 1989/1990* (Paris: La Documentation Française).

Le Gall, G. (1992). "L'effet immigration," pp. 119–136 in SOFRES, *L'état de l'opinion 1991* (Paris: Seuil).

────── (1984). "Une élection sans enjeu, avec conséquences," *Revue politique et parlementaire* 86, pp. 9–47.

Leggewie, C. (1993). *Druck von rechts, wohin treibt die Bundesrepublik?* (Munich: Beck).

────── (1989). *Die Republikaner: Phantombild der neuen Rechten* (Berlin: Rotbuch Verlag).

Lehideux, M. (1993). *Pour en finir avec le chômage,* Paris.

Le Pen, J.-M. (1989). *L'Espoir* (Paris: Albatros).

────── (1985). *Pour la France* (Paris: Albatros).

Lewis-Beck, M. S. and Mitchell, G. E. (1993). "French Electoral Theory: The National Front Test," *Electoral Studies* 12 (June) 112–127.

Lipietz, A. (1992). *Towards a New Economic Order* (New York: Oxford University Press).

────── (1991). "Governing the Economy in the Face of International Challenge: From National Developmentalism to National Crisis," pp. 17–42 in J. F. Hollifield and G. Ross (eds) *Searching for the New France* (New York/London: Routledge).

Lindbeck, A., Molander, P., Persson, T., Peterson, O., Sandmo, A., Swedenborg, B., and Thygesen, N. (1993), "Options for Economic and Political Reform in Sweden," *Economic Policy* 16 (April) 220–246.

Linder, W. (1992). "Die Schweiz zwischen Isolation und Integration," *Aus Politik und Zeitgeschichte* B47-48 (November) 20–31.

Lipset, S. M. (1981). *Political Man,* 2nd. ed. (Baltimore: Johns Hopkins University Press).

────── and Rokkan, S. (1967). "Cleavage Structures, Party Systems and Voter Alignments: An Introduction," pp. 1–64 in S. M. Lipset and S. Rokkan (eds) *Party Systems and Voter Alignments* (New York: Free Press).

Listhaug, O. (1993). "The Dynamics of Political Trust," paper prepared for presentation at the meeting of the ESF-project "Beliefs in Government," Budapest, March.

Loch, D. (1991). *Der schnelle Aufstieg des Front National* (Munich: tuduv-Verlagsgesellschaft).

Longchamp, C. (1991). "Politisch-kultureller Wandel in der Schweiz," pp. 49–101 in F. Plasser and P. A. Ulram (eds) *Staatsbürger oder Untertanen?* (Frankfurt/Bern/New York/Paris: Peter Lang).

―――― and Hardmeier, S. (1992). *Analyse der Nationalratswahl 1991*, VOX 16, no. 43, January.

Mabille, X., Lentzen, E., and Blaise, P. (1991). *Les élections législatives du 24 novembre 1991*, Courrier hebdomadaire, no. 1335–1336.

Mannheimer, R. (1993). "The Electorate of the Lega Nord," pp. 85–107 in G. Pasquino and P. McCarthy (eds) *The End of Post-War Politics in Italy* (Boulder/San Francisco/Oxford: Westview Press).

―――― (1992). "Gli elettori e simpatizzanti della Lega Lombarda dopo le elezioni politiche del 1992," paper presented at the Annual Conference of the American Political Science Association, Chicago.

―――― (1991). "Chi vota Lega e perché," pp. 122–158 in R. Mannheimer (ed) *La Lega Lombarda* (Milan: Feltrinelli).

Marchand, O. (1992). "La main-d'oeuvre étrangère en France," *Revue française des affaires sociales* 46 (December) 71–82.

Marklund, S. (1990). "Structures of Modern Poverty," *Acta Sociologica* 33 (2) 125–140.

Maurin, E. (1991). "Les étrangers: und main-d'æuvre à part?" *Economie et statistique* 242 (April) 39–50.

Mayer, N. (1992). "Des élection sans vainceur," *French Politics and Society* 10 (Spring) 1–12.

―――― (1991). "Le Front National," pp. 113–119 in *Bilan: Politique de la France* (Paris: Hachette).

―――― (1989). "Le vote FN de Passy à Barbès," pp. 249–267 in N. Mayer and P. Perrineau (eds) *Le Front national à découvert* (Paris: Presses de la Fondation nationale des sciences politiques).

―――― (1987). "De Passy à Barbès: Deux visages du vote Le Pen à Paris," *Revue française de science politique* 37 (December) 891–905.

―――― and Perrineau, P. (1992). "Why Do They Vote For Le Pen?" *European Journal of Political Research* 22 (July) 123–141.

―――― and Perrineau, P. (1989). *Le Front national à découvert* (Paris: Presses de la Fondation nationale de sciences politiques).

McCarthy, P. (1993). "The State's Will to Survive and the Discontent of its Citizens: A Reading of Domestic French Politics," *SAIS Review* 13 (Fall) 29–62.

Melotti, U. (1990). "L'immigrazione straniera in Italia; dati, cause, tipi," *Inchiesta* 20 (October/December) 27–36.

Meny, Y. (1993). *Government and Politics in Western Europe*, 2nd. ed., revised by A. Knapp (Oxford: Oxford University Press).

Mermet, G. (1990). *Francoscopie 1991* (Paris: Larousse)

Micossi, S. and Tullio, G. (1992). "Squilibri di bilancio, distorsioni economiche e *performance* di lungo periodo dell' economia italiana," *Rivista di Politica Economica* 82 (July) 39–91.

Miller, A. H. and Listhaug, O. (1993). "Ideology and Political Alienation," *Scandinavian Political Studies* 16 (2) 167–192.

Miller, A. H. and Listhaug, O. (1990). "Political Parties and Confidence in Government: A Comparison of Norway, Sweden and the United States," *British Journal of Political Science* 29 (3) 357–386.

Mingione, E. (1993). "Italy: The Resurgence of Regionalism," *International Affairs* 69 (April) 305–318.

Minkenberg, M. (1992). "The New Right in Germany: The Transformation of Conservatism and the Extreme Right," *European Journal of Political Research* 22 (July) 55–81.

———— and Inglehart, R. (1989). "Neoconservatism and Value Change in the USA: Tendencies in the Mass Public of a Postindustrial Society," pp. 81-109 in J. Gibbins (ed) *Contemporary Political Culture* (Newbury Park: SAGE).

Mitra, S. (1988). "The National Front in France—A Single-Issue Movement?" *West European Politics* 11 (April) 47–64.

Möller, K. (1993). "Zusammenhänge der Modernisierung des Rechtsextremismus mit der Modernisierung der Gesellschaft," *Aus Politik und Zeitgeschichte* B46-47 (November) 3–9.

Mölzer. A. (1990). *Jörg! Der Eisbrecher* (Klagenfurt: Suxxes).

Moioli, V. (1991). *Il tarlo delle leghe* (Trezzo sull' Adda: Comedit2000).

———— (1990). *I nuovi razzismi* (Rome: Edizioni Associate).

Molitor, U. (1992). *Wählen Frauen anders?* (Baden-Baden: Nomos).

Müller, S. (1992). "Plädoyer für Menschen," *Kommune* 10 (December) 20–24.

Natale, P. (1991). "Lega Lombarda e insediamento territoriale: un' analisi ecologica," pp. 83–121 in R. Mannheimer (ed) *La Lega Lombarda* (Milan: Feltrinelli).

Natale, L. (1990). "Gli stranieri nelle carceri italiane: dati e interpretazioni," *Polis* 4 (August) 325–352.

Natter, E. and Riedlsperger, A. (ed) (1988). *Zweidrittelgesellschaft* (Vienna: Europaverlag).

Neu, V. and Zelle, C. (1992). *Der Protest von Rechts*, Interne Studie Nr. 34/1992, Konrad-Adenauer-Stiftung, Sankt Augustin.

Nielsen, H. J. (1976). "The Uncivic Culture: Attitudes Towards the Political System in Denmark," *Scandinavian Political Studies* 11, pp. 147–155.

Noelle-Neumann, E. (1993). *Rechtsextremismus in Deutschland,* Institut für Demoskopie Allensbach, Allensbach.

——— (1989). *Die Republikaner* (Allensbach: Institut für Demoskopie Allensbach).

Notermans, T. (1993). "The Abdication from National Policy Autonomy: Why the Macroeconomic Policy Regime has Become So Unfavorable to Labor," *Politics & Society* 21 (June 1993) 133–167.

OECD (1991). *SOPEMI 1990* (Paris: OECD).

——— (1989). *Economies in Transition* (Paris: OECD).

Offe, C. (1987). "Challenging the Boundaries of Institutional Politics: Social Movements Since the 1960s," pp. 63–105 in C. S. Maier (ed) *Changing the Boundaries of the Political* (Cambridge: Cambridge University Press).

Olsen, E. (1984). "The Dilemmas of the Social-Democratic Labor Parties," *Daedalus* 113 (Spring) 169–194.

Oswalt, W. (1989). "Die FPÖ—ein Modell für Europa?" pp. 78–93 in M. Kirfel and W. Oswalt (eds) *Die Rückkehr der Führer. Modernisierter Rechtsradikalismus in Westeuropa* (Vienna: Europa Verlag).

Ottomani, M. (1992). *Brigate rozze* (Naples: Tullio Pironti).

Paci, M. (1992). *Il mutamento della struttura sociale in Italia* (Milan: Il Mulino).

Pappi, F. U. (1990). "Die Republikaner im Parteiensystem der Bundesrepublik," *Aus Politik und Zeitgeschichte,* B21/90 (May) 37–44.

Parlement Européen (1991). *Rapport élaboré au nom de la commission d'enquete su le racisme et la xénophobie* (Luxembourg: Communautés européennes).

Pasquino, G. (1993). "Introduction: A Case of Regime Crisis," pp. 1–11 in G. Pasquino and P. McCarthy (eds) *The End of Post-War Politics in Italy* (Boulder/San Francisco/Oxford: Westview Press).

——— (1991). "Meno partiti più Lega" *Polis* 3 (December) 555–564.

Pelinka, A. (1992). "Österreich: Was bleibt von den Besonderheiten?" *Aus Politik und Zeitgeschichte* B47-48 (November) 12–19.

——— (1989). "Alte Rechte, neue Rechte in Österreich," *Die Neue Gesellschaft/Frankfurter Hefte* 36 (February) 103–109.

Perrineau, P. (1990). "Le Front national d'une élection l'autre," *Regards sur l'actualité* 161 (May) 17–32.

——— (1988). "Front national: l'écho politique de l'anomie urbaine," *Esprit* 136/137 (March/April) 22–38.

Piel, E. (1992). *Wieviel Politikverachtung verträgt der Staat? Aktuelles demoskopisches Material zur sogenannten "Politikverdrossenheit"* (Allensbach: Institut für Demoskopie Allensbach).

Piore, M. and Sabel, C. (1984). *The Second Industrial Divide* (New York: Basic Books).

Plasser, F. (1986). "Die Nationalratswahl 1986: Analyse und politische Konsequenzen," *Österreichische Monatshefte* 42 (August) 9–26.

Plasser, F. and Ulram, P. A. (1994). *Wählerstrukturen und Entscheidungsmotive bei den Landtagswahlen am 13. März 1984 in Kärnten, Salzburg und Tirol,* Zentrum für angewandte Politikforschung und Fessel + GfK - Institut, Vienna.

——— (1992). "Überdehnung, Erosion und rechtspopulistische Reaktion," *Österreichische Zeitschrift für Politikwissenschaft* 21 (2) 147–164.

——— (1991). "'Die Ausländer kommen!'" pp. 311-323 in A. Khol, G. Ofner and A. Stirnemann (eds) *Österreichisches Jahrbuch für Politik 1990* (Vienna: Verlag für Geschichte und Politik).

——— (1991a). "Politisch-kultureller Wandel in Österreich," pp. 103–153 in F. Plasser and P. A. Ulram (eds) *Staatsbürger oder Untertanen? Politische Kultur Deutschlands, Österreichs und der Schweiz im Vergleich* (Frankfurt, Berne, New York, Paris: Peter Lang).

——— (1991b). "Analyse der Wiener Gemeinderatswahlen 1991," pp. 97–120 in A. Khol, G. Ofner, and A. Stirnemann (eds) *Österreichisches Jahrbuch für Politik '91* (Oldenbourg: Verlag für Geschichte und Politik).

——— (1991c). "Exit Poll GRW Wien '91," Vienna, Fessel + GFK Institut.

——— (1990). "Abstieg oder letzte Chance der ÖVP?" *Österreichische Monatshefte* 46 (July) 6–15.

——— (1990a). "Politische Kultur in Österreich," *Österreichische Monatshefte* 46 (January) 19–22.

——— (1989). "Wahltag ist Zahltag. Populistischer Appell und Wählerprotest in den achtziger Jahren," *Österreichische Zeitschrift für Politikwissenschaft* 18 (2) 151–164.

——— (1989a). "Major Parties on the Defensive," pp. 69–91 in A. Pelinka and F. Plasser (eds) *The Austrian Party System* (Boulder, San Francisco, London: Westview Press).

Plasser, F., Sommer, F., and Ulram, P. A. (1990). *Analyse der Nationalratswahl 1990,* mimeo, Vienna.

Plasser, F., Ulram, P. A., and Graushuber, A. (1992). "The Decline of 'Lager Mentality' and the New Model of Electoral Competition in Austria," *West European Politics* 15 (January) 16–44.

Poche, B. (1991/92). "The Lombard League: From Cultural Autonomy to Integral Federalism," *Telos* 90 (Winter) 71–81.

Pontussen, J. (1992). "Sweden," pp. 425–510 in M. Kesselman and J. Krieger, *European Politics in Transition,* 2nd. ed. (Lexington, MA: D. C. Heath).

Powell, B. J., Jr. (1986). "American Voter Turnout in Comparative Perspective," *American Political Science Review* 80 (March) 17–43.

Radcliff, B. (1992). "The Welfare State, Turnout, and the Economy: A Comparative Analysis," *American Political Science Review* 89 (June) 444–454.

Ranger, J. (1989). "Le cercle des sympathisants," pp. 135–148 in N. Mayer and P. Perrineau (eds) *Le Front national à découvert* (Paris: Presses de la Fondation nationale des sciences politiques).

Rattinger, H. (1993). "Abkehr von den Parteien? Dimensionen der Parteiverdrossenheit," *Aus Politik und Zeitgeschichte* B11/93 (March) 24–35.

Reich, R. (1992). *The Work of Nations* (New York: Vintage Books).

Reiter, E. (1992). "Die Europapolitik der Freiheitlichen," pp. 87–100 in A. Khol, G. Ofner and A. Stirnemann (eds) *Österreichisches Jahrbuch für Politik 1992* (Vienna: Verlag für Geschichte und Politik).

Die Republikaner (1992). *Die Republikaner für Baden-Württemberg,* Landtagwahlprogramm '92, Stuttgart.

———— (1990). *Parteiprogramm,* Bonn.

———— (1987). *Programm der Republikaner 1987,* Munich.

Ricolfi, L. (1993). "Lo spazio politico e la collocazione della Lega," pp. 127–154 in A. Cavalli and A. de Lillo (eds) *Giovanni anni 90* (Bologna: Il Mulino).

Riedlsperger, M. (1993). "Mit der 'dritten Kraft' in die Dritte Republik," mimeo, Department of History, California Polytechnic University.

———— (1992). "Heil Haider! The Revitalization of the Austrian Freedom Party since 1986," *Politics and Society in Germany, Austria and Switzerland* 4 (3) 18–58.

Ritter, M. (1990). *Sturm auf Europa* (Munich: v. Hase & Koehler).

Ritzer, G. (1993). *The McDonaldization of Society* (Thousand Oaks: Pine Forge Press).

Ronge, V. (1993). "Ost-West-Wanderungen nach Deutschland," *Aus Politik und Zeitgeschichte* B7/93 (February) 16–28.

Room, G. J. and Hennigsen, B. (1990). *Neue Armut in der Europäischen Gemeinschaft* (Frankfurt/New York: Campus).

Room, G. J., Lawson, R., and Laczko, F. (1989) " 'New Poverty' in the European Community," *Policy and Politics* 17 (April) 165–176.

Roth, D. (1993). "Gibt es eine Wiedergeburt des Rechtsradikalismus?" mimeo, Forschungsgruppe Wahlen e.V., Mannheim.

———— (1990). "Die Republikaner. Schneller Aufstieg und tiefer Fall einer Protestpartei am rechten Rand," *Aus Politik und Zeitgeschichte* B37–38/90 (September), 27–39.

———— (1989). "Sind die Republikaner die fünfte Partei?" *Aus Politik und Zeitgeschichte,* B41–42/89, (October) 10–20.

Saffran, W. (1991). "State, Nation, National Identity, and Citizenship: France as a Test Case," *International Political Science Review* 12 (July) 219–238.

Sauer, W. (1967). "National Socialism: Totalitarianism or Fascism?" *American Historical Review* 73 (December) 404–424.

Savelli, G. (1992). *Che cosa vuole la Lega* (Milan: Longanesi).

Schain, M. (1990). "Immigration and Politics," pp. 253–268 in P. A. Hall, J. Hayward, and H. Machin (eds) *Developments in French Politics* (New York: St. Martin's Press).

———— (1987). "The National Front in France and the Construction of Political Legitimacy," *West European Politics* 10 (April) 229–252.

Scharpf, F. W. (1993). "Soziale Gerechtigkeit im globalen Kapitalismus," *Die Neue Gesellschaft/Frankfurter Hefte* 40 (June) 544–547.

Scharsach, H.-H. (1992). *Haider's Kampf* (Vienna: Orac).

Schedler, A. (1993). "Die demoskopische Konstruktion von 'Politikverdrossenheit'," *Politische Vierteljahresschrift* 34 (September) 414–435.

Scheuch, E. K. and Klingemann, H. D. (1967). "Theorie des Rechtsradikalismus in westlichen Industriegesellschaften," *Hamburger Jahrbuch für Wirtschafts- und Gesellschaftspolitik* 12, pp. 11–29.

Scheuch, K. and Scheuch, U. (1992). *Clinquen, Klüngel und Karrieren* (Reinbek: Rowohlt).

Schiesser, G. (1992). "Die Schweizer Auto-Partei," *Die Neue Gesellschaft/Frankfurter Hefte* 39 (April) 330–335.

Schmitter Heisler, B. (1991). "A Comparative Perspective on the Underclass," *Theory and Society* 20, pp. 455–483.

Schmollinger, H. W. (1989). "Die Wahl zum Abgeordnetenhaus von Berlin am 29. Januar 1989," *Zeitschrift für Parlamentsfragen* 20 (October) 309–322.

Schönhuber, F. (1987). *Trotz allem Deutschland* (Munich/Vienna: Langen Müller).

Schröter, W. (1994). "Dem Teufel der Tüftler gehen die Ideen aus," *Kommune* 12 (January) 9–12.

Schulte, A. (1990). "Multikulturelle Gesellschaft: Chance, Ideologie oder Bedrohung?" *Aus Politik und Zeitgeschichte* B23–24 (June) 3–15.

Schulze, G. (1993). *Die Erlebnisgesellschaft: Kultursoziologie der Gegenwart* (Frankfurt: Campus).

Schultze, R.-O. (1992). "Weder Protest noch Parteienverdrossenheit," *Die Neue Gesellschaft/Frankfurter Hefte* 39 (October) 886–892.

Shields, J. G. (1991). "The Politics of Disaffection: France in the 1980s," pp. 69–90 in J. Gaffney and E. Kolinsky (eds) *Political Culture in France and Germany* (London/New York: Routledge).

Smith Jespersen, M. P. (1989). "A Danish Defense Dilemma: The Election of May 1988," *West European Politics* 12 (January) 189–195.

SOFRES (1993). *L'état de l'opinion 1993* (Paris: Seuil).

Starzacher, K., Schacht, K., Friederich, B., and Leif, T. (eds) (1992). *Protestwähler und Wahlverweigerer: Krise der Demokratie?* (Cologne: Bund).

Statera, G. (1993). *Come votano gli italiani* (Milan: Sperling & Kupfer).

Statistisches Bundesamt (ed.) (1992). *Datenreport 1992* (Bonn: Bundeszentrale für politische Bildung).

Statistisches Landesamt der Freien und Hansestadt Hamburg (1993). *Analyse der Hamburger Wahlen am 19. September 1993.* Hamburg.

Stirnemann, A. (1992). "Gibt es einen Haider-Effekt?" pp. 137–185 in A. Khol, G. Ofner, and A. Stirnemann (eds) *Österreichisches Jahrbuch für Politik 1992* (Oldenbourg: Verlag für Geschichte und Politik).

—— (1988). "Die Freiheitlichen—Abkehr vom Liberalismus?" pp. 165–201 in A. Khol, G. Ofner, and A. Stirnemann (eds) *Österreichisches Jahrbuch für Politik* (Oldenbourg: Verlag für Geschichte und Politik).

Stöss, R. (1990). "Parteikritik und Parteiverdrossenheit," *Aus Politik und Zeitgeschichte* B21/90 (May) 15–24.

Stooß, F. and Weidig, I. (1990). "Der Wandel der Tätigkeitsfelder und -profile bis zum Jahr 2000," *Mitteilungen aus der Arbeits- und Berufsforschung* 23 (1) 22–33.

Strom, K. and Leipart, J. Y. (1989). "Ideology, Strategy and Party Competition in Postwar Norway," *European Journal of Political Research* 17 (3) 263–288.

—— and de Rotstein (1991). "The Radical Right and the Contemporary Scandinavian Experience," paper presented at the Conference on the Radical Right in Western Europe, University of Minnesota, Minneapolis.

Svensson, P. and Togeby, L. (1991). "The Political Mobilization of the New Middle Class in Denmark during the 1970s and 1980s," *West European Politics* 14 (4) 149–168.

—— (1991a). *Hojrebolge* (Arhus: Forlaget Politica).

Swyngedouw, M. (1993). "Nieuwe breuklijnen in de Vlaamse politiek?" pp. 85–112 in M. Swyngedouw, J. Billiet, A. Carton, and R. Beerten (eds) *Kiezen is verliezen* (Leuven: Acco).

—— (1992). *Waar vor je waarden: De opkomst van Vlaams Blok en Agalev in de jaren tachtig* (Leuven: ISPO/University of Leuven).

—— (1992a). "National Elections in Belgium: The Breakthrough of the Extreme Right in Flanders," *Regional Politics & Policy* 2 (Autumn) 62–75.

—— (1991). "Het Vlaams Blok in Antwerpen: Een analyse van de verkiezingsuitslagen sinds 1985," pp. 93–114 in H. De Schampheleire and Y. Tannassekos (eds) *Extreem rechts in West-Europa* (Brussels: VUB Press).

——, Beerten, R., Billiet, J., and Carton, A. (1993). "Partijkeuze verklaren," pp. 15–25 in M. Swyngedouw, J. Billiet, A. Carton, and R. Beertens (eds) *Kiezen is verliezen* (Leuven: Acco).

—— and de Winter, L. (1991). "Het Vlaams Blok in de Europese verkiezingen van 1984 en 1989," pp. 115–127 in H. De Schampheleire and Y. Tannassekos (eds) *Extreem rechts in West-Europa* (Brussels: VUB Press).

Taggart, P. (1992). "Green Parties and Populist Parties and the Establishment of New Politics in Sweden," paper presented at the Annual Conference of the American Political Science Association, Chicago.

Taguieff, P.-A. (1990). "The New Cultural Racism in France," *Telos* 83 (Spring) 109–122.

——— (1984). "La rhétorique du national-populisme," *Mots* 9 (October) 113–139.

Therborn, G. (1992). "Swedish Social Democracy and the Transition from Industrial to Postindustrial Politics," pp. 101–123 in F. Fox Piven (ed) *Labor Parties in Postindustrial Societies* (New York: Oxford University Press).

Thränhardt, D. (1988). "Die Bundesrepublik Deutschland—ein unerklärtes Einwanderungsland," *Aus Politik und Zeitgeschichte* B24/88 (June) 3–13.

Tresmontant, R. (1991). "Chômage: les chances d'en sortir," *Economie et statistique* 241 (March) 41–50.

Tribalat, M. (1986). "La population étrangère en France," *Regards sur l'actualité* 118 (February) 33–44.

Turner, B. S. (1989). "From Postindustrial Society to Postmodern Politics: the Political Sociology of Daniel Bell," pp. 199–217.

Uterwedde, H. (1993). "Französische Wirtschaftspolitik in den neunziger Jahren. Veränderte Rahmenbedingungen und neue Handlungsansätze," *Aus Politik und Zeitgeschichte* B32/93 (August) 3–9.

——— (1991). "Wirtschafts- und Sozialpolitik unter Mitterrand 1981-1991," *Aus Politik und Zeitgeschichte* B47–48/91 (November) 16–25.

Valen, H. (1990). "The Storting Election of 1989: Polarization and Protest," *Scandinavian Political Studies* 13 (3) 277–290.

———, Aardal, B., and Vogt, G. (1990). *Endring og kontinuitet: Stortingvalget 1989* (Oslo: Central Bureau of Statistic).

——— and Martinussen, W. (1977). "Electoral Trends and Foreign Politics in Norway: The 1973 Storting Election and the EEC Issue," pp. 39–71 in K. Cerny (ed) *Scandinavia at the Polls* (Washington, D.C.: American Enterprise Institute).

Vandermotten, C. and Vanlaer, J. (1991). "Immigration et vote d'extrême-droite en Europe Occidentale et en Belgique," mimeo, Université Libre de Bruxelles, Brussels.

van der Eijk, C., Franklin, M., Mackie T., and Valen, H. (1992). "Cleavages, Conflict Resolution and Democracy," pp. 406–431 in M. Franklin, T. Mackie, Henry Valen et al. *Electoral Change: Responses to Evolving Social and Attitudinal Structures in Western Countries* (Cambridge: Cambridge University Press).

Vaughan, M. (1991). "The Extreme Right in France: 'Lepenisme' or the Politics of Fear," pp. 211–233 in L. Cheles, R. Ferguson, and M. Vaughan (eds) *Neo-Fascism in Europe* (London/New York: Longman).

Veen, H.-J. (1989). "The Greens as a Milieu Party," pp. 31–59 in E. Kolinsky (ed) *The Greens in West Germany* (Oxford/New York/Munich: Berg).

————, Lepsky, N., and Mnich, P. (1992). *Die Republikaner-Partei zu Beginn der 90er Jahre,* Interne Studie 14/1991–1992, Forschungsinstitut der Konrad-Adenauer-Stiftung, Sankt Augustin.

Vester, M. (1993). "Das Janusgesicht sozialer Modernisierung," *Aus Politik und Zeitgeschichte* B26–27/93 (June) 3–19.

————, von Oertzen, P., Geiling, H., Hermann, T., and Müller, D. (1993). *Soziale Milieus im gesellschaftlichen Strukturwandel* (Cologne: Bund-Verlag).

Vimercati, D. (1990). *I lombardi alla nuova crociata* (Milan: Mursia).

Vincent, J.-M. (1985). "Pourquoi l'extrême droite," *Les Tempes Modernes* 41 (April) 1773–1779.

Vlaams Blok (1991). *Uit zelfverdediging,* Verkiezingsprogramma 1991, Brussels.

———— (n. d.). *Manifest van het rechtse Vlaams-nationalisme,* Brussels.

von Beyme (1988). "Right-Wing Extremism in Post-War Europe," *West European Politics* 11 (April) 1–18.

Wasserman, R. (1992). "Plädoyer für eine neue Asyl- und Ausländerpolitik," *Aus Politik und Zeitgeschichte* B9/92 (February) 13–20.

Werner, J. (1992). *Die Invasion der Armen* (Mainz and Munich: v. Hase & Koehler).

Whitney, C. R. (1991). "Europeans Look for Ways to Bar Door to Immigrants," *The New York Times* December 29, 1991, pp. 1, 8.

Wiesendahl, E. (1992). "Volksparteien im Abstieg," *Aus Politik und Zeitgeschichte* B34–35/92 (August) 3–14.

Wildenmann, R. (1989). *Volksparteien: Ratlose Riesen?* (Baden-Baden: Nomos Verlagsgesellschaft).

Wilgren, J. (1887). "International Migration: New Challenges to Europe," *Migration News* 36 (2) 3–35.

Wilke, G. (1990). *Arbeitslosigkeit: Diagnosen und Therapien* (Bonn: Bundeszentrale für politische Bildung).

Woods, D. (1992). "The Centre No Longer Holds: The Rise of Regional Leagues in Italian Politics," *West European Politics* 15 (April) 56–76.

Worcester, K. (1989). "Ten Years of Thatcherism: The 'Enterprise Culture' and the Democratic Alternative," *World Policy Journal* 6 (Spring) 297–320.

Wright, E. O. and Cho, D. (1992). "State Employment, Class Location, and Ideological Orientation: A Comparative Analysis of the United States and Sweden," *Politics & Society* 20 (June) 167–196.

Ysmal, C. (1991). "Les cadres du Front national: les habits neufs de l'extrême droite," pp. 181–197 in SOFRES, *L'état de l'opinion 1991* (Paris: Seuil).

INDEX